DISARMAMENT

& NUCLEAR TESTS

1960-63

INTERIM HISTORY

This new series of popularly priced books — which we call Interim History — was created by Facts on File to bridge the chasm between today's newspapers and the definitive histories that will probably be written anywhere from five years to several decades from now.

The researcher, student or interested citizen has no difficulty in getting most of the facts of what is happening in the world right now. Newspapers, magazines, radio and television deluge him with more information than he can possibly digest.

Similarly, it is easy to find adequate accounts of the events of the past — provided that one does not mean the immediate past. Any good library can supply, on a moment's notice, a superb collection of painstakingly researched histories of World Wars I and II, of the War of the Roses and the American Civil War (especially the Civil War), of the Franco-Prussian War and the Boxer Rebellion, and of hundreds of less bellicose periods.

But to ask for a detailed retelling of a major series of events that took place only two or three years ago may well be like asking for the moon — and even a request for the moon may soon be easier to fulfill. A collection of newspaper articles about a current topic may take weeks to compile and still may prove disappointingly inadequate. True, a definitive history of the subject will probably be written some day — or year — but that knowledge is small consolation when we need information now.

Facts on File is attempting to bridge the gap with this new series of books — Interim History. We hope it will prove of value in the interim — in the years between the date on today's newspaper and the publication date of the future histories of these times.

Each volume of Interim History will consist of a journalistic account of the events in a single field during a few recent years. As a rule the material will be taken verbatim — or with minor changes — from the various volumes of News Year and Facts on File and, where appropriate, from other acceptable sources.

DISARMAMENT

& NUCLEAR TESTS

1960-63

Compiled by the Editors of
Facts on File and News Year

Lester A. Sobel, Editor-in-Chief

FACTS ON FILE   **NEW YORK**

DISARMAMENT & NUCLEAR TESTS 1960-63

© Copyright, 1964, by Facts on File, Inc.

Library of Congress Catalog Card No. 64-56719
ISBN 0-87196-153-9

9   8   7   6   5

PRINTED IN THE UNITED STATES OF AMERICA

Contents

Disarmament & Nuclear Tests 1960-63

The development of nuclear weapons added urgency to the long search for a way to achieve an international agreement on abolishing war and ending the costly burden of armament. It also introduced a new element—the need to prevent further radio-active contamination of the atmosphere from atomic tests.

Representatives of the nuclear powers met frequently during the years 1960-63 in an effort to work out agreements to control or abolish conventional and nuclear weapons. In 1963 they finally signed a treaty prohibiting nuclear weapons tests in the atmosphere, in space and under water. But mutual fears and suspicions still ruled out any agreement on general disarmament.

This book tells how the negotiators for the East and West met repeatedly and disagreed almost as often during the 4-year period 1960-63. It also records details of many other events involved in the effort to bring about international disarmament and to free the world of the menace of mass-destruction weapons. Except for some editorial revision, largely minor, the material of this book comes directly from the pages of the 4 volumes of News Year that cover the period involved.

Mounting East-West competition in nuclear-armed missiles gave added impetus in 1960 to worldwide demands for new attempts at arms limitation. A 10-nation disarmament conference was convened in Geneva Mar. 15 but ended in disagreement June 27. Geneva talks on a treaty to ban nuclear weapons tests continued through their 3d year with no sign of progress although the 3 major nuclear powers—the U.S., USSR and Britain—continued a self-imposed moratorium on such tests. France, however, tested 3 nuclear devices in 1960. A projected Big-3 summit conference on disarmament and other East-West problems convened in Paris May 16 but was broken up within 3 hours in a dispute over the U.S.' use of U-2 'spy planes' for military reconnaissance of Soviet territory.

Pre-Geneva Developments

Khrushchev Hints Troop Cuts. Soviet Premier Nikita S. Khrushchev said at a Kremlin New Year's reception Jan. 1 that the USSR might "disarm unilaterally" if its recent proposal for disarmament did not win Western acceptance.

Addressing 1,500 Soviet officials & foreign diplomats, Khrushchev added: Why "should we not reduce our armed forces more and rely on rocket & nuclear weapons to defend our borders?" "The number of troops," he declared, "does not matter so much in the age of rockets." Referring to the USSR's space rocket successes in 1959, Khrushchev made it clear that he expected missile-borne weapons to make up for any further unilateral cut in Soviet military manpower.

In an exchange of New Year's messages with Pres. Eisenhower, made public Jan. 4, Khrushchev & Marshal Kliment Y. Voroshilov, chairman of the Supreme Soviet Presidium (equivalent to Soviet president), voiced hopes that 1960 would bring a "new triumph of reason" and solution of "the most important problem of our time—the general & complete disarmament & the liberation of mankind from the burden of armament." Mr. Eisenhower replied that the U.S. "seeks the achievement of a just & lasting peace in a world where all questions are settled by peaceful means alone."

USSR Reduces Forces. A 1,200,-000-man reduction of Soviet armed forces—from 3,623,000 men to 2,423,-000—was proposed Jan. 14 by Premier Khrushchev and was approved unanimously by the USSR's Supreme Soviet (Parliament) the next day.

Khrushchev stressed the fact that the Soviet troop reduction was made possible by the USSR's increasing nuclear missile forces. "In our country," he asserted, "the armed forces have been to a considerable extent transferred to rocket & nuclear arms. These arms are being perfected and will continue to be perfected until the day they are banned."

"The air force & the navy have lost their previous importance," and their conventional arms are "not being reduced but replaced," Khrushchev said. "Almost the whole of the air force is being replaced by rocket equipment. We have by now cut down sharply and . . . will continue to cut down & even discontinue the manufacture of bombers & other obsolete machinery." "In the navy," he continued, "the submarine fleet assumes great importance, whilst above-water ships can no longer play" their former role.

Khrushchev emphasized that "we already possess so many nuclear weapons, both atomic & hydrogen, and the necessary rockets for sending these weapons to the territory of a potential aggressor, that should any madman launch an attack on our state or on other Socialist states, we would be able literally to wipe the . . .

An entire Soviet army division is demobilized in town square of Osipovie near Minsk, White Russia. Soviet Premier Khrushchev, proposing the uni lateral military manpower reduction, told the Supreme Soviet Jan. 14 tha Soviet might was shifting from men to rockets.   (Wide World photo

countries which attack us off the face of the earth."

Alluding to Soviet discovery of a new superweapon, he boasted that, "though the weapons we have now are formidable, . . . the weapon we have today in the hatching stage is even more perfect & even more formidable." This new Soviet arm, "in the portfolio of our scientists & designers, is a fantastic weapon."

Khrushchev's proposal for reducing Soviet troop strength was embodied in a law passed unanimously by the Supreme Soviet Jan. 15. A formal appeal to "the parliaments & governments of all the nations of the world" to emulate the Soviet action was approved unanimously by the Supreme Soviet the same day.

Chinese Role. U.S. State Secy Christian A. Herter asserted Jan. 21 that Communist Chinese participation in an East-West disarmament accord was "inevitable" if such an agreement were to be effective. Herter, testifying at a closed session of the Senate Foreign Relations Committee, made it clear, however, that U.S. & Red Chinese participation in an arms agreement would not imply U.S. recognition of Peiping.

A State Department statement said later the same day that if "substantial progress is made toward controlled disarmament" in forthcoming 10-nation arms talks in Geneva, "then it would be logical to consider participation in such a disarmament program by other countries, including Red China."

Communist Chinese Foreign Min. Chen Yi, addressing a National People's Congress meeting in Peiping, said Jan. 21: "China is ready . . . to commit itself to international obligations to which it agrees. However, any . . . disarmament agreement which is arrived at without [Chinese] . . . participation" "cannot . . . have any binding force on China."

Pres. Eisenhower said at a news conference Mar. 16 that as international disarmament developed, the world "unquestionably [would] have to take into account the armaments of Red China," although "there has to be a very great deal of progress before we are into the stage of worrying about Red China."

Herter Urges Arms Accord. An appeal for an East-West disarmament system that would end the danger of nuclear war by miscalculation was voiced Feb. 18 by State Secy. Herter.

Addressing the National Press Club in Washington, Herter asserted that the world faced 2 major dangers from the East-West arms race:

• "Spiraling competition in strategic delivery systems with ever shorter reaction times, [which] could lead to war by miscalculation. Such miscalculations might . . . cause an international crisis to develop into general [unintended] war."
• "The proliferating production of nuclear weapons, [which] might eventually enable almost any country, however irresponsible, to secure these weapons. . . . The more nations that have the power to trigger off a nuclear war, the greater the chance that some nation might use this power in haste or blind folly."

Herter said that in the 10-nation Geneva disarmament talks, the West would "insist on inspection procedures that will permit verification" of disarmament measures required by any international pact. He stressed that any proposed agreement would be measured "by one practical yardstick: Would United States & free world security be greater—or less?"

Geneva Arms Talks Open

10-Nation Group Meets. The first full-scale East-West disarmament negotiations in 2½ years were convened in Geneva Mar. 15 by Western & Soviet delegations to a 10-nation Committee on Disarmament.

The Geneva meeting was opened by UN Undersecretary Dragoslav Protitch, representing Secy. Gen. Dag Hammarskjöld, after the 5 Western & 5 Soviet delegations had agreed to be seated alphabetically around a U-shaped conference table in Geneva's Palais des Nations. Chairmanship of the conference was to rotate daily among participating states on an alphabetical basis.

Western delegation chiefs: Frederick M. Eaton (U.S.); David Ormsby-Gore (Britain); Jules Moch (France); Gen. E. L. M. Burns (Canada); Gaetano Martino (Italy).

Soviet delegation chiefs: Valerian A. Zorin (USSR); Marian Naszkowski (Poland); Jiri Nosek (Czechoslovakia); Eduard Mejinescu (Rumania); Milko Tarabanov (Bulgaria).

Messages from Secy. Gen. Hammarskjöld, Pres. Eisenhower & Soviet Premier Khrushchev were delivered to the opening session by Protitch and the U.S. & Soviet delegation chiefs.

Red Troop Strength 1927-59

Khrushchev Jan. 14 gave the Supreme Soviet the following review of Soviet troop strength since 1927:

1927—"After the civil war . . . the number of service personnel was cut to 586,000. . . ."

1937—"As the result of . . . aggression in the Far East & the growth of fascism in Germany . . . [Soviet forces] amounted to 1,433,000. . . ."

1941—"The outbreak of World War II & the growing danger of a . . . German invasion compelled . . . [an increase] to 4,207,000. . . ."

1945—Soviet forces totaled 11,365,000 by the end of World War II.

1948—Postwar demobilization cut manpower to 2,874,000.

1955—"NATO threat & atomic blackmail" compelled a buildup to 5,763,000 men.

1959—Soviet forces totalled 3,623,000 men.

Major points of the 3 messages:

Hammarskjöld—"In creating this new forum as 'a useful means of exploring . . . avenues of possible progress,' the 4 powers [U.S., Britain, France, USSR] explicitly recognized the 'ultimate responsibility for disarmament . . . rests with the United Nations' and expressed the hope that 'the results achieved in these deliberations would provide a useful basis for consideration . . . in the United Nations.' . . . Your deliberations, therefore, take place with the full endorsement & support" of the UN.

Eisenhower—The U.S. "is prepared to explore every possible avenue to find a way toward general disarmament. We must not be pessimistic because of the lack of success in past . . . negotiations. Nor should we . . . expect immediate, dramatic & far-reaching strides. . . . Rather, it should be our objective . . . to contribute by carefully balanced, phased & safeguarded arms control agreements to the ultimate objective of a secure, free & peaceful world in which . . . disputes will be settled in accordance with the . . . [UN] Charter."

Khrushchev—"The 10-nation committee is entrusted with the most important & responsible task—to work out within the briefest possible period practical ways of carrying out general & complete disarmament. . . . It is precisely general & complete disarmament that is the most secure & reliable means of eliminating wars forever from the life of human society. The Soviet Union is fully resolved to carry out general & complete disarmament. It has demonstrated its desire to back up concrete deeds this determination by the recent decision to further reduce its armed forces by 1,200,000 men."

Other statements at the opening session centered on a unified Western disarmament plan made public on the eve of the conference.

Western Arms Plan. The draft Western disarmament plan was contained in a working paper transmitted to Soviet bloc delegations and made public in Geneva Mar. 14.

The unified 3-stage Western plan had been worked out in Paris Mar.

Arms Talks Background

The 10-nation disarmament committee was established by the U.S., USSR, Britain & France Sept. 7, 1959 to renew East-West disarmament negotiations on a formal basis outside the UN.

Full-scale East-West disarmament talks had been dormant since a 5-nation subcommittee of the UN Disarmament Commission recessed deadlocked sessions in London Sept. 6, 1957. Other aspects of the East-West arms race had been considered in diplomatic exchanges and conferences on preventing surprise attacks & banning nuclear tests, but no general disarmament talks had taken place since the London talks.

The 10-nation committee had been proposed & explored at the 1959 Big 4 foreign ministers' Geneva conference on Germany and was sanctioned by a joint U.S.-Soviet resolution voted Nov. 20, 1959 by the UN General Assembly. The Geneva meeting was arranged in an exchange of notes in Dec. 1959.

No Nobel Peace Prize

The Norwegian Parliament's 5-member Nobel Peace Prize Committee announced in Oslo Oct. 28 that it would present no Nobel Peace Prize for 1960. It set aside the award money ($43,627) for possible presentation in 1961. It was the 17th time an award had not been made since the prize was established in 1901.

7-10 by the U.S., British, French, Canadian & Italian delegations. Submitted to the NATO Permanent Council in Paris Mar. 10, the plan provided for conventional & nuclear disarmament under strict controls designed to lead to elimination of all means of mass destruction. It was to be supervised by an International Disarmament Organization.

The Western program was a combination of disarmament proposals advanced by British Foreign Secy. Lloyd before the UN General Assembly Sept. 17, 1959, by State Secy. Herter in his Feb. 18 address to the National Press Club and by French disarmament delegate Jules Moch during Western talks prior to the Geneva conference.

THE WESTERN WORKING PAPER

(Text of Western proposals, with minor deletions)

Stage I—"The following measures are proposed . . [to] be undertaken forthwith:

"A. The establishment of an International Disarmament Organization (IDO) by progressive steps following a joint study of the composition & functions of such an organization & its relationship to the United Nations. . . .

"B. Prior notification to the IDO of proposed launchings of space vehicles and . . . cooperative arrangements for communicating to the IDO data obtained from . . . tracking facilities.

"C. The collection of information on present force levels . . . and on armaments pertaining to land, sea & air forces possessed by the various powers. . . .

"D. The coordinated reduction or limitation of force levels & conventional armaments upon the establishment of . . . verification by the IDO as follows:

"1. Initial force-level ceilings to be 2,500,000 for the Soviet Union & . . . for the United States, and agreed appropriate force levels for certain other states.

"2. Each state . . . shall place in storage depots, within its own territories and under the supervision of the IDO, agreed types & quantities of conventional armaments. . . .

"E. The submission by the various states to the IDO of data relating to . . . the amount of their military expenditures and the percentage of their gross national product earmarked for military expenditures. . . .

"F. Joint studies . . . on the following subjects:

"1. Measures to assure . . . that no nation shall place into orbit or station in outer space weapons of mass destruction, including provision for on-site inspection.

"2. Measures to assure . . . prior notification of missile launchings, . . . and . . . declarations to the International Disarmament Organization of launching sites & places of manufacture of such missiles.

"3. Measures to . . . discontinue the manufacture of fissionable materials for weapons purposes.

"4. Arrangements . . . to transfer . . . fissionable material from past production to non-weapons uses, including stockpiling.

"5. Measures to give . . . greater protection against surprise attack with effective verification procedures including aerial inspection, ground observers, . . . mobile ground teams, overlapping radar, [&] notification of aircraft flights. . . .

"6. Measures to verify budgetary information submitted . . . to the IDO.

"7. Means of preventing aggression and preserving world peace & security, as national armaments are reduced, by an international organization . . . of, or linked to the United Nations.

"8. . . . extending [of] a disarmament agreement . . . to include other states having significant military capabilities."

Stage II—"The following measures will be undertaken as rapidly as possible upon successful completion of the relevant preparatory study: . . .

"A. The prohibition against placing into orbit or stationing in outer space of vehicles capable of mass destruction, to be effective immediately after the installation & effective operation of an agreed control system. . . .

"B. Prior notification to the IDO of proposed launchings of missiles . . . and declarations of locations of launching sites, and places of [missile] manufacture, with agreed verification. . . .

"C. The cessation of production of fissionable materials for weapons purposes immediately after the installation & effective operation of an agreed control system, . . . conditional upon satisfactory progress in . . . conventional disarmament.

"D. Agreed quantities of fissionable material . . . to be transferred . . . to non-weapons uses . . . upon the installation & effective operation of an agreed control system to verify the cessation of [fission] production . . . for weapons. . . .

"E. Establishment of appropriate measures to give participating states greater protection against surprise attack. . . .

"F. A disarmament conference with other states having significant military capabilities called to consider their accession to the . . . agreement. . . .

"G. Force-level ceilings for all militarily significant states and appropriate inspection & verification measures to go into effect simultaneously with the establishment of force-level ceilings of 2,100,000 for the U.S. & USSR. At the same time, each [state] . . . shall agree to place in storage depots agreed types & quantities of armaments in agreed relation to the . . . ceilings.

"H. . . . measures to verify budgetary information.

"I. Further . . . development of the . . . [IDO].

"J. Initial establishment of the international organization to preserve world peace."

Stage III—These "additional measures which are regarded as necessary for achieving the ultimate [disarmament] goal:

"A. Reduction of national armed forces & armaments by progressive safeguarded steps . . . to levels required by internal security and fulfillment of [UN] obligations . . . to the end that no single nation or group of nations can effectively oppose enforcement of international law.

"B. Measures toward this objective, phased to coincide with the buildup of international law enforcement capability to preserve world peace, and with the extension of the IDO to provide necessary inspection & control, will include:

"1. Prohibition of production of nuclear, chemical, biological & other weapons of mass destruction.

"2. Further reduction of . . . stocks of nuclear, chemical, biological & other weapons of mass destruction; further transfer of fissionable materials to peaceful use, and further steps . . . to achieve the final elimination of these weapons.

"3. Measures to insure the use of outer space for peaceful purposes only.

"4. Control of the production of agreed categories of military missiles & existing national stocks and their final elimination.

"5. Establishment of effective international control over military budgets.

"6. Completion of the establishment of international . . . arrangements to preserve world peace.

"7. Final reduction of military manpower & armaments . . . including the disposition of surplus armaments.

"8. Control over the production of all remaining types of armaments. . . ."

USSR Vs. West's Plan. The Western plan was attacked by Soviet delegate Zorin at the meeting's opening session Mar. 15 on grounds that it made necessary "a prolonged study of various technical problems and forms of control over armaments . . . leaving the practical solution of the question of general disarmament for an indefinitely far-off future." Zorin said that only Soviet Premier Khrushchev's plan for "general & complete disarmament under international control" would "deliver nations from the threat of nuclear rocket war."

Zorin charged that certain "circles" in the West still were taking steps to intensify the arms race by preparing to establish "a joint [NATO] nuclear force," by seeking West German military bases in Spain and by seeking to evade a nuclear test ban.

U.S. chief delegate Eaton, alluding to Khrushchev's total disarmament plan, retorted that "we would only deceive ourselves & those millions who are hungering for peace if we were to place our name on some grand but hollow design, some ambitious but unenforceable scheme, some unrealistically timed program of disarmament."

West Asks Space-Weapon Ban. An international ban on earth satellites bearing nuclear bombs was proposed by British delegate Ormsby-

Gore Mar. 16 as the Geneva conferees began their closed working sessions. (Summaries of major developments at closed sessions were given to reporters at news conferences held daily by each delegation.)

Zorin outlined to the meeting control measures proposed in Khrushchev's plan for total disarmament in 4 years. He made it clear that the USSR favored a control system that would be expanded with each new stage of disarmament but saw the achievement of total disarmament as a unified problem and would not accept an agreement on nuclear satellites alone.

French chief delegate Jules Moch, speaking for the West, asked Communist delegates Mar. 18 if they would accept Western demands for a full census of world military manpower & armaments from rifles to battleships. He pressed Zorin to tell precisely what the USSR meant by its repeated calls for total disarmament under "international control."

USSR Offers A-Arms Priority. A Soviet offer to revise the order of disarmament proposed by the Khrushchev plan and to give priority to control & limitation of nuclear weapons was made by Zorin Mar. 21.

Zorin reportedly said conventional disarmament had been given priority in the Khrushchev plan because the Western powers, at the last East-West disarmament conference (in 1957), had demanded prior conventional arms limitation to protect themselves from the USSR's mass ground forces. He reportedly offered to place nuclear disarmament ahead of conventional arms control if the West preferred. Zorin's proposal was outlined to newsmen by Aleksei A. Roshchin, his chief Geneva aide.

Zorin said Mar. 21 that the USSR objected to the West's 3-stage disarmament plan because: (1) the 2d-stage reduction of U.S. & Soviet armed forces to 2,100,000 men was less comprehensive than the West's 1957 proposals for cutting U.S. & Soviet forces to 1,700,000 men; (2) participating states would not be prevented explicitly from withdrawing their arms from the disarmament depots established on their own territories; (3) no specific time limit was placed on completing any stage of the plan.

A-Delivery, Bases Discussed. A warning that effective nuclear disarmament no longer could be based on sequestration of the actual weapons was voiced Mar. 22 by French delegate Moch. Reiterating French views that nuclear weapons had become so widespread and easily concealed that there could be no effective way to insure that nuclear powers had deprived themselves of all such weapons, Moch called for nuclear disarmament through rigid control & limitation of missiles & other means of delivery of nuclear weapons. He said control & limitation of missiles was verifiable while control of warheads was not.

Replying to repeated Communist demands for early dismantling of the U.S.' network of foreign bases, Eaton told Zorin that U.S. bases had been established only to defend "ourselves & those of our allies who wish to be associated with us and welcome our troops as part of their defenses." "The time may come," he said, "when they need not be employed . . . [and] then there need be no doubt . . . that those forces would be withdrawn."

East's Arms Control Views. Soviet demands for strict but unspecified controls over international disarmament were outlined by Zorin Mar. 23-25.

Zorin said Mar. 23 that the USSR favored "strict" "control & inspection" of compliance with a proposed disarmament pact and of the disarmed world of the future. He cited recent Khrushchev statements to show that the USSR would permit international inspectors to enter its territory to enforce provisions of Khrushchev's plan for "general & complete disarmament" within 4 years. He said, however, that control & inspection must be phased to specific disarmament measures and must not precede them, as the West proposed.

Questioned by Western delegates on the USSR's attitude toward control measures, Zorin Mar. 24 rejected any aerial inspection of Soviet territory prior to attainment of general disarmament. He reiterated Soviet contentions that premature & unwarranted inspection measures would constitute "espionage." Asked by Eaton Mar. 25 to begin immediate negotiation of detailed functions of an international arms control & inspection organization, Zorin demanded that they proceed on the principle of "no controls without disarmament as well as no disarmament without controls."

West's Control Views. Western proposals for an International Disarmament Organization (IDO) to supervise the carrying out of a disarmament pact were outlined to the conference Mar. 28 by Italian delegate Francesco Cavaletti.

Under the Western plan, the IDO, to be directed by a 14-member executive committee composed of the major East-West powers & others chosen by a council of all arms pact signatories, would grow in functions & power as each disarmament step in a pact was implemented. The IDO would be veto-free to "insure that no member can thwart the inspection & control provisions" of the treaty.

Initial IDO functions would include (a) amassing of information on satellite & missile launchings; (b) a census of armed forces & military budgets; (c) testing of procedures for reduction of arms & manpower; (d) creation of systems to end nuclear weapons production & verify the transfer of fission material from military to peaceful use; (e) creation of machinery to prevent surprise attacks.

USSR Eases on 4-Year Limit. Soviet delegation spokesmen indicated Mar. 30 that the USSR was prepared to discuss extension of its 4-year time limit for total world disarmament.

The Soviet concession came after Ormsby-Gore of Britain & Moch of France had attacked the 4-year limit Mar. 29 as unrealistic. Ormsby-Gore, asserting that the West's plan could be implemented faster, noted that the Soviet program called for a world disarmament conference that might last a year before accomplishment of any disarmament. Moch said the Soviet plan was "a wish, but not a real program."

The Soviet delegation statement, made outside the conference, said that "if the West proposes other time limits, we would be ready to consider them." It warned, however, that the 4-year limit would have to be re-

placed by some other "strict" deadline to prevent the delay of disarmament "indefinitely."

Space Plea Renewed by West. Appeals for immediate negotiation of a ban on orbiting nuclear weapons were reiterated by Western delegates Apr. 1 but were rejected by Soviet negotiators.

Western delegates asserted that a force of 30 international inspectors could observe operations effectively at the few U.S. & Soviet sites capable of satellite launchings and prevent the arming of space vehicles with nuclear weapons.

Zorin refused Apr. 4 to commit the USSR to a pact controlling space weapons unless the U.S. agreed to accept an agreement liquidating its foreign military bases. Zorin said the West was attempting to hobble Soviet military power by wiping out its claimed lead in missile weaponry but leaving untouched the vast Western system of foreign bases.

Khrushchev Plan Rejected. The Khrushchev plan for total disarmament was rejected Apr. 5 by Western delegates led by Moch of France.

Moch told the Soviet bloc that its total disarmament scheme "does not offer a basis of acceptable compromise" on disarmament "even with amendments that fail to modify its substance." Rejecting proposals for disarmament before inspection within a 4-year period, Moch made it clear that the West would not negotiate on the basis of the Soviet plan and awaited specific Eastern suggestions for gradual & verified disarmament. Moch also rejected "partial measures" proposed by Khruschev in his 1959 UN speech as "tactical shifts" designed to wreck the NATO military system.

Eaton warned that, if carried out, the Soviet plan for total disarmament would result in "anarchy." He asserted that "a world without an international police force in operation at the end of a general process of disarmament could easily result in the enslavement of small nations by their larger neighbors."

East Offers 'Principles.' Zorin suggested Apr. 7 that both sides put aside their conflicting disarmament plans and approach the problem anew on the basis of the principles of the 1959

UN General Assembly resolution on disarmament.

Zorin prefaced his suggestion with a formal rejection of the West's plan for graduated disarmament. He then proposed that since both plans had been turned down, a fresh approach could be made through negotiation on the basis of Western & Soviet statements of principles for an acceptable disarmament accord.

A Soviet statement of "5 basic principles" for a disarmament agreement was presented Apr. 8 and immediately rejected by the Western delegations as the Khrushchev plan in a new form. The Soviet statement contained all major provisions of the Khrushchev plan and an additional section calling on all signatories to renounce first use of nuclear weapons in the event of war.

THE SOVIET PROPOSAL

(Text of the Soviet bloc's 5 basic principles for general disarmament, with minor deletions)

"The . . . states participating in the 10-nation Committee on Disarmament, being guided by the resolution 'On General & Complete Disarmament' of the . . . UN General Assembly of Nov. 20, 1959, accept as an urgent practical task the implementation of general & complete disarmament of all states on the basis of the following principles, in conformity with which a treaty on general & complete disarmament should be worked out:

"(1) General & complete disarmament includes the disbandment of all armed forces, the liquidation of all armaments, the cessation of all kinds of military production, the liquidation of all alien bases on foreign territories, the withdrawal from these territories of foreign troops & their disbandment, the prohibition of nuclear, chemical, bacteriological & rocket weapons, the cessation of production of such weapons & the destruction of their stockpiles, the abolition of organs & institutions designed for organizing military activities in states (general staffs, war ministries & their local organs), the prohibition of military training, the liquidation of military training establishments & the discontinuance of the appropriation of funds for military purposes.

"(2) General & complete disarmament is carried out according to an agreed sequence by stages & is completed within a strictly defined time limit—within 4 years.

"(3) The implementation of all measures . . . [for] general & complete disarmament is carried out under international control whose scope should correspond to the scope & nature of disarmament measures implemented at each stage. For the organization of control & inspection over disarmament, an international control organ is set up, with the participation of all states, which functions . . . [under] the treaty on disarmament.

"(4) After the implementation of the program of general & complete disarmament, states shall retain at their disposal only strictly limited contingents of police (militia) agreed for each country & equipped with small firearms & designed exclusively for the maintenance of internal order & the protection of the personal security of citizens.

"(5) "The implementation by states of the program of general & complete disarmament cannot be interrupted or made dependent on the fulfilment of any conditions . . . not provided for by the treaty.

"In case of attempts . . . to violate the treaty on general & complete disarmament, the question of such a violation shall be submitted for immediate consideration by the Security Council & the UN General Assembly for taking measures against the violator.

"The . . . participating . . . [states] express their confidence that . . . general & complete disarmament, in accordance with the outlined principles, will forever remove the threat of war and will insure to mankind durable peace.

"As an act of goodwill for the purpose of creating appropriate conditions for an early conclusion of a treaty on general & complete disarmament, the participants in the . . . committee that possess nuclear weapons solemnly declare that they renounce that they will be the first to use such weapons."

French A-Weapon Warning. French delegate Moch warned the conference Apr. 13 that it would have to achieve "nuclear disarmament, combined with conventional disarmament," or risk "peace & civilization."

Moch, pressing French proposals for control of nuclear weapons by elimination of missiles & other means of delivery to a target, asserted: "We are afraid that if we delay too long, the 4 nuclear powers, whose maturity removes all risk of universal annihilation, will be joined in the near future by other nations which will not be elements of peace & stability." Moch said France's development of a nuclear bomb without help showed the absurdity of "pseudo-secrets" and proved that "nothing will long enchain Prometheus."

Rejecting an appeal Apr. 13 by Eduard Mejinescu of Rumania for Western acceptance of the proposed renunciation of first use of nuclear weapons, Eaton called the renunciation a "pious statement" that would "deceive the world & expose weaker countries" to aggressors.

West Offers A-Weapons Halt. Western delegates offered Apr. 14 to end production of atomic & hydrogen weapons and to permit international inspection of Western A-bomb plants.

Speaking for the West, U.S. delegate Eaton appealed to the USSR to agree on a verifiable halt in nuclear weapons production as the first step toward nuclear disarmament and an accord on general disarmament. Eaton, rejecting Soviet demands for an unenforcable ban on possession & use of such weapons, said the West saw "nuclear disarmament as . . . a series of actions in which we first must deal with those measures that appear verifiable." Eaton listed the U.S.' major atomic materials plants, challenged the USSR to make public its nuclear factory sites and urged an internationally supervised shut-down of the U.S. & Soviet plants.

Installations listed by Eaton were in Oak Ridge, Tenn; Hanford, Wash.; Aiken, S.C.; Portsmouth, O.; Paducah, Ky. No Soviet list was forthcoming.

Manpower Inspection Asked. A Western plan for creation of mobile international inspection teams to check on compliance with agreements for the reduction of national armed forces was presented to the conference Apr. 21 but was rejected by the USSR.

The Western proposal, introduced by Eaton, provided for mixed U.S.-Soviet inspection teams to begin work immediately after U.S.-Soviet agreement to limit their armed forces to 2½ million men. Inspection would be extended to other countries as they accepted specific manpower ceilings during a 2d-phase reduction of U.S. & Russian forces to 2,100,000. The teams would be based in predetermined military districts of the U.S. & USSR and would carry out "visiting programs" 4 times yearly to verify troop strengths listed for parts of each district. The ground inspection would be supplemented by aerial checks of troop movements and spot checks of warships & crews in their home ports.

The military census plan was rejected by Soviet delegate Zorin the same day on grounds that it would pinpoint deployment of existing armed forces and that it amounted to control without disarmament.

Western Arms 'Principles.' The The West's basic principles & conditions for general disarmament were presented to the conference Apr. 26 by French chief delegate Moch.

The Western principles:

● Disarmament measures must be formulated "progressively," beginning with the least difficult, and be applied in stages without a time limit.

● Conventional & nuclear disarmament must be interrelated & balanced so that neither East nor West would be given military superiority.

● Disarmament must be supervised by an international agency linked with the UN and must provide for an international force to keep peace.

● An arms pact must provide for preservation of outer space for peaceful purposes and for elimination of mass destruction weapons.

The Western principles immediately were rejected by Zorin as "disappointing" and unrelated to the problem of total disarmament.

Adjournment. The conferees recessed Apr. 29 until June 7 after failing to agree on a communiqué summarizing the conference's 32 sessions. The adjournment was intended to permit consideration of the disarmament problem at the Paris summit meeting.

USSR Offers Revised Plan. A revised plan for "general & complete disarmament" containing inspection & control measures demanded by the West was offered to the world June 2 by the Soviet government.

Transmitted to the U.S., Britain, & France and to UN Secy. Gen. Hammarskjöld June 2 for circulation to the 82 UN member states, the proposal was submitted formally to the 10-Nation Committee on Disarmament June 7 when it reconvened in Geneva.

The proposal, an amended version of Premier Khrushchev's total disarmament plan presented to the UN Sept. 18, 1959, was accompanied by a draft of "basic clauses" for a treaty embodying its features.

The 3-stage Soviet plan called for:

● An international control organization, within the framework of the UN, to begin work on a treaty and to supervise each stage of disarmament. The control organization would be ruled by a control council made up of representatives of participating Western, Soviet & other states. Council decisions would be made by a simple majority or ⅔ vote except in "specially provided cases" — which presumably would be subject to veto.

● Supervision of all disarmament measures by ground & aerial inspection. International teams would be stationed in each participating state and would be allowed free access to any area for on-site inspection of compliance with the treaty. The control organization would carry out aerial inspection, but unilateral surveillance flights by aircraft or satellites would be forbidden. On completion of disarmament, peace would be enforced by national contingents under UN Security Council orders.

● A first-stage ban on the production, stockpiling or use of nuclear weapons and destruction of all missiles, strategic aircraft, submarines, cannon & "all means of delivering such weapons." This proposal, originally suggested by France, was coupled with a proposed first-stage liquidation of all foreign military bases & stockpiles. The 2d stage of disarmament would limit the U.S. & Soviet armed forces to 1,700,000 men each and prohibit all other mass destruction weapons. The 3d stage would eliminate all national forces except limited militias.

THE REVISED SOVIET PROPOSAL

(Abridged text of the USSR's "Basic Clauses· of a Treaty on General & Complete Disarmament")

"(1) General & complete disarmament shall provide for: Disbandment of all armed forces maintained by states & the prohibition of their re-establishment in any form; prohibition of stockpiling, destruction of all stockpiles and cessation of production of all types of armaments, including atomic, hydrogen, chemical, biological & other weapons of mass destruction; destruction of all vehicles for the delivery of weapons of mass destruction; elimination of military bases of all kinds . . .; abolition of . . . compulsory military service, . . . of war ministries & general staffs and . . . discontinuance of the appropriation of funds for military purposes . . .; after general & complete disarmament has been achieved, states shall . . . [keep only] strictly limited police (militia) contingents of agreed size for each country, . . . with light infantry weapons . . . [to maintain] internal order. . . .

"(2) General & complete disarmament shall be carried out by all states simultaneously over an agreed & strictly defined period of time; the process of disarmament shall proceed gradually in 3 successive stages, in such a manner that no state shall at any stage obtain military advantages. . . .

"(3) All disarmament measures . . . shall be carried out under strict & effective international control, as follows: (a) Immediately after the signing of the treaty there shall be set up a preparatory commission . . . [to establish] an international organization [to control] . . . disarmament. (b) The control organization shall be established within the [UN's] framework. . . . It shall consist of all states parties to the treaty, whose representatives . . . shall elect a control council composed of . . . the socialist countries, . . . states at present members of the Western . . . alliances, & . . . neutral states. Except in specially provided cases, decisions of the control council on questions of substance shall be taken by a ⅔ majority, and decisions on questions of procedure by simple majority. (c) The control council shall be responsible for the practical direction of the control system. . . . (d) The control organization shall have its staff in all countries parties to the agreement, such staff being recruited on an international basis with due regard to the principle of equitable geographical distribution.

. . . Each party to the treaty shall be required to allow the control officers & inspection teams in their territories prompt & free access to any place where disarmament measures subject to control are being carried out or . . . in which on-the-spot inspection of such measures is to take place. . . . (e) The staff . . . shall enjoy . . . immunities as are necessary for . . . unimpeded control of the execution of the disarmament agreement. (f) . . . The control organization shall at each stage have powers commensurate with the scale & nature of the disarmament measures.

"The basic disarmament measures shall be spread over the 3 stages . . . as follows:

"**FIRST STAGE:** 1. Nuclear weapons shall be eliminated from the arsenals of states, their manufacture shall be discontinued and all means of delivering such weapons shall be destroyed, including: strategic & operational-tactical rockets, self-propelled missiles of all types, all military aircraft capable of delivering nuclear weapons; surface warships capable of being used to carry nuclear weapons; submarines of all classes & types; all artillery systems & other means which may be used as carriers of atomic or hydrogen weapons.

"2. All foreign troops shall be withdrawn from the territories of other states to within their own national boundaries. Foreign military bases & stores of all kinds . . . shall be eliminated.

"3. . . . The launching into orbit or the placing in outer space of special devices, the penetration of warships beyond the limits of territorial waters and the flight beyond the limits of their national territory of military aircraft capable of carrying weapons of mass destruction shall be prohibited.

"4. Rockets shall be launched exclusively for peaceful purposes . . . subject to agreed verification measures, including on-the-spot inspection of the launching sites. . . .

"5. States possessing nuclear weapons shall undertake not to transmit such weapons or information necessary for their manufacture to states which do not possess such weapons . . .

"6. States shall correspondingly reduce their expenditures for military purposes.

"7. . . . International on-the-spot control shall be established over the destruction of missiles, military aircraft, surface warships, submarines & other devices which may be used to carry atomic & hydrogen weapons.

"International inspection teams shall be sent to . . . supervise the abolition of . . . [foreign] bases and the withdrawal of troops and military personnel to within their own national frontiers; control shall also be established at airports & harbors. . . . Under the supervision of the international control organization, missile-launching installations shall be destroyed, with the exception of those retained for . . . peaceful purposes.

"The control organization shall have the right freely to inspect all undertakings, plants, factories & dockyards . . . in order to prevent the organization of clandestine manufacture of armaments which could be used as carriers of atomic & hydrogen weapons. . . .

"The . . . teams . . . shall have the right to make a complete inspection of rocket devices to be launched for peaceful purposes and to be present at their launching. . . .

"8. . . . A joint study shall be made of measures . . . [to end] the production of nuclear, chemical & biological weapons. . . .

"9. The first stage shall be completed in approximately one year to 18 months. . . .

"**SECOND STAGE:** 1. Complete prohibition of nuclear, chemical, biological & other weapons of mass destruction, and also cessation of the production & destruction of all stockpiles of [such] weapons. . . .

"2. Reduction of the armed forces of all states to agreed levels, the armed forces of the . . . [U.S. & USSR] to not more than 1,700,000 men. The conventional weapons & ammunition thus released shall be destroyed, and the military equipment destroyed or used for peaceful uses. . . .

"3. . . . . Representatives . . . shall verify on the spot the destruction of all . . . nuclear, chemical & biological weapons. The control organization shall have the right to inspect all undertakings which extract atomic raw materials or which produce or use atomic materials or atomic energy. . . .

"International on-the-spot control shall be effected over the disbanding of troops & the destruction of armaments.

"The duties of control officers shall include: supervision of the . . . disbanding of military units & formations, and the removal & destruction of a substantial proportion of conventional armaments, military equipment & ammunition. . . .

"The control organization shall have free access to all material relating to the budgetary allocations of states for military purposes. . . .

"4. . . . . A joint study shall be undertaken of . . . measures . . . to be carried out during the 3d stage. . . .

"5. . . . The international control organization shall ascertain [& report on] to what extent the 2d-stage measures have been carried out. . . .

"**THIRD STAGE:** 1. The completion of the disbandment of the armed forces of all states. States shall retain at their disposal only strictly limited contingents of police (militia), the size of which shall be agreed upon for each country and which shall be equipped with small arms and be used for the maintenance of internal order & the protection of the personal security of citizens.

"2. All remaining types of conventional armaments & ammunition, . . . shall be destroyed or used for peaceful purposes.

"3. Military production shall be wound up at all factories . . . with the exception of a strictly limited output of small arms . . . [for] police (militia). . . .

"4. War ministries, general staffs & all military & paramilitary establishments & organizations shall be abolished. . . . States shall enact legislation prohibiting the military education of young people & abolishing military service in all its forms.

"5. The appropriation of funds for military purposes in any form . . . shall be discontinued. . . . [These] funds . . . shall be used to reduce or abolish taxation . . . to subsidize national economies & to [aid] . . . under-developed countries.

"6. . . . The international control organization shall send control officers to verify on the spot the abolition of war ministries, general staffs & all military & paramilitary establishments . . . [and] discontinuance of the appropriation of funds for military purposes.

"The control organization may, as necessary, institute a system of aerial observation & aerial photography over the territories of states.

"7. After completion of the program of general & complete disarmament, the control organization . . . shall exercise permanent surveillance over the fulfillment by states of the obligations they have assumed. The control council shall have the right to send mobile inspection teams to any point . . . in the territories of states.

"States shall communicate to the control organization particulars of the points at which contingents of police (militia) are stationed . . . and all transfers of large contingents of police (militia) near the state frontiers. . . .

"8. The further measures worked out to insure compliance . . . shall take effect.

"9. . . . States shall undertake to place at the disposal of the Security Council as necessary formations from [their] . . . police (militia). . . ."

UN ASKS RENEWED TALKS. The UN Security Council May 27 approved by 9-0 vote (Poland & the USSR abstaining) a resolution calling on the U.S., Britain, France & USSR to resume negotiations on "general and complete disarmament under effective international control," on the discontinuance of all nuclear weapons tests under an . . . international control system," and on "measures to prevent surprise attack."

The resolution was submitted May 23 by Argentina, Ceylon, Ecuador & Tunisia. It was opposed by Soviet Foreign Min. Andrei A. Gromyko, who said at a UN news conference May 28 that the USSR would not accept "open sky" surveillance because "a country which is not preparing for an aggressive war does not need information on . . . other countries." U.S. Amb.-to-UN Henry Cabot Lodge Jr. replied May 28 that "it is the country that will never attack that would like to know when the attack is coming."

Soviet Plan Attacked. The USSR's revised draft disarmament treaty was submitted to the 10-nation committee when it resumed meetings in Geneva June 7 after the collapse of the East-West summit meeting. It was presented by chief Soviet delegate Zorin in an address in which he lauded provisions for simultaneous abolition of foreign bases & means for delivering nuclear weapons on grounds that such bases primarily were intended to bring nuclear weapons "nearer to the frontiers of Socialist states."

U.S. chief delegate Eaton, who had welcomed the Soviet draft June 10 for its "hopeful signs of positive movement" toward the West's disarmament position, launched the Western attack on the Soviet plan June 15.

Concentrating on the Soviet draft's provision for liquidation of foreign military bases and elimination of military missiles & other means for the delivery of nuclear weapons in the first stage of disarmament, Eaton said: "Even if total . . . [U.S.] & Soviet force levels were . . . about the same, the immediate withdrawal of

[U.S.] . . . forces from Europe would unbalance the military situation in favor of the Soviet Union. With all aircraft & ships capable of carrying nuclear weapons also eliminated, . . . the return of . . . [U.S.] forces to Europe would not be feasible and the smaller nations of Europe would be at the mercy of their larger Eastern neighbor."

USSR Quits Arms Talks

Geneva Sessions Suspended. Negotiations of the Geneva committee were suspended June 27 when Soviet Deputy Foreign Min. Zorin led the 5 Communist delegations in a walkout from the conference.

Zorin told newsmen that the conference was "finished" and no longer would be attended by the USSR. He formally announced the Soviet government's withdrawal from the committee's meetings later the same day.

The Soviet walkout, concerted in advance with other Communist delegates, came minutes after Eaton told Zorin that a revised Western disarmament plan would be presented to the conference within a few days.

In a statement read to the conference immediately after the opening of its 47th session, Zorin informed the Western delegations that the USSR was withdrawing from the talks because the West had refused to negotiate seriously on the revised Soviet plan for total world disarmament. He charged the Western delegations with using the Geneva talks "as a smoke-screen to camouflage the armament race launched by the West" and with seeking arms "control without disarmament."

The meeting ended in confusion when the day's chairman, Marian Naszkowski of Poland, declared the committee's work "discontinued" after the last Communist delegate had spoken. British delegate Ormsby-Gore assumed the chairmanship when the Communist delegates had left the conference room. Declaring the committee still in session, he opened the meeting to the press to hear denunciations of the Soviet walkout by Eaton & Jules Moch of France. The Western delegates reconvened the committee June 28, but adjourned when the Soviet bloc representatives failed to appear.

New U.S. Arms Plan. A revised U.S. proposal for phased general disarmament under international supervision was submitted to the conference by Eaton June 27 after the Communist nations had withdrawn.

The proposal tabled by Eaton contained a draft of disarmament principles & outlined provisions for a 3-stage disarmament treaty in which emphasis was placed on measures against surprise attack and on destruction of missiles & other vehicles for nuclear weapons delivery, strict supervision of each phase of disarmament, and enforcement of the post-disarmament peace by an international force controlled by the UN. The plan contained a detailed timetable under which a treaty embodying first-stage disarmament provisions would be negotiated by the 10-nation committee but a treaty containing 2d- & 3d-stage provisions would be submitted to a world arms conference.

THE REVISED U.S. PROPOSAL

(Abridged text of the revised U.S. plan for controlled general disarmament in 3 stages)

"**INTRODUCTION:** The ultimate goal is a secure & peaceful world of free & open societies in which there shall be general & complete disarmament under effective international control and agreed procedures for the settlement of disputes in accordance with the principles of the United Nations Charter.

"General & complete disarmament in a secure, free & peaceful world requires:

"1. The disbanding through progressive stages, of all armed forces of all states and the prohibition of their re-establishment in any form whatsoever, except for those contingents of agreed size required for the purpose of maintaining internal order & insuring the personal security of citizens and for agreed contingents for the international peace force.

"2. The cessation of the production of all kinds of armaments, including all means for delivering weapons of mass destruction, and their complete elimination from national arsenals, through progressive stages, except for those armaments agreed upon for use by an international peace force and agreed remaining national contingents.

"3. Strict & effective international control, from beginning to end, of the carrying out of all disarmament measures, to insure that there are no violations.

"4. The establishment of effective means for enforcement of international agreements and for the maintenance of peace.

"**CONTROLLING PRINCIPLES:** 1. Disarmament under effective international control shall be carried out in such a manner that at no time shall any state, whether or not a party to a treaty, obtain military advantage over other states as a result of the progress of disarmament.

"2. General & complete disarmament shall proceed through three stages containing balanced, phased & safeguarded measures with each measure being carried out in an agreed and strictly defined period of time, under the supervision of an

International Disarmament Control Organization, within the framework of the United Nations.

"3. Each measure within each stage shall be initiated simultaneously by all participating states upon completion of the necessary preparatory studies and upon establishment of the arrangements and procedures necessary for the International Disarmament Control Organization to verify the measure on an initial & continuing basis.

"4. Transition from one stage to the next shall be initiated when the Security Council of the United Nations agrees that all measures in the preceding stages have been fully implemented. . . .

"5. The treaties shall remain in force indefinitely subject to the inherent right of a party to withdraw and be relieved of obligations thereunder if the provisions of the treaty . . . are not fulfilled and observed.

"6. The International Disarmament Control Organization shall comprise all participating states whose representatives shall meet as a conference periodically as required. There shall in addition be a control commission and a director general. . . .

"7. The specific arrangements, procedures and means required for effective . . . verification of satisfactory performance of each measure by the International Disarmament Control Organization shall be specified in the treaties. These shall provide for all necessary means required for effective verification of compliance with each step of each measure. . . .

"**TASK OF THE 10-NATION COMMITTEE ON DISARMAMENT:** The task of the 10-nation committee on disarmament is to work out a treaty for general & complete disarmament under effective international control governed by the foregoing controlling principles as follows:

"1. Negotiate & agree upon a treaty . . . embodying the first stage of the program. This stage shall consist of those initial and controllable measures which can & shall be undertaken without delay by the states participating in the committee. . . .

"2. In the course of negotiating such a treaty, arrange for & conduct the necessary technical studies to work out effective control arrangements for measures to be carried out in the program. . . .

"3. After reaching agreement on a treaty on the first stage of the program, prepare for submission to a world disarmament conference an agreed draft treaty on the second and third stages of the program as set forth below. . . .

"4. Thereupon, arrange for a world-wide conference of all states . . . [for] (a) Accession to the treaty covering Stage I by states which have not already done so: (b) Accession to the treaty covering Stages II & III by all states.

"**STAGE I:** 1. An international disarmament control organization shall be established within the framework of the United Nations, and expanded as required by the progressive implementation of general & complete disarmament.

"2. The placing into orbit or stationing in outer space of vehicles carrying weapons capable of mass destruction shall be prohibited.

"3. To give greater protection against surprise attack, (a) prior notification to an International Disarmament Control Organization of all proposed launchings of space vehicles and missiles and their planned tracks; (b) the establishment of a zone of aerial & ground inspection in agreed areas including the U.S. & USSR; (c) exchange of observers on a reciprocal basis at agreed military bases, domestic & foreign.

"4. Declaration of and institution of on-site inspection at mutually agreed operational air bases, missile launching pads, submarine & naval bases in order to establish a basis for controls over nuclear delivery systems in subsequent stages.

"5. Initial force level ceilings shall be established as follows: 2,500,000 for the U.S. & the USSR and agreed appropriate force levels for certain other states. After the accession to the treaty of other militarily significant states . . . force levels of 2,100,000 shall be established for the U.S. & the USSR and agreed . . . levels . . . for other militarily significant states.

"6. Agreed types and quantities of armaments . . . shall be placed in storage depots by participating states within their own territories, under supervision by the International Disarmament Control Organization pending their final destruction or conversion to peaceful uses.

"7. The production of fissionable materials for use in weapons shall be stopped upon installation and effective operation of the control system found necessary to verify this step by prior technical study, and agreed quantities of fissionable materials from past production shall be transferred . . . to non-weapons uses. . . .

"8. The submission by the various states to the International Disarmament Control Organization of data relating to: The operation of their financial system as it affects military expenditures, the amount of their military expenditures, and the percentage of their gross national product earmarked for military expenditures. . . .

"**STAGE II:** 1. Force levels shall be further reduced to 1,700,000 for the U.S. & USSR and ro agreed appropriate levels for other states.

"2. Quantities of all kinds of armaments of each state, including nuclear, chemical, biological & other weapons of mass destruction . . . and all means for their delivery shall be reduced to agreed levels. . . . Agreed categories of missiles, aircraft, surface ships, submarines & artillery designed to deliver nuclear & other weapons of mass destruction shall be included in this measure.

"3. Expenditures for military purposes shall be reduced in amounts bearing a relation to the agreed reductions in armed forces and armaments.

"4. An international peace force, within the United Nations, shall be progressively established and maintained with agreed personnel strength & armaments sufficient to preserve world peace when general & complete disarmament is achieved.

"**STAGE III:** 1. Forces & military establishments of all states shall be finally reduced to those levels required for the purpose of maintaining internal order and insuring the personal security of citizens and of providing agreed contingents of forces to the international peace force.

"2. The international peace force & remaining agreed contingents of national armed forces shall be armed only with agreed types & quantities cf armaments. All other remaining armaments, including weapons of mass destruction & vehicles for their delivery & conventional armaments shall be destroyed or converted to peaceful uses.

"3. Expenditures for military purposes by all states shall be further reduced. . . .

"4. There shall be no manufacture of any armaments except for agreed types & quantities for use by the international peace force & agreed remaining national contingents. . . ."

USSR Asks UN Arms Action. A memorandum from Soviet Foreign Min. Gromyko to UN Secy. Gen. Hammarskjöld asked June 27 that the disarmament question be placed on the agenda of the UN General Assembly session beginning in September. The memorandum, delivered by Soviet Rep.-to-UN Arkady A. Sobolev, reiterated charges that the 10-nation Disarmament Committee's work had been sabotaged by the Western powers' "endless procrastination" in negotiations on the USSR's disarmament proposal. It noted, as an indication of Soviet readiness to compromise, that the revised Soviet arms plan had "unreservedly accepted France's view that the means of delivering nuclear weapons should be prohibited & destroyed first."

Notes from Soviet Premier Krushchev to Pres. Eisenhower, Prime Min. Macmillan, Pres. de Gaulle, Canadian Prime Min. Diefenbaker & Italian Premier Tambroni charged June 27 that all Western participants in the Geneva talks bore responsibility for the deadlock but that the U.S "above all" had caused the breakdown in negotiations.

West Urges Renewed Talks. In a series of replies June 29-July 2 to Khrushchev's charges that the West had caused the breakdown of the Geneva negotiations, the U.S., Britain & France rejected Khrushchev's allegations and called on the USSR to resume participation in meetings of the 10-nation committee.

The U.S. note was delivered in Moscow July 2 as a government communication rather than as a personal reply by Pres. Eisenhower to Khrushchev. It suggested that the USSR consider continuing "the task of serious negotiation" on disarmament. It rejected as "wholly inaccurate the Soviet version of events within the 10-nation Disarmament Committee" and questioned the USSR's "true motivation in torpedoing the conference." It charged that the USSR had quit the Geneva talks in the knowledge that the U.S. was about to submit a revised disarmament plan incorporating several Soviet proposals.

A note from French Pres. de Gaulle to Khrushchev July 2 denied that the Soviet plan for the destroying of missiles & other means of delivering nuclear weapons was a reasonable variation of the French plan for "control" of such "vehicles." He said that it had "already become difficult . . . to control the total elimination of nuclear charges & bombs. . . . Furthermore, to destroy all the rockets & all the airplanes and prevent construction of others would appear to be . . . inapplicable in our century, which

is essentially that of airplanes, rockets & . . . satellites."

British Prime Min. Macmillan told Khrushchev in a note June 29 that the USSR's walkout from the Geneva talks immediately before submission of the U.S.' revised arms plan was "incomprehensible" and an indication that "you did not want to know what we were going to propose."

UN Secy. Gen. Hammarskjöld urged the Western powers June 30 to allow "the dust to settle" before trying to re-start the East-West disarmament negotiations through the UN. Commenting on U.S. delegation efforts to revive the discussion in the UN Disarmament Commission—composed of all 82 UN member states—Hammarskjöld warned that an over-hasty commission meeting would risk "getting stuck in the rehashing" of old talks.

Khrushchev Bars New Talks. Western plans for resumption of the disarament talks were rejected by Khrushchev in letters delivered to Macmillan, de Gaulle & Canadian Prime Min. Diefenbaker July 23 & made public July 25. A similar rejection was delivered to the U.S. Embassy in Moscow July 25 (published July 27). All of the Soviet replies charged that the U.S. disarmament plan tabled on the day of the Soviet walkout was insincere, contained no specific timetable for accomplishment and was designed to give the West a military advantage over the USSR.

UN Commission Called. The 82-nation UN Disarmament Commission was summoned to meet at UN headquarters in New York Aug. 16 despite Soviet efforts to block the meeting and return the disarmament problem to the UN General Assembly.

The commission was summoned Aug. 9 by Secy. Gen. Dag Hammarskjöld at the request of its chairman, Luis Padilla Nervo, after a majority of the commission's members had agreed to a U.S. request July 22 that it meet to discuss the failure of the Geneva arms talks. Soviet UN delegates, led by First Deputy Foreign Min. Vasily V. Kuznetsov, had carried out a lobbying campaign against the commission meeting and had warned neutralist nations that the Soviet bloc might boycott its sessions.

Commission for New Talks. The commission met Aug. 16-18 and voted to urge the "earliest possible continuation" of the big-power talks on "general and complete disarmament under effective international control."

The appeal was contained in a resolution introduced by Ecuador, India, Mexico, Sweden, the UAR & Yugoslavia and approved by a show of hands at the end of the commission's 3-day meeting. The resolution reaffirmed the UN's "ultimate responsibility . . . in the field of disarmament" and recommended that the problem be placed on the General Assembly's agenda.

At the commission's opening session Aug. 16, U.S. Amb.-to-UN Lodge suggested that negotiations resume on the basis of these new U.S. proposals for reducing world nuclear arsenals:

● The transfer, "on a reciprocal basis," of 30,000 kg. (66,000 lb.) of "weapons grade U-235" from each nation's "existing weapons stocks to peaceful purposes" under international control.

● The "shutdown, one by one, under international inspection, [of] our major plants producing enriched uranium & plutonium, if the Soviet Union will shut down equivalent facilities."

Lodge told the commission that the use of 30,000 kg. of U-235 in "modern nuclear weapons would generate an explosive force well over 1,000 times greater than that of all the high explosive bombs dropped by all the warring powers during World War II." He said that "the transfer of that amount to peaceful uses by the United States, and an equal amount by the Soviet Union, would mean an immediate & sizable reduction in the nuclear threat" and "would be a real & a practical measure of disarmament." Lodge offered the plan for reciprocal closure of nuclear factories as an alternative if the proposal for transfer of fission stocks was not acceptable to the USSR.

Both U.S. proposals were rejected Aug. 16 by Kuznetsov. He asserted that the withdrawal of even so huge an amount of U-235 from weapons use would leave tremendous nuclear weapons potential in the hands of the U.S. & USSR.

The Drive to Ban Tests

No man-made nuclear explosions were known to have taken place since Nov. 3, 1958, when the Soviet Union ended its test program with a low-yield atomic explosion in the southern USSR.

The 3 powers had voluntarily—and unilaterally—renounced nuclear tests in connection with the Geneva conference on a treaty to ban tests, which was convened Oct. 31, 1958. Major steps that led to the moratorium on atomic tests:

● *The USSR announced an indefinite suspension of its nuclear tests Mar. 31, 1958 and called on the U.S. and Britain to match its action. The Soviet declaration was reiterated in notes sent by Soviet Premier Nikita S. Khrushchev to U.S. Pres. Dwight D. Eisenhower and British Prime Min. Harold Macmillan Apr. 4, 1958, but it was rejected by Mr. Eisenhower in a reply Apr. 8, 1958.*

● *The U.S. and British proposed Aug. 22, 1958 that tests be suspended for a one-year period during which negotiations would be started on a treaty to ban weapons tests. The proposal, made in notes to Khrushchev from Mr. Eisenhower and Macmillan, was rejected on the ground that a one-year suspension was insufficient.*

● *The U.S. and Britain ended their nuclear test programs Oct. 31, 1958, coincidentally with the Geneva talks. They pledged not to resume tests for one year unless the USSR did so. The Soviet Union, which had resumed testing Sept. 30, 1958, halted its series Nov. 3, 1958. Pres. Eisenhower warned Nov. 7 that the U.S. would "reconsider" its suspension if the USSR continued tests.*

● *The Western test suspension was extended to Dec. 11, 1959 in announcements made by the U.S. Aug. 26 and Britain Aug. 27, 1959. But the U.S. moratorium was ended by Pres. Eisenhower Dec. 29, 1959 in a statement that said the U.S. would observe a "voluntary suspension" of tests as long as the Geneva talks showed progress.*

● *The Soviet test suspension was continued despite the U.S. announcement. Khrushchev, in an interview granted Dec. 30, 1959 and broadcast Jan. 3*

1960 by Moscow radio, declared that the USSR "has already suspended all tests of hydrogen and atomic weapons" and would conduct no more "unless the Western powers do so."

Khrushchev Doubts Cheating. Khrushchev declared Jan. 14 that an agreement to halt all nuclear weapons tests was feasible despite Western fears that it could be violated by the carrying out of clandestine underground tests.

Addressing the USSR Supreme Soviet (Parliament) in Moscow, Khrushchev asserted that any nation daring to violate the pact would be condemned by the world. He said: The U.S. held "that underground blasts can be camouflaged so as to defy detection by any instruments. . . . But even if today we do not have guarantees that all explosions will be recorded accurately & completely, the conclusion of an agreement to end tests would place great responsibility on the parties to it. And it goes without saying that they all will have to abide strictly by it. If some side violates the assumed commitments . . . [they] will cover themselves with shame."

U.S. Ready for Tests. The U.S. Atomic Energy Commission reported Jan. 30 that its Nevada test grounds had been in "stand-by-readiness" to resume nuclear tests ever since the cessation Dec. 31, 1959 of the U.S.' test moratorium.

The AEC, in its annual report to Congress, said that during 1959 "emphasis continued on research & development activities designed to improve & increase the [U.S.] arsenal of nuclear weapons." It reported that: special attention had been given to the development of small nuclear weapons; 37 nuclear submarines & 3 nuclear surface vessels were in use, under construction or authorized; U.S. uranium production had increased by 30% during 1959.

Geneva Talks Resumed. U.S., British & Soviet delegates reopened in Geneva Jan. 12 the 14-month-old conference on a treaty to discontinue nuclear weapons tests. Chief representatives of the 3 powers: James J. Wadsworth (U.S.), Sir Michael Wright (Britain), Semyon K. Tsarapkin (USSR).

Opening statements by the 3 delegations made it clear that no partici-

pating power had moderated its position contributing to the deadlock in which the conference recessed Dec. 19, 1959. Tsarapkin insisted that the USSR still favored the signing of a test-ban treaty as quickly as possible with further study later of the problem of detecting small underground nuclear detonations. Wadsworth stressed that the U.S. would not sign a test-ban treaty until the problems of underground test detection and treaty enforcement & safeguards had been dealt with effectively.

Closed conference sessions were begun following the opening session.

Detection Dispute. Detonations of conventional explosives in an abandoned Winnfield, La. salt mine indicated that small nuclear weapons tests could be muffled underground, U.S. AEC officials reported Feb. 4 at Senate Disarmament Subcommittee hearings. They reported that the tests had shown that seismic effects of such detonations were reduced by as much as 150 times. Dr. James B. Fisk, delegate to 1958 Geneva nuclear test detection talks, said in the hearings that Soviet scientists approached the "brink of absurdity" when they insisted that nearly all underground tests could be detected & identified.

Dr. Edward Teller, University of California physicist who played a major scientific role in U.S. development of the H-bomb, told a Fordham College alumni meeting in New York Jan. 26 that "we can agree to stop testing in the atmosphere . . . the oceans & in that part of the earth's surface where nuclear explosions can be reliably identified." But he warned that tests in outer space & under special conditions underground could not be detected.

A Pravda article signed by 7 Soviet scientists headed by Prof. Yevgeni K. Federov, chief Soviet scientific adviser at the Geneva talks, charged Feb. 8 that U.S. nuclear test detection data presented to the Geneva conference had been erroneous & distorted. The Soviet scientists asserted that American detection experts had underestimated the magnitudes of U.S. underground tests used to check the detection theories. They said that Soviet experts were convinced they could detect tremors from such tests and "compare [them] with assurance" with natural earthquakes.

U.S. Offers Limited A-Ban. A U.S. offer to join in an East-West treaty banning all controllable & detectable nuclear tests was made public by Pres. Eisenhower Feb. 11 and was presented to the USSR the same day at the 3-power Geneva conference.

A White House statement said that the U.S. plan would:

● Ban "all nuclear weapons tests in the atmosphere . . . in the oceans . . . in those regions in space where effective controls can now be agreed . . . [&] all controllable nuclear weapons tests" underground.

● Permit, "through a joint program of research & experimentation, the ban to be systematically extended to remaining areas underground, where adequate control measures are not now possible to incorporate."

● Allay "worldwide concern over possible increases in levels of [test-caused] radioactivity, since it discontinues all tests which can release radioactivity into the atmosphere."

The U.S. plan specifically would ban "all underground tests above the present limit (or threshold) of detection & identification." It defined banned underground tests as those "which cause seismic magnitude readings of 4.75 or more." As presented in Geneva, the plan contained provisions for up to 40 on-site inspections annually of unidentified seismic events that might be caused by clandestine nuclear tests on Soviet, U.S. or British territory.

Pres. Eisenhower said at a Feb. 11 news conference that the U.S. had faced "the most difficult of all problems in this disarmament thing when we put all our attention on . . . nuclear testing & nuclear use." He described the U.S. proposal as a "good one" which "ought to lead . . . to even a better one."

France detonated its first nuclear device Feb. 13 at a test site near Reggan, deep in the Sahara desert. The French government, in a statement issued Mar. 22 at the 10-nation Geneva disarmament conference, said that it would not join the Geneva nuclear test ban talks because these were an attempt to perpetuate "discrimination

for the benefit of the powers which have already made a sufficient number of [atomic] tests."

Soviet Inspection Plan. The U.S. proposal was rejected by Soviet Geneva delegate Tsarapkin, who proposed instead Feb. 16 a Soviet plan to permit a limited quota of on-site inspections of suspicious seismic events within the USSR.

Tsarapkin, who had labelled the U.S. plan "unacceptable" & a "step backward" Feb. 11, charged the next day that it was part of a Western "conspiracy" to wreck the Geneva negotiations and resume nuclear tests.

The Soviet plan presented by Tsarapkin Feb. 16 was based upon a cessation of all nuclear tests but contained what was considered a major concession—acceptance of on-site inspection of any Soviet seismic event deemed suspicious by Western standards. The Soviet plan would accept the Western detection standards as the basis for inspection for a 2-to-3-year period during which Western & Soviet experts would attempt to establish precise & agreed detection standards. Tsarapkin made clear, however, that the USSR would insist on a relatively small annual quota for such inspections.

Tsarapkin refused Feb. 17 to tell how many on-site inspections the USSR would permit annually on its territory. He said the USSR would discuss the question only after the West had accepted in principle the Soviet proposals for a test ban in conjunction with the inspection quota. He announced Feb. 26 that the USSR would agree to participate in a joint U.S.-British-Soviet research program to improve the detection of underground nuclear tests on condition that the program was carried out with conventional explosives and was preceded by a treaty to ban all tests.

'Ike' Plan Accepted. The USSR offered Mar. 19 to accept Pres. Eisenhower's proposal of a treaty to ban all nuclear tests except small underground ones considered unverifiable by Western scientific standards.

The Soviet offer was conditional on Western acceptance of a joint pledge to explode no nuclear devices for an indefinite period during which the U.S., USSR & Britain would engage in joint research to improve detection of underground tests.

The Soviet proposal was presented at the 188th Geneva test-ban session and was made public by Tsarapkin at a news conference later Mar. 19. It specifically recommended:

● A treaty banning all nuclear tests in the earth's atmosphere, under water, in space & underground, except underground detonations that produced seismographic readings of less than 4.75.*

● A treaty annex requiring a moratorium on all tests, including underground detonations smaller than the 4.75 seismic magnitude, while the 3 powers carried out, with conventional explosives, joint studies on improving detection methods.

Tsarapkin again refused to tell the Western delegations exactly how many annual on-site inspections of unverified seismic events the USSR would permit on its own territory under any test-ban treaty. Tsarapkin stressed Soviet views that an annual quota of on-site inspections would have to be politically determined because scientific detection data showed too much variance to form the basis for determining such inspection needs.

Replying to Western queries on the Soviet proposal, Tsarapkin indicated Mar. 21 that a 4- to 5-year moratorium on small underground tests would allow completion of joint research in improving test detection.

Western Reaction. Statements issued Mar. 19 by the U.S. State Department & British Foreign Office pledged serious study of the Soviet proposal.

The U.S. & Britain announced Mar. 24 that Prime Min. Macmillan would fly to the U.S. to meet with Pres. Eisenhower to discuss the Western reply to the Soviet proposal.

U.S. State Secy. Christian A. Herter said at a Washington news conference Mar. 25 that although the Soviet proposal "recognizes for the first time that we are unwilling to . . . ban . . . explosions which could not be detected & which are conducted underground," it contained these objectionable features: (1) the proposed moratorium on small underground tests evidently would be made part of the treaty & would extend for 4 to 5 years instead

of the one to 2 years reportedly favored by the U.S.; (2) the lack of a clearcut plan for control & inspection of banned tests as well as the "question as to what should be done for those tests below the [4.75 seismic] threshold."

The N.Y. Times reported Mar. 25 that, at a meeting with Herter & CIA Dir. Allen W. Dulles, AEC Chrmn. John A. McCone & Defense Secy. Thomas S. Gates Jr. had opposed acceptance of the Soviet bid or any change in the U.S.' past refusals to ban all nuclear tests.‡

AEC Chrmn. McCone told newsmen Mar. 22 that "we must not . . . in my opinion expose ourselves to a long-range [test] moratorium in areas which cannot be safeguarded." Other U.S. reaction: Chrmn. Clinton P. Anderson (D., N.M.) of the Joint Congressional Atomic Energy Committee denounced the Soviet plan as "a phony" Mar. 22 and urged the U.S. to break off the Geneva talks unless the USSR agreed to negotiate satisfactory test controls; Sen. Hubert H. Humphrey (D., Minn.) said Mar. 23 that the plan offered a basis for a workable agreement banning tests and that the "deadlock can be broken if the Soviet Union were now willing to accept about 20 [on-site] inspections a year . . . & if this country were willing to accept a moratorium on small underground tests"; Dr. Hans Bethe, Cornell University scientist & U.S. adviser on the Geneva talks, asserted Mar. 23 that the Soviet bid contained "major concessions" to the Western powers' previous demands; Sen. Albert Gore (D., Tenn.) charged Mar. 28 that James J. Wadsworth, chief U.S. delegate in the Geneva nu-

---

* Underground nuclear detonations below the 4.75 seismic level, of a force equivalent to the explosion of 19,000 tons of TNT (19 kilotons), were considered by the West to be indistinguishable frequently from normal earth tremors. The Soviet proposal apparently would ban all nuclear detonations in space up to & beyond 175,000 miles, the point at which the West believed such explosions to be unverifiable with current detection techniques.

‡ An AEC announcement made Mar. 16 with the express approval of Pres. Eisenhower disclosed that the U.S. was preparing a 10-kiloton underground nuclear detonation under the Project Plowshare program to determine the feasibility of nuclear blasts for peaceful purposes. The test, if given final approval by Pres. Eisenhower, was to be carried out early in 1961 in a salt bed 25 miles southeast of Carlsbad, N.M.

clear talks, had misled public opinion by permitting a delegation statement to describe the Soviet plan as an acceptance of the U.S.' Feb. 11 proposals without mentioning the USSR's demand for a moratorium on small underground tests.

'Ike'-Macmillan Terms. In a joint statement issued Mar. 29 after 2 days of talks at Camp David, Md., Pres. Eisenhower & British Prime Min. Macmillan offered to accept the Soviet proposal for a limited treaty banning nuclear tests and a moratorium on small underground tests on condition that the USSR accepted in advance the strict inspection & control of treaty provisions and a joint research program on improvement of underground test detection.

The joint statement said that "as soon as this [test-ban] treaty has been signed and arrangements made for a coordinated research program for . . . progressively improving control methods for [verifying] events below a seismic magnitude of 4.75, they [Pres. Eisenhower & Macmillan] will be ready to institute a voluntary moratorium of agreed duration on nuclear weapons tests below the threshold . . . by unilateral declaration of each of the 3 powers."

It declared the "earnest desire" of Britain & the U.S. "to achieve . . . the total prohibition of all nuclear weapons tests, under effective international control." It said that problems to be solved before the signing of a treaty included "an adequate quota of on-site inspections, the composition of the control commission, control post staffing and voting matters, as well as arrangements for peaceful purposes detonations."

The President, meeting newsmen Mar. 30 after the Camp David talks, said the "driving force" behind his effort for a test-ban treaty was the "dangerous . . . spreading of this knowledge" to new nuclear powers.

Mr. Eisenhower said a voluntary U.S. moratorium on small nuclear tests would be a "Presidential action" and "if that period went beyond . . . [his] term of office, I personally think it would have to be reaffirmed by a successor . . . to be effective."

The Eisenhower-Macmillan offer was presented at the Geneva talks Mar. 31.

Test Detection Study Set. Western suggestions that Soviet & Western scientists meet to formulate a joint research program for improving detection of underground nuclear tests were accepted Apr. 14 by the USSR.

The Western proposal was presented in Geneva Apr. 12 by the U.S.' Wadsworth with the support of Britain's Sir Michael Wright. It called for U.S., British & Soviet scientists to begin technical talks in Geneva May 11 to outline a detection research program to be carried out as a condition for a temporary 3-power ban on all nuclear tests, including those the West considered undetectable by current scientific standards.

The scientific meeting would try to decide on (a) the length of the joint research program, a prime factor in fixing the duration of the voluntary moratorium; (b) which specific projects would be carried out jointly and which separately but on a coordinated basis; (c) requirements for the exchange of experts, scientific data & instrumentation affecting the program.

The West's proposal was accepted by Soviet chief delegate Tsarapkin Apr. 14 before the conference began an 11-day recess.

USSR Accepts Joint A-Tests. The USSR May 3 accepted Western proposals for joint underground nuclear detonations as part of an East-West scientific program to improve methods for detecting such tests.

Soviet envoys announced that the USSR "reluctantly" would agree to a "strictly limited number of joint underground nuclear explosions" as part of the research program. Chief delegate Tsarapkin said the detonations should be confined to detection research needs. Rejecting Western suggestions that the tests be carried out nationally under 3-power observation, Tsarapkin demanded that they be conducted "jointly" by Western & Soviet scientists.

U.S. Plans Buried A-Tests. Pres. Eisenhower announced May 7 that the U.S. planned to resume underground nuclear tests as part of an expanded Project Vela program to improve the "capability to detect & identify underground nuclear explosions."

A White House statement said that the Vela program, based on recommendations of the (Dr. Lloyd V.) Berkner panel on seismic improvement, would be allocated $66 million in fiscal 1961 to carry out "an experimental program of underground detonations encompassing . . . high explosive &, where necessary, nuclear explosions." It said that "a series of [nuclear] explosions of various sizes in differing types of geological formations" were planned but that all would be "carried out under fully contained conditions" with "no radioactive fallout." Administration officials stressed that Vela detonations would not be used to test nuclear weapons.

Soviet objections to the resumption of U.S. nuclear tests were made clear at the 3-power Geneva talks May 9.

Mr. Eisenhower told newsmen May 11 that there had been a "misunderstanding" of his announcement that the U.S. planned to expand its Project Vela program for improving nuclear test detection. The President said the proposed detonations would "not have anything to do either with weapons development or the Plowshare project" for the development of peaceful uses of nuclear explosions. Indicating that no nuclear explosions were planned under the expanded Vela program, Mr. Eisenhower said that the U.S. was not currently "involved in any nuclear explosions" except under proposals for cooperative U.S.-British-Soviet detonations to test underground detection techniques.

U.S. 6-Year Plan. A U.S. plan for setting up a nuclear test control-&-inspection system in 3 stages within 6 years after the signing of a treaty was presented to the Geneva conference May 12.

The U.S. plan, based on the detection system approved by the 1958 Geneva conference of nuclear experts, called for completion of a network of 21 control posts in the USSR, 23 in the U.S. & one in Britain during the first stage, ending 3 years after adoption of the treaty. The control system would be extended to cover all of the Northern Hemisphere during the 2d stage and the entire world during the 3d stage, ending 6 years after treaty approval.

The conference recessed for 2 weeks beginning May 12 to permit discussion of the nuclear test problem by the projected Paris summit meeting. The meetings were resumed in Geneva May 27 after the collapse of the Paris talks.

Experts' Report. The panel of U.S., British & Soviet scientists charged with formulating a joint East-West research program for the detection of underground tests reported to the full conference May 31. The report, drawn up after panel meetings begun May 11, disclosed that the U.S. planned to carry out 12 underground nuclear explosions under its Project Vela test detection program. Soviet scientists were said to have objected specifically to 7 of the planned U.S. tests—5 of them intended to check theories that tests could be muffled in large underground chambers and 2 of them of "baby" nuclear devices that the USSR said had military applications.

Technical safeguards to insure that the U.S. was not using the 12 test detonations for purposes of weapons development were offered to the USSR June 2 but were rejected the same day by Tsarapkin, who insisted that Soviet scientific observers be given the right to detailed examination of the devices used in the test series. The U.S. had offered: (1) to use only previously-tested devices; (2) to deposit them under international supervision before the tests; (3) to permit Soviet observers to carry out their own instrumentation of the detonations; (4) to refrain from "diagnostic" instrumentation of the tests necessary for military research.

USSR Vs. Mock A-Blast. A U.S. invitation for Soviet scientific observers to attend an underground nonnuclear explosion designed to explore peaceful uses of nuclear detonations was rejected June 27 by Tsarapkin.

The invitation was extended to Britain & the USSR June 14 by U.S. chief delegate Wadsworth and was accepted by Britain the same day. Tsarapkin rejected the invitation on the ground that the test was not relevant to the Geneva negotiations. He added that since the USSR was planning no such tests, either nuclear or non-nuclear, Western scientists would not be invited to visit Soviet test areas.

U.S. Asks A-Test 'Pool.' The U.S. offered July 12 to join with Britain and the USSR in contributing nuclear test devices to a joint "pool" that would be open to inspection by both sides and would be used for research on seismic detection of underground test explosions.

The U.S. offer was made in order to meet Soviet charges that the U.S.' proposed test program for detection of underground nuclear detonations could be used for perfecting new types of small nuclear weapons. Under the U.S. plan, each of the 3 participating countries would contribute equal numbers of outmoded nuclear devices to the joint pool and would be free to inspect any of the devices. The pool would be placed under international guard, and each of the 3 nations then could withdraw any devices they wished to carry out detection tests under international supervision.

The U.S. proposal was rejected by Tsarapkin July 19 in an address to the World Federation of UN Associations in Geneva. Tsarapkin commented that if the U.S. and Britain deemed it necessary to re-test seismic detection theories, the USSR would be prepared to inspect the nuclear devices used by them. He made clear that the USSR would not permit Western inspection of its devices. The U.S. was notified of the USSR's formal rejection of the plan Aug. 2.

Inspection Quota Accepted. The U.S. announced at the talks July 13 that it accepted plans for a fixed annual quota of on-site inspections of possible clandestine nuclear tests by the U.S., Britain & USSR. It also submitted proposals for determining the quota of on-site inspections (minimum: 2) to be required of later signatories of a test ban pact.

A quota of 3 on-site inspections annually of possible nuclear detonations on the territory of the U.S., Britain & USSR was proposed by Tsarapkin July 26. Tsarapkin said that the quota of 3 inspections would include on-site investigations of seismic tremors both above & below 4.75 seismographic intensity, the lowest level considered detectable with current scientific techniques. He asserted that the U.S.' proposal for a quota of 20 annual on-site inspections for each of the 3 nuclear powers was unrealistic & unacceptable. The Soviet

> **169 U.S. DETONATIONS.** The Atomic Energy Commission disclosed Aug. 27 that the U.S. had detonated 169 nuclear devices and bombs since 1945. Only 134 previously had been disclosed or listed. AEC spokesmen said that the earlier lists included all nuclear detonations considered "significant" but that the 169 figure included the Hiroshima and Nagasaki bombs and several small safety tests.

quota offer was rejected the same day by Wadsworth & Wright as inadequate and no deterrant to any country willing to risk violating a test ban treaty.

The 3 delegations announced Aug. 11 their agreement that the proposed international detection & control system should be fully operational within 6 years after the signing of the projected draft treaty. A Soviet timetable submitted by Tsarapkin called for the setting up of 68 control posts —15 in the USSR—within 4 years after the treaty was signed. A Western timetable presented by Wadsworth provided for 47 posts—21 in the USSR—within 3 years after the treaty was signed.

U.S. Weighs Talks' Progress. Warnings that the U.S. doubted the progress of the 3-power Geneva talks on a nuclear test ban pact and might be forced to resume underground nuclear tests were voiced by State Secy. Herter Aug. 9 and by Pres. Eisenhower Aug. 10.

Herter, reminding newsmen that the U.S. had not been bound by a nuclear test moratorium since Jan. 1, said: "We have not done so . . . in the hope that we would be able to reach a satisfactory agreement" in Geneva; "the negotiations have dragged," however, and there would have to be "a time limit" on the talks to prevent "indefinite negotiations."

Mr. Eisenhower told newsmen the next day that the Geneva talks had been "very disappointing & discouraging" and that if it became evident "that progress is not possible, . . . we [will] have to take care of ourselves." In a presumed reference to AEC plans for resumption of underground testing, the President said that he would keep his "one promise"—that he would "not allow anything to be exploded in the atmosphere" in future nuclear tests.

Underground Moratorium Asked. A proposal for a 27-month moratorium on small underground nuclear test detonations was presented by the U.S. Sept. 27 when the delegates resumed sessions after a vacation recess begun Aug. 22.

The plan was submitted by Charles C. Stelle, acting head of the U.S. delegation. Stelle stressed, however, that the U.S. offer was conditional on the signing of a 3-power treaty banning all other forms of nuclear testing and on implementation of a coordinated seismic research program on detection of small underground tests. Stelle warned that unless the USSR agreed to the proposed coordinated seismic research, the U.S. would resume its own detection work and presumably end its voluntary nuclear test suspension.

Tsarapkin rejected the U.S.-proposed moratorium Oct. 5 as insufficient to permit settlement of the underground detection dispute. He reiterated Soviet demands for a 4- to 5-year moratorium on testing.

(Sen. Hubert H. Humphrey [D., Minn.], a leading advocate of an international agreement to suspend nuclear tests, called Oct. 2 for the resumption of U.S. tests, "if necessary for weapons development," if the Geneva talks failed to produce agreement by June 1961. Humphrey, who blamed both Soviet & Western negotiators for the conference's "lengthy delays," said that the U.S. "cannot indefinitely accept a situation whereby its tests have stopped and there is no agreement & no control system to verify that the Soviet Union has also stopped its tests.")

Kennedy & Nixon. The issue was discussed by the U.S. Presidential candidates, Sen. John F. Kennedy, & Vice Pres. Richard M. Nixon, during a TV debate Oct. 21. Kennedy said the next President "should make one last effort to secure an agreement on the cessation of [nuclear] tests. . . . We should go back to Geneva . . . & try once again. . . . I don't think that even if that effort fails that it will be necessary to carry on tests in the

atmosphere. . . . They can be carried out underground . . . [&/or] in outer space. . . . But I'm most concerned about the whole problem of the spread of atomic weapons. . . ."

Nixon pointed out that "there's been a moratorium on testing as a result of the fact that we have been negotiating" on test inspection. He said: He had "reached the conclusion that the Soviet Union is actually filibustering" & "may be cheating." "I don't think we can wait until the next President is inaugurated and then all the months of negotiating. . . . I think that immediately after this election we should set a timetable— the next President working with . . . Pres. Eisenhower— . . . to break the Soviet filibuster."

Conference Recessed. The U.S., British & Soviet negotiators concluded their 273d session Dec. 5 and recessed the talks until Feb. 7, 1961.

The adjournment had been requested by the U.S. to eliminate the possibility of binding Pres.-elect Kennedy to Eisenhower Administration decisions. U.S. delegate Stelle pledged Dec. 5 that "a thorough review of U.S. policy toward this conference will have been made by . . . February." Soviet chief delegate Tsarapkin asserted Dec. 5 that the USSR had "emptied its pockets" and that it was up to the U.S. to make concessions and break the 2-year Geneva deadlock.

Stelle Nov. 22 had rejected as "absurdly low" the Soviet offer of 3 on-site inspections annually of suspected nuclear detonations in the USSR. He urged the USSR Dec. 5 to review its inspection quota offer and accept control provisions without which, he said, the U.S. could not sign a test-ban treaty. He warned that the U.S. would not agree to observe indefinitely the voluntary test moratorium in effect since Nov. 1958.

A-Weapons Spread

French Test Succeeds. French scientists successfully detonated France's first atomic bomb—a plutonium device with an estimated force of 20,000 to 100,000 tons of TNT—at 7 a.m. Feb. 13 atop a 350-foot steel tower 28 miles south of Reggan, in the Sahara.

France thus became, after the U.S.,

the Soviet Union & Britain, the world's 4th nuclear power.*

The bomb tested at Reggan, officially described as an "atomic device," was believed to have been too cumbersome for use as a weapon.†

The Reggan test was carried out by a task force commanded by Maj. Gen. Charles Ailleret, head of a special interservice weapons development group. It was witnessed by Pierre Guillaumat, minister delegate for atomic affairs, & by Brig. Gen. Albert Buchalet, commander of the civil-military group that had built the bomb.

The device, triggered electrically from a command post 10 miles away in Hamoudia after a 30-minute countdown, produced a mushroom-shaped cloud, which drifted southeastward over a desolate desert region. The detonation was recorded & measured by cameras, rockets & other equipment, and the cloud & surrounding atmosphere were monitored for radioactivity by jet aircraft. A statement by Armed Forces Min. Pierre Messmer said the monitoring had given "assurance that no inhabited center had been threatened or touched by radioactive fallout." The test site was located 750 miles south of Algiers & 650 miles east of Casablanca.

Pres. de Gaulle, in a jubilant message to Guillaumat at the Reggan site, declared: "Hurrah for France! Since this morning she is stronger & prouder. From the bottom of my heart, thanks to you & to those who have . . . achieved this magnificent success." De Gaulle said "the security of populations of the Sahara & of the neighboring countries has been . . . assured."

A de Gaulle statement issued by the Armed Forces Ministry declared that as a result of the test, "France, thanks to her own national effort, can reinforce her defensive potential, that of the [French] Community & . . . of the West." France, he said, was in a "better position to further its action toward the conclusion of agreements among the atomic powers with a view to achieving nuclear disarmament."

Test Criticized. News of the Sahara A-test brought a wave of criticism of France for carrying it out despite a 1959 UN General Assembly resolution opposing it and in view of the U.S.-British-Soviet efforts to write a treaty banning all tests.

Pres. Eisenhower said at a Washington news conference Feb. 17 that France, as was "only natural," had been impelled by "matters of pride & prestige" to develop its own atomic bomb. Mr. Eisenhower expressed hope that "the larger nations that have already done this thing" would reach agreements to spare "other nations . . . the expense of going into this kind of an armaments race" and to "stop this whole thing in its tracks."

A Soviet government statement issued Feb. 13 via Tass "deplored" the test as an affront to "world public opinion" and a factor complicating "the solution of the total . . . disarmament problem, the over-riding problem of the day." It warned that "if nuclear explosions should continue, the Soviet government will . . . not . . . fail to draw the proper conclusions for the sake of safeguarding its . . . security."

Prime Min. Kwame Nkrumah of Ghana denounced the French test with "horror" Feb. 13 and ordered all French assets in Ghana frozen "until such time as the effects on the population of Ghana of the present . . . & future experiments" were known.

Morocco charged France Feb. 15 with ignoring its repeated protests against any Saharan nuclear test. It revoked the 1956 French-Moroccan diplomatic cooperation treaty and recalled Amb.-to-France Abdellatif Ben Jalloun.

De Gaulle asserted Feb. 27 in a speech in Le Vigan that France was ready to renounce the production & possession of nuclear weapons "with great joy if those who already possess the bomb . . . also renounce it." He declared that, faced with the "totalitarian threat that is dividing the world into 2 camps," France was ready to stand with the camp of freedom "not as a protege but as an ally" possessing full "means of defense."

De Gaulle had told a Narbonne rally Feb. 26 that foreign criticism of the

---

* The U.S. had detonated the world's first atomic bomb near Almagordo, N.M. July 16, 1945; the USSR its first Aug. 29, 1949, and Britain its first at the Monte Bello Islands, off Australia, Oct. 3, 1952.

† Plutonium for the French bomb was produced by the Marcoule, France nuclear center. The Marcoule center currently was undergoing expansion and, newsmen reported, would be capable of producing enough plutonium for 15 bombs a year.

Feb. 13 French nuclear test was "hysterical" and that some countries 'which said nothing about the 199 preceding [nuclear] explosions accuse us of wanting to poison humanity."

2d French A-Bomb Detonated. A "limited-power" plutonium bomb described as compact & capable of being modified for military use was detonated by French technicians Apr. 1 near Reggan.

The bomb, reportedly of an explosive force equal to 19,000 tons of TNT, was exploded at ground level 13 miles south of the point at which the first French nuclear device was tested Feb. 13. The government announced that the bomb was tested with precautions to insure that "fallout presents no danger to the population."

The French Atomic Energy Commission announced Apr. 2 that it was ready to fill Armed Forces Ministry orders for plutonium bombs that could be carried by aircraft. Government statements issued in Paris & at UN headquarters Apr. 4 said that the 2d Reggan explosion had completed France's plutonium bomb research project.

(22 Asian & African states formally requested Mar. 14 that the UN General Assembly be called into special session to consider the question of French nuclear tests. UN Secy. Gen. Hammarskjöld announced Apr. 14 that only 36 member states, less than the majority required, had supported the request.)

3d French A-Test. France set off its 3d nuclear explosion Dec. 27. The test, reportedly of an operational atomic weapon, was made near Reggan.

A communiqué issued by the French Armed Forces Ministry, in charge of test site operations, described the test as "a nuclear explosion of limited power." It said all precautions had been taken to minimize fallout.

It was reported from Paris Dec. 27 that the device tested was a plutonium bomb with an explosive force equivalent to 10,000 to 14,000 tons of TNT. It was detonated atop a steel tower surrounded by test animals & military equipment.

Brig. Gen. Jean Thiry, commander of the test task force, told newsmen Dec. 27 that France's nuclear weapons

program was designed to produce a maximum of technological progress with a minimum of test detonations. Thiry said: "Our method of . . . perfecting the nuclear arm remains based on the principle of doing many things by calculation and thus avoiding a multiplication of tests." He said France would "spend less money & advance relatively faster than did the other nuclear powers."

The French detonation was denounced in statements issued by the USSR, East Germany, Morocco & Japan, which filed a formal protest. U.S. State Department spokesman Lincoln White said Dec. 27 that the French test was not unexpected but that U.S. policy remained opposed to "proliferation of atomic capabilities."

'Cheap' A-Bomb Process. An inexpensive process for the production of uranium-235, which could be used for nuclear weapons, was ordered classified as a state secret Oct. 12 by the West German government.

Knowledge of the process first was made public in the U.S. Oct. 10 by Sen. Albert Gore (D., Tenn.). Gore termed the process a major reason for an appeal issued the previous day by Sen. John F. Kennedy (Mass.) for a renewed U.S. effort at the Geneva test-ban talks.

The process, developed by the Degussa Chemical Co. of Frankfurt, was based on use of a centrifuge to separate fissionable uranium-235 from heavier, non-fissionable uranium-238. The centrifuge technique had been discarded by Allied scientists during World War II in favor of the gaseous diffusion method for separation of fissionable uranium. Research by West German scientists reportedly had perfected the centrifuge technique and made it a feasible way for technically advanced countries to become nuclear powers and produce fissionable materials for nuclear weapons without huge financial outlays required by current production methods.

The West German government announced Oct. 12 that it had asked the Federal Patents Office to declare the centrifuge process a state secret to prevent other countries from acquiring it. (The N.Y. Times reported Oct. 10 that Degussa already had sold 2 experimental nuclear centrifuges to West German concerns & one to the Brazilian government.)

'Neutron Bomb' Warning. Ex-Atomic Energy Commissioner Thomas E. Murray warned in a Nov. 3 letter to both U.S. Presidential candidates that the USSR might have been developing & testing a "fantastic" new atomic weapon "as radically different from the H-bomb as the H-bomb was from the Hiroshima-type A-bomb." Murray said the voluntary A-test moratorium had prevented the U.S. from bringing the new weapon, for which the U.S. had "conceptual designs," to the testing stage. He said that the weapon, described elsewhere as a "neutron bomb" reportedly being developed at the AEC's Livermore, Calif. weapons center, was "primarily anti-personnel in destruction & effect." It was reported that the prospective weapon produced deadly radiation without the blast, heat or fallout of A- or H-bombs.

Israel Denies A-Bomb Program. The Israeli government denied Dec. 20-21 that it had begun work on a nuclear reactor to produce plutonium for an Israeli atomic bomb.

The Israeli denials were made by Amb.-to-U.S. Avraham Harman at a meeting with State Secy. Herter in Washington Dec. 20 and by Premier David Ben-Gurion in a Knesset address Dec. 21. Ben-Gurion said the secret reactor, reported in the U.S. to have been planned for weapons purposes, was being built in the Negev near Beersheba "exclusively for peaceful purposes" & that it would "serve the needs of industry, agriculture, science & health." Ben-Gurion said the reactor, to be of 24,000 - thermal-kilowatt capacity, would be open to inspection by friendly nations after completion in 3-4 years.

The suspected Israeli A-bomb project first was mentioned publicly by U.S. AEC Chrmn. John A. McCone Dec. 18 on NBC-TV's Meet the Press program. McCone confirmed reports that the U.S. feared Israel might be building facilities capable of producing plutonium for military uses. Washington officials reported Dec. 19 that the nature of the Beersheba plant, concealed by Israel, had been discovered by long-range photography. They said the plant apparently was designed to produce plutonium that could be used for either power or weapons.

The French Foreign Ministry denied Dec. 19 that any French technical aid given Israel in the nuclear energy field was being used for weapons purposes. French officials confirmed that Israel had been given nuclear aid, but it was not known whether the Beersheba reactor was included in this program.

UAR Pres. Nasser said in Port Said Dec. 23 that any attempt by Israel to build an atomic bomb would result in war with the UAR. "We would not permit Israel to make an atomic bomb," he declared. "We would confront the base of aggression even if we had to mobilize 4 million men."

(The UAR reported Dec. 11 that West Germany had agreed to build an atomic reactor in the UAR.)

A-Bomb Spread Seen Near. Warnings that many nations had the capability to produce nuclear weapons within a few years—and that an atomic war almost certainly would result from the spread of such weapons—were voiced at the annual meeting of the American Association for the Advancement of Science, convened in New York Dec. 26.

Sir Charles P. Snow, British physicist & author, said at the meeting Dec. 27 that "a dozen or more states" had the scientific & engineering personnel to equip themselves "with fission & fusion bombs" within 6 years. Snow, who based his estimate on "engineering truth" and the fact that "it is relatively easy to make plutonium," warned: "We know . . . that if enough of these weapons are made—by enough different states—some of them are going to blow up" "through accident, or folly, or madness." Snow predicted that if at the end of 6 years "China & several other states have a stock of nuclear bombs, within at the most 10 years, some . . . bombs are going off."

Snow appealed to the U.S. to accept a limited "agreement on the stopping of nuclear tests" as a step toward the possible "restriction of nuclear armaments." He said the U.S. was "not going to get the 99.9% 'security' that it has been asking for" because it was scientifically unobtainable, but the alternatives were "a finite risk" or "a certainty of disaster."

A symposium on Communist Chinese science, sponsored by the National Science Foundation in conjunction with the AAAS meeting, was told Dec. 26 by T. C. Tsao of Columbia University that the world should not be surprised "if the Chinese explode an atomic bomb or launch a rocket soon."

Pre-Summit Events

Visits Exchanged. Soviet and Western leaders intensified their personal contacts during the early months of 1960 in preparation for the scheduled summit conference.

Italian Pres. Giovanni Gronchi, the first Italian chief of state to visit Russia in 50 years, spent 5 days in the USSR Feb. 6-11 for political talks with Khrushchev.

Khrushchev paid an 11-day state visit to France Mar. 23-Apr. 3 for conferences with de Gaulle.

De Gaulle visited England Apr. 5-8. Addressing both houses of Parliament Apr. 7 he said that France wanted all "stocks of nuclear weapons to be destroyed, the installations where they are made to be used for different purposes, the rockets & the aircraft capable of carrying them . . . [&] the fixed or floating bases from which these vehicles of death can be launched, to be placed under surveillance." France then would "give up the [atomic] tests & the capital expenditures" necessary to create a French nuclear arsenal, he pledged.

De Gaulle visited Canada Apr. 18-22 and the U.S. Apr. 22-29 for intensive discussions with Pres. Eisenhower. Outlining French hopes for an East-West "détent," de Gaulle told reporters at the National Press Club Apr. 23: "It seems to me that the efforts to reach a détente should focus on nuclear weapons and . . . [should] be limited to reciprocal control of rockets, strategic aircraft & ships capable of carrying nuclear weapons." In this area "I think it is still possible to do something practical."

In an address Apr. 25 before a joint session of Congress, de Gaulle reiterated his belief that "there is no other hope for the future of our species" than "to destroy these [nuclear] weapons by common consent, . . . not to manufacture any others [and] to open up all territories to reciprocal

supervision." De Gaulle warned that "failing the renunciation of atomic armaments by those states who are provided with them," France "will be obliged to equip itself with such armaments. . . . [And] how many others will attempt to do the same?"

U.S. U-2 Downed Over USSR. An American U-2 jet plane was shot down near Sverdlovsk, in the central USSR, May 1 while making one of a series of reconnaissance flights begun by the U.S. over Soviet territory in 1956.

The bitterness of the Soviet reaction to the incident was attributed to the fact that the flight had been undertaken immediately before the summit meeting—planned to begin in Paris May 16—and to the U.S. admission that U.S. planes had been flying over the USSR for 4 years.

The May 1 mission, initially denied by the U.S., was admitted after the USSR announced its capture of the U-2 pilot, ex-U.S. Air Force First Lt. Francis Gary Powers, 30, of Jenkins, Ky. Powers at first was described by the U.S. as a civilian pilot employed by the Lockheed Aircraft Corp. to fly the U-2 for a weather research project of the National Aeronautics & Space Administration. It soon became known, however, that Powers had been flying reconnaissance missions for the Central Intelligence Agency from a U.S. airbase at Incirlik, near Adana, Turkey.

Paris Meeting Collapses

The Paris summit conference collapsed at its opening session May 16 when Soviet Premier Khrushchev refused to begin talks unless Pres. Eisenhower formally apologized for the sending of U.S. reconnaissance planes over the USSR. Efforts of British Prime Min. Harold Macmillan and French Pres. Charles de Gaulle to persuade Khrushchev to continue the conference failed May 17 despite Mr. Eisenhower's assurances that the flights had been suspended after the U-2 incident and would not be resumed.

Khrushchev Rejects Talks. The heads-of-government meeting began May 16 in Paris' Elysée Palace. It adjourned indefinitely 3 hours later after Khrushchev had delivered a denunciation of U.S. policy and had refused to continue the conference unless Pres. Eisenhower made amends for the U-2 incident.

Making clear that he considered Mr. Eisenhower personally responsible for the U.S.' military reconnaissance of the USSR and the deterioration of U.S.-Soviet relations, Khrushchev withdrew his invitation for the President's scheduled June visit to the USSR and suggested that the summit talks be postponed for "approximately 6 to 8 months." He said the "provocative flights of American military planes" had deprived the USSR of the "possibility to receive the President with the proper cordiality with which the Soviet people receive welcome guests."

Khrushchev stated these 3 conditions—to be met by the U.S.—for possible continuance of the Paris meetings:
● Condemnation of "the inadmissible provocative actions of the United States Air Force with regard to the Soviet Union."
● Assurances that the U.S. government would "refrain from continuing such actions" against the USSR.
● Punishment by the U.S. of "those who are directly guilty" of ordering and carrying out the flights.

Without waiting for Mr. Eisenhower's reply, Khrushchev said that the U.S.' policy, justifiable "only when states are in a state of war," had doomed "the summit conference to failure in advance." Khrushchev declared that he could not "be among the participants in negotiations where one of them has made treachery the basis of his policy with regard to the Soviet Union." "Reasonable agreements are possible, but . . . not at this . . . time," he said. For a summit meeting to have a chance of success, the U.S. would have to confess "that it has committed aggression and admits that it regrets it," he declared.

Eisenhower's Reply. In a statement issued after adjournment of the meeting, Pres. Eisenhower made public the substance of his reply to Khrushchev's terms for further summit sessions.

Mr. Eisenhower, disclosing that he had been forewarned of Khrushchev's bellicose attitude by de Gaulle & Macmillan, said he had replied that:

● The U.S. had made clear "that these activities [the U-2 flights] had no aggressive intent but rather were to assure the safety of the United States & the free world against surprise attack by a power which boasts of its ability to devastate . . . [others] by missiles . . . with atomic warheads."

● The U.S. had made "no . . . threat" to continue the spy flights. "In point of fact, these flights were suspended after the recent incident and are not to be resumed. Accordingly, this cannot be the issue" endangering the conference.

● He had come to Paris to seek agreements that would "eliminate the necessity for all forms of espionage." If the conference's failure prevented this, the U.S. planned to submit to the UN a proposal for the creation of a UN "aerial surveillance to detect preparations for attack."

● "Mr. Khrushchev was left in no doubt . . . that his ultimatum would never be acceptable to the United States." Khrushchev was asked to drop the U-2 incident or to meet privately with Mr. Eisenhower, but he "brushed aside all . . . reason" and "made [it] apparent that he was determined to wreck the . . . conference."

Mediation Fails. Macmillan & de Gaulle failed May 16-17 in efforts to persuade Khrushchev to resume the talks without a U.S. apology for the U-2 incident.

Macmillan, acting immediately after the conference adjourned May 16, called on Mr. Eisenhower & de Gaulle and then on Khrushchev to convey their views and ascertain Khrushchev's position on resuming the talks. Macmillan met with Pres. Eisenhower & de Gaulle early May 17 and then conferred privately with Mr. Eisenhower again during a visit to a Paris suburb where the latter had lived as NATO supreme commander.

At midday May 17, de Gaulle invited Mr. Eisenhower, Macmillan & Khrushchev to meet "to ascertain whether it is possible for the summit conference to begin the study of the questions which we agreed should be taken up." Mr. Eisenhower & Macmillan accepted the invitation, but Soviet aides replied that Khrushchev would attend only if given assurances the meeting was considered preliminary to & not part of a summit conference.

The meeting summoned by de Gaulle was begun by the 3 Western leaders at 3 p.m. without Khrushchev. A statement issued by Khrushchev an hour later and conveyed to the Western leaders said that he would be ready to "participate in the summit conference" only if the U.S. had "come to the decision to condemn the treacherous incursion . . . into the airspace of the Soviet Union, publicly express regret over these incursions, punish those who are guilty and give assurances" they "will not be repeated."

A final conference statement was drafted by de Gaulle with the approval of Mr. Eisenhower & Macmillan and was issued before the end of their meeting at 5 p.m. It said that the Western leaders had met to discuss whether "the summit conference could begin" but that in "the absence of Mr. Khrushchev," the "planned discussions could not take place."

Khrushchev Press Conference. At a tumultuous 2½-hour news conference held in Paris May 18 before his departure for East Berlin, Khrushchev angrily denounced the U.S. & Pres. Eisenhower.

In a preliminary statement read at the press conference, Khrushchev rejected attempts to "lay the blame on us for the alleged refusal of the Soviet Union to take part in the meeting." He said:

● "We are ready to take part in the [summit] conference if the United States government makes up publicly for the insult inflicted upon our country by its aggressive actions. . . . We are still not sure that the espionage flights . . . will not be repeated." If they are repeated, "we shall shoot these planes down, we shall administer shattering blows at the bases whence they come and at those who have set up those bases and actually dispose of them."

● The U.S.' renunciation of U-2 flights was "merely a temporary suspension of flights 'til Jan. 1961." "Eisenhower said at the preliminary meeting on May 16 that what he had meant . . . was that they would not

be resumed for the remainder of his tenure as President." "But international relations can not be built on the term of office of this or that official, for what would then be the worth of any international agreement?"

● "The Soviet people" & "public opinion . . . would not understand us if we contented ourselves with the American President's dodges and the 'favor' he 'graciously' did us by stopping flights" temporarily. "Would . . . you yourselves feel safe listening to the drone of an alien military plane over your heads?" "We will not tolerate insults. . . .'"

● "Eisenhower's statement" that he planned to submit a new "open skies" plan to the UN "looked like a threat." The "Pentagon" has "apparently decided to send planes with the same aims but under the United Nations flag. It is to be hoped that the United Nations is . . . not a branch of the Pentagon and will decline this humiliating role."

Khrushchev, flanked by Foreign Min. Gromyko & Defense Min. Marshal Malinovsky, gave these answers to reporters' questions:

Spy flights—He had been about to raise the matter of U.S. espionage flights over the USSR in his 1959 Camp David talks with Pres. Eisenhower but "became apprehensive and . . . thought there was something fishy about this friend of mine [Mr. Eisenhower]." "I was right, because when we caught them red-handed, they say they are not thieves." "Wouldn't it be better . . . to take the American aggressors by the scruff of the neck . . . and give them a little shaking and make them understand they must not commit . . . aggression against the Soviet Union."

New summit talks—Despite his disappointment with Pres. Eisenhower, "we are convinced that persons will come to power in the United States who will [be] . . . in favor of reaching mutually acceptable agreements." "If, however, they should elect someone who would not understand [this] . . . necessity, . . . we have waited & we can wait [again]."

A-ban, disarmament — "We shall continue our [A-test ban] negotiations in Geneva. . . . But if Eisenhower threatens that he will continue [nuclear] testing, then we, too, will follow suit." "The disarmament negotiations are another matter" because the Western powers "do not want disarmament but . . . control over armaments, which is in other words the collection of espionage information. We will not agree to this."

'Ike' Report to Nation. Pres. Eisenhower spoke from the White House May 25 in a nationwide radio-TV report on the U-2 incident & the failure of the summit conference.

The President's address was considered his answer to domestic & foreign charges that the U.S. had blundered in its handling of the U-2 incident and had given Khrushchev an excuse for wrecking the conference.

Mr. Eisenhower placed the blame for the summit failure directly on Khrushchev, but he pledged that Western leaders would continue "a careful search for common interests between the Western allies & the Soviet Union on specific problems."

Major points made by the President:

Need for espionage—"Our safety & that of the free world demand . . . effective systems for gathering information about the military capability of other powerful nations, especially those that make a fetish of secrecy. . . . This has long been one of my most serious preoccupations. It is part of my grave responsibility, in the overall problem of protecting the American people, to guard ourselves & our allies against surprise attack. . . . I take full responsibility for approving all the . . . programs undertaken by our government to secure & evaluate military intelligence."

U-2 timing & statements—"As to the timing [of the May 1 flight], the question was really whether to halt the program & thus forego the gathering of important information that was essential & that was likely to be unavailable at a later date. . . . When a nation needs intelligence activity, there is no time when vigilance can be relaxed." When the interception of the U-2 became known, a "covering statement" was issued "to protect the pilot, his mission & our intelligence processes. . . . When later the status of the pilot was definitely established, and there was no further possibility of avoiding exposure of the project, the

factual details were set forth."

Halting of flights—U.S. statements, particularly the one issued May 9 by State Secy. Herter, made clear that American espionage efforts would go on but did "not . . . say that these particular flights would be continued." Before leaving for the summit meeting, "I had directed that these U-2 flights be stopped. Clearly their usefulness was impaired. Moreover [they] . . . could not but complicate the relations of certain of our allies with the Soviets. I wanted no public announcement of this decision until I could personally disclose it at the summit meeting in conjunction with . . . proposals [for] . . . a system of [UN] aerial surveillance."*

Soviet reaction—Despite U.S. assurances that the U-2 flights had been halted, Khrushchev maintained "extreme demands" for an apology that "obviously" the President would not make. "He knew, of course, by holding to those demands, the Soviet Union was scuttling the summit conference. In torpedoing the conference, Mr. Khrushchev claimed . . . high moral indignation over alleged American acts of aggression." But the flights had been under way for "4 years" and, "in his Paris press conference, . . . Khrushchev confirmed that he knew of these flights when he visited the United States." "It is apparent that the Soviets had decided [in advance of the summit meeting] . . . that my trip to the Soviet Union should be canceled and that nothing constructive from their point of view would come out of the summit conference."

Mr. Eisenhower declared that "to build a more sane & hopeful reality," the U.S. must adhere to the following policy: "(1) We must keep up our strength, and hold it steady for the long pull. . . . We can make it clear to everyone there can be no gain in the use of pressure tactics or aggression against us & our allies. (2) We must continue businesslike dealings with the Soviet leaders on outstanding issues and improve the contacts between our own & the Soviet peoples, making clear that the path of reason

*In an apparent reference to the U.S.' Midas missile-warning & Samos photo-reconnaissance satellite programs, Mr. Eisenhower said another reason for ending U-2 flights was that "new techniques, other than aircraft, are constantly being developed."

& common sense is still open if the Soviets will but use it. (3) To improve world conditions in which human freedom can flourish, we must continue to move ahead with positive programs at home & abroad, in collaboration with free nations everywhere" & in support of the UN.

De Gaulle Proposals. In a televised address to the French people, Pres. de Gaulle May 31 briefly reviewed the failure of the summit conference and outlined proposals to recreate conditions for an East-West accommodation.

Conceding that the U.S.' May 1 U-2 flight over the USSR had been "ill-timed," de Gaulle held that "this was not sufficient reason for refusing to open the discussion of the affairs of the world at the summit." "At the very moment when Moscow had launched a new space vehicle passing over the West 18 times a day," he declared, "it seemed excessive to require public apologies & reparations from Washington because a single-engine plane, equipped with a camera, had attempted to cross Soviet territory, considering that the plane had been shot down . . . and that the guarantee that the act would not be re-peated had been received."

De Gaulle said the division of the world into 2 rival camps, either of which was capable of wiping out "a large part of humanity . . . in a few hours," made "exorcising this monstrous peril" more important than any "territorial disagreement or ideological dispute." To accomplish this he proposed that the world act to meet these 3 conditions:

● "The first is a détente, . . . the bettering of international relations, putting a stop to provocative actions & speeches, and increasing trade & cultural exchanges . . . in order that a more peaceful atmosphere might be created." Otherwise, war might start again "because the archduke was dead or someone wanted Danzig."

● "The 2d condition is a specific degree of controlled disarmament, preferably aimed at the devices capable of carrying bombs to strategic distances, in order that the possibility . . . suddenly to provoke general destruction might vanish."

● "The 3d condition is a beginning of organized cooperation between East & West devoted to the service of man either by helping in the progress of under-developed peoples or by collaborating in the . . . scientific research on which depends the future of all."

Within this framework, France intended to remain "ready to defend herself," de Gaulle declared. He said: "She shall remain an integral part of the Atlantic alliance"; "she too must acquire a nuclear armament"; "she must be sole mistress of her resources & her territory"; but France also would work "to build Western Europe into a political, economic, cultural & human group, organized for action, progress & defense," foreseeing "the probable evolution of [a] political regime" & a "European entente from the Atlantic to the Urals."

Macmillan Bars Shift. A continued policy of close British cooperation with the U.S. and pursuit of fruitful East-West summit talks was pledged May 30-June 2 by Prime Min. Macmillan.

Addressing Parliament, Macmillan reaffirmed May 30 the potential value of "summitry" in dealing with the USSR on matters "where conclusions cannot be reached except by heads of government." "We must," he said, "utilize all the means available—diplomatic, ministerial . . . for negotiation at any suitable time." Macmillan made it clear, however, in a speech June 2 at a Conservative rally, that Britain would not "be swayed from one tack to another by every changing gust of the wind from Moscow, blowing hot or cold."

U.S. Would Renew Talks. At his first Washington news conference since the breakdown of the conference, Pres. Eisenhower declared July 6 his continued readiness to resume international discussions on any problems in East-West relations.

Mr. Eisenhower said he had "made sure . . . there is a clear understanding on the part of the Soviets that we are ready to talk any time, honestly & without any equivocation," on "disarmament, nuclear testing, liberalizing movements . . . and all that sort of thing."

The President also said:

● The apparent divergence in Soviet

& Chinese views on the inevitability of war was due to the fact that certain Communist states had grown "more productive," had "accumulated wealth" and had found that "their views as to the methods they will use to dominate the world might be changed." This growth had not yet affected China, and it remained "much more belligerent & . . . quarrelsome."

● Khrushchev's recent statement that he expected to see the entire world ruled by communism was proof that "the Communists have never retreated one step from their conviction . . . that the Communist flag ought to fly over the whole world from pole to pole." But Khrushchev made it clear "in that same statement that he wasn't talking about doing it by violence or by war."

● It was "worthwhile" to continue efforts to achieve a nuclear test ban agreement with the USSR. The U.S. had renounced its test ban but the decision to resume underground U.S. tests "in the interests of our own security & defense" would be made only "when we see what happens" at the Geneva test-ban talks.

USSR Renews Summit Bid. Premier Khrushchev told British Prime Min. Macmillan Aug. 5 that he would be willing to attend a new East-West summit meeting on the problems of Germany, Berlin & disarmament after the U.S. Presidential elections.

Khrushchev, in a reply dated Aug 4 to a Macmillan letter of July 19, rejected Macmillan's professed confusion about Soviet aims. He declared that Macmillan's condemnation of the USSR for current East-West tension was the result of "an utterly wrong & unrealistic view of the developments taking place." He warned that the USSR would (1) retaliate against further Western spy flights by shooting down the planes & taking "steps against the bases & countries from whose territories these aggressive raids are made," and (2) sign a peace treaty with East Germany to remove "the prime factor that produces the cold war . . . the German question."

Khrushchev's letter recited a list of allegedly hostile acts against the USSR: the U-2 flight; the West's alleged violation of the Potsdam treaty "obligation to prevent the re-armament & remilitarization of Germany," and "the military blocs & American bases established around the Soviet Union." The message warned that "the circumstances which can breed dangerous accidents must be removed. We must not wait until a madman will, owing to his lack of reason, make a fateful move and trigger off a 3d world war. . . ."

The failure of the summit conference, followed by heightened East-West tensions, generated a U.S. political controversy. Democrats assailed the Eisenhower Administration for launching the U-2 flight such a short time before the Paris talks. They said the Administration had blundered in its handling of the incident after the USSR's disclosure of the pilot's capture. The accusations, made largely by liberal Democrats and rejected by Republicans, were examined by the Senate Foreign Relations Committee and were upheld in a committee report criticizing the Administration's actions. Inevitably, the controversy was linked to the approaching U.S. Presidential election campaign.

Nixon Defends Policy. The Republican defense of the Administration's actions in the U-2 affair was launched by Vice Pres. Richard M. Nixon in a televised interview made before the summit collapse. (The Administration's major statement in defense of its U-2 policies was made personally by Pres. Eisenhower in his radio-TV report to the nation on returning from Paris.)

Interviewed by David Susskind on the TV program "Open End" in New York the night of May 15-16, Nixon defended the U.S.' use of reconnaissance flights over the USSR to bar aggression. Speaking before the collapse of the summit conference, Nixon urged the summit conferees to "put surprise attack at the top of [their agenda] . . . so that such flights" would "not be necessary in the future." "We have to" protect the nation by assuring that there would be "no gap" in U.S. intelligence information, Nixon said. "I was privy to and do indorse" the Administration policy of making U-2-type reconnaisssance, Nixon declared. Such flights were "the only way we can get" certain kinds of information.

Nixon also told Susskind: The U-2 flight "clearly demonstrates the feasibility of the [President's] 'open-skies' proposal"; the "immense advantages" of summit conferences were that they meant "talking & not fighting"; he "agree[d] with our career diplomats when they take a very dim view of personal summitry" and prefer leaving diplomatic negotiations to the professionals; but "when you're dealing with Mr. Khrushchev & others who head totalitarian countries, you have to have personal summitry because he's the man . . . who makes these decisions" & "who insisted upon this."

Nixon, during a pre-Presidential campaign visit to Auburn, N.Y. May 17, charged that Khrushchev had used the U-2 incident "as an excuse, not a reason" to walk out of the summit conference.

Stevenson Vs. 'Blunders.' Adlai E. Stevenson May 12 described as "blunders" both the U-2 incident & Pres. Eisenhower's decision to resume underground nuclear detection tests "on the very eve of" the summit conference. Addressing a Chicago Conference on World Tensions, Stevenson said that "no one questions the necessity of gathering intelligence for our security" but that the timing of the U-2 flight was bad. He raised the question of whether such "blunders" might not "carelessly, accidentally, trigger the holocaust." He noted, however, that "this is no time for partisan censure."

Stevenson said at a Cook County Democratic fund-raising dinner in Chicago May 19 that although Khrushchev wrecked this [summit] conference" with "his impossible demand" that the President "apologize & punish those responsible for the spy plane flight, . . . we handed Khrushchev the crowbar & sledgehammer to wreck the meeting." "Without our series of blunders," Stevenson said, "Mr. Khrushchev would not have had a pretext for making his impossible demand & wild charges." He said: "There is no question about national unity in a time of crisis. But errors must be corrected. It is the duty of responsible opposition in a democracy to expose & criticize

carelessness & mistakes, especially in a case of such national & world importance. We cannot sweep this whole sorry mess under the rug in the name of national unity."

Senate GOP leader Everett M. Dirksen (Ill.) charged May 23 that "a well-placed, well-timed torpedo" fired by Stevenson had wrecked the summit talks in advance. Dirksen said Stevenson had given a pre-summit interview to a French newspaper, which quoted Stevenson as proposing, in effect, extraordinary concessions to Russia on the German problem, disarmament & other matters. Stevenson May 23 reiterated earlier denials of such an interview and denied that he favored concessions such as were reported. The alleged interview was published in the May 15-16 edition of the "Paris Presse-l'Intransigeant" by reporter Robert Boulay.

Democrats Vs. Soviet View. Assertions of Khrushchev that "broad sections of the [American] public & many prominent political figures in the United States are seriously concerned about the [Eisenhower Administration's] foreign policy" were rejected by Senate Democratic leader Lyndon B. Johnson (Tex.) June 2 as an attempt to divide the American people and cripple bipartisan policy.

The Khrushchev statement was contained in a personal message cabled May 31 to Johnson, House Speaker Sam Rayburn (D., Tex.), Chrmn. Fulbright of the Senate Foreign Relations Committee and Adlai Stevenson. The message, made public June 2 by Johnson, reiterated charges that Pres. Eisenhower had wrecked the summit conference by his refusal to make amends for U.S. aerial reconnaissance over the USSR.

The Khrushchev message was in reply to a personal appeal by the 4 Democrats for immediate resumption of the Paris summit meetings. The Democratic appeal had been conveyed to Khrushchev in Paris May 17.

Johnson told the Senate June 2 that Khrushchev's message was an "arrogant denial of the facts" that showed the USSR to be responsible for the collapse of the summit talks. Asserting that Khrushchev confessedly was incapable of understanding U.S. bipartisanship on world issues,

Johnson said: "It is equally obvious that he does not understand that Americans . . .—Republican or Democratic—will stand united against him in his effort to divide the country & weaken the hopes of freedom."

UN 'Summit' Session

World Leaders in N.Y. Views on disarmament were exchanged by world leaders in New York at the UN General Assembly's 1960 session, which convened Sept. 20.

The session was transformed into an unprecedented world summit meeting by the presence of Khrushchev and a host of leaders from Communist, neutralist and Western countries. This transformation was an outgrowth of the failure of the Paris summit conference and of the break-up of the 10-nation Geneva disarmament conference. The disarmament issue, however, was only one of many problems taken up at the session.

The UN summit session had been suggested by the USSR Aug. 1 in a letter to Luis Padilla Nervo, Mexican chairman of the UN Disarmament Commission. The Soviet letter asserted that the 10-nation Geneva disarmament committee's task—talks on "general and complete disarmament"—had been fixed by the 1959 Assembly and that the disarmament question should be returned to the Assembly for discussion by Khrushchev, Pres. Eisenhower and other world leaders. The Soviet government announced Sept. 1 that Khrushchev personally would lead the Soviet delegation to the 15th Assembly.

The Soviet proposal for a gathering of world political leaders at the UN was opposed by the U.S. as an empty gesture and an attempt to avoid genuine East-West negotiations. The U.S. held that a mammoth summit meeting would be incapable of sober discussion and was intended primarily to serve as a propaganda platform for Khrushchev and other Soviet bloc leaders. Despite the U.S.' opposition, many world leaders said they would attend.

Eisenhower's Address. Pres. Eisenhower went to New York Sept. 22 to present to the Assembly a U.S. program to settle world problems through common action in the U.N.

The President, the first chief of state to address the current Assembly session, announced U.S. readiness to join with other UN members in programs of aid to less-developed nations, elimination of nuclear weapons, peaceful use of outer space, creation of a UN surveillance force to supervise world disarmament and establishment of standby UN forces to keep the peace.

Among Mr. Eisenhower's remarks:

Disarmament — Negotiations on "general disarmament," broken off by the Soviet walkout from the 10-nation disarmament committee's Geneva meetings, "can & should soon be resumed." "We should not have to wait until we have agreed on all the detailed measures . . . before we begin to move toward disarmament." The new talks should "deal particularly with 2 pressing dangers—that of war by miscalculation & that of mounting nuclear weapons stockpiles."

The "danger of war by miscalculation could be reduced, in times of crisis, by the intervention, when requested by any nation seeking to prove its own peaceful intention, of an appropriate United Nations surveillance body. The . . . methods can be left to the experts." The U.S. was "prepared to submit to any international inspection, provided only that it is effective & truly reciprocal."

The danger "posed by the growth & prospective spread of nuclear weapons stockpiles" can be reversed by negotiation of "a system for terminating, under verifiable procedures, all production of fissionable materials for weapons purposes." The U.S. was willing to join in immediate negotiations for this and would agree to (a) termination of fission production as soon as an inspection system was in operation and (b) reciprocal U.S.-Soviet transferral of nuclear material to international stockpiles. The U.S. was "willing to match the USSR in shutting down [without delay] major plants producing fissionable materials. one by one, under international inspection & verification."

Peaceful use of space—In order to assure that "outer space be preserved for peaceful use & developed for the benefit of all mankind" rather than becoming "another focus for the arms race," the U.S. proposed these agreements to control space: (1) "celestial bodies are not subject to national appropriation" or "sovereignty"; (2) "nations . . . shall not engage in warlike activities on these bodies"; (3) "no nation will put into orbit or station in outer space weapons of mass destruction"; "all launchings of space craft should be verified in advance by the United Nations"; (4) "international cooperation for constructive peaceful uses of outer space under the United Nations."

Khrushchev's Address. Khrushchev addressed the Assembly Sept. 23. His remarks on disarmament: The USSR was submitting to the UN a revised draft plan for general & complete disarmament which "in many respects . . . meets halfway the position of the Western powers." (The Soviet text was similar to the USSR's June 2 Geneva disarmament draft. It provided for reduction of U.S. & Soviet armed forces to 1,700,000 men each in the first stage of disarmament rather than the 2d stage, as accepted in the U.S.' draft disarmament plan issued June 27.) "The Soviet Government is deeply convinced that only a radical solution of the disarmament problem which would provide for the complete prohibition of nuclear weapons . . . [would deliver] mankind from the threat of nuclear war."

Macmillan's Address. An appeal for the return of trust necessary for East-West negotiations was voiced by Macmillan Sept. 29 in an Assembly address that was subjected to outbursts by Khrushchev.

Macmillan, declaring that there no longer was any purpose in "recrimination" for the collapse of the Paris summit meeting, was interrupted by Khrushchev, who waved his arm & shouted: "You send your planes over our territory, you are guilty of aggression!" Macmillan was interrupted for the 2d time as he reviewed Soviet objections to Western demands for disarmament controls; Khrushchev called out: "You accept our proposals on disarmament & we will accept any form of controls!"

Macmillan made this disarmament proposal: As a first step, "a group of technical experts, scientific, military & administrative," should be appointed to prepare a report on

"what measures of inspection & control would be effective & fair to all countries." Their report, which "would not at this stage be political & controversial," would "provide a basis for political action, just as . . . was the scientists' report which had provided a basis for the Geneva conference on [nuclear] tests." "It would enable the statesmen . . . to translate into action what the technicians tell us is technically possible." Any acceptable disarmament agreement must provide "effective verification" and (a) "prevent the use of outer space for military purposes," (b) halt the production & "clandestine storage" of nuclear weapons, and (c) insure against "surprise attack."

'Ike'-Khrushchev Talks Sought. An appeal for UN indorsement of a new summit meeting of Pres. Eisenhower & Khrushchev was made Sept. 30 by leaders of 5 neutralist states.

The appeal was contained in a draft resolution presented to the Assembly by Indonesian Pres. Sukarno & Indian Prime Min. Nehru with the joint sponsorship of Presidents Tito of Yugoslavia, Nkrumah of Ghana & Nasser of the United Arab Republic.

The proposal immediately was opposed by the U.S. & other delegations on grounds that it would force the 2 leaders into a personal meeting that would stand no chance of success due to Soviet intransigence.

The resolution had been transmitted to Mr. Eisenhower, Khrushchev & Assembly Pres. Boland the previous day in letters from the 5 leaders urging immediate consideration of the proposal by the U.S., USSR & UN General Assembly. Formally introducing the draft in the UN Sept. 30, Sukarno appealed for its adoption by a unanimous UN to make clear "the full force of the world's concern" over mounting East-West tension. "The opportunity may not come again," he warned.

U.S. Rejects Appeal. Pres. Eisenhower told the neutralists Oct. 2 that he saw "nothing in the words or actions of the . . . Soviet which gives me reason to believe that the meeting [would hold] . . . promise."

In letters to Nehru, Nasser, Tito, Nkrumah & Sukarno, the President reiterated his personal pledge "to meet with anyone at any time if there is any serious promise of productive results." He made it clear, however, that Khrushchev's repeated threats of "rocket retaliation" against the U.S. & other nations and his refusal to permit investigation of the July 1 shooting down of a U.S. RB-47 reconnaissance jet had made proposed summit talks useless. He asserted that the disputes responsible for current world tension were of "vital concern to other nations as well" and were "beyond personal or official relations between any 2 individuals."

Mr. Eisenhower suggested that if the USSR were ready to begin serious negotiations on disarmament or any other important issue, it could do so through the UN or normal diplomatic channels. He said he would not "participate in a mere gesture which . . . might convey a thoroughly misleading & unfortunate impression to the peoples of the world."

USSR Sets Conditions. Khrushchev replied Oct. 3 that he was prepared to meet with Pres. Eisenhower only if Mr. Eisenhower apologized in advance for the U-2 & RB-47 flights.

Khrushchev, lauding the 5 neutralists' motives in proposing a new summit meeting, informed them that "we are ready to establish contacts & enter into negotiations with [Pres. Eisenhower] . . . having in mind that the United States . . . will find courage to condemn the above-mentioned acts [U-2 & RB-47 flights] that brought about a deterioration of the Soviet-American relations and will show goodwill toward the . . . improvement of these relations."

Neutralists Withdraw Draft. The 5-nation neutralist draft resolution proposing an Eisenhower-Khrushchev meeting was withdrawn Oct. 6 by Nehru. It was abandoned after the Assembly, in a complex series of maneuvers by the neutralists & by Western powers seeking to avoid an Eisenhower-Khrushchev meeting, had voted Oct. 5 to delete the draft's reference to the 2 leaders.

Khrushchev TV Interview. In an impromptu pledge to Americans Oct. 9, Khrushchev declared "categorically" that "we shall never start a war, so you can sleep in peace."

Khrushchev's pledge came at the end of a 2¼-hour interview conducted by David Susskind on his WNTA-TV "Open End" program from a studio at UN headquarters.

Khrushchev devoted a major part of the broadcast to a recitation of the Soviet version of events surrounding the U-2 incident & collapse of the summit talks. He compared the U.S.' alleged attitude with Soviet professions of peace and of willingness to negotiate settlement of all outstanding world problems. He declared his willingness to meet personally with Pres. Eisenhower's successor and indicated that he would not expect an apology for the U-2 incident as a precondition to the meeting.

Walkout Threatened. In his farewell appearance at the Assembly, Khrushchev. threatened Oct. 13 to order a Soviet boycott of disarmament talks unless they were limited to his proposals for total world disarmament.

Reading to the Assembly a Soviet draft resolution that reiterated his 1959 plan for "general & complete disarmament," Khrushchev warned that the USSR would withdraw from the Assembly's Political Committee, the UN Disarmament Commission & the 10-nation (Geneva) Committee on Disarmament unless the Political Committee "works out specific directives, at least on the basic principles of disarmament" as outlined in the Soviet paper. Brushing aside British Rep.-to-UN David Ormsby-Gore's efforts to interrupt, Khrushchev warned that Britain, "the well-known . . . unsinkable aircraft carrier, would cease to exist on the very first day of . . . war." Referring to the U.S., he said: "If you want war, keep provoking it and you'll get it."

Khrushchev ended his 25-day visit to the UN Assembly and flew from New York to Moscow Oct. 13-14 aboard a Soviet TU-114 airliner.

Khrushchev's departure from New York marked the virtual end of the UN "summit" session. Most neutralist leaders had preceded him home; most Soviet-bloc chiefs left at about the same time. The Soviet UN delegation leadership was assumed by Deputy Foreign Min. Valerian Zorin, who had been named Sept. 24 to replace Arkady A. Sobolev as the USSR's permanent representative at the UN.

Reporting to the Russian people on his UN visit, Khrushchev told an audience in Moscow's Luzhniki Sports Palace Oct. 20 that he had achieved "considerable results" by attracting important world leaders to the UN's debates. He declared that the Soviet draft resolution against colonialism had been a "great success" and that only the opposition of Western leaders, particularly Macmillan, had prevented rapid approval of Soviet disarmament proposals.

National Leaders' Views

The UN "summit" session was used by leaders & representatives of many nations as a forum for their countries' views.

Among opinions presented:

Yugoslav Pres. Tito (Sept. 22)— Yugoslavia supported Soviet proposals for disarmament, the halting of nuclear weapons tests, and destruction of all A-weapon stockpiles.

Mindful of the fact that "the piling up of ever more destructive weapons in itself leads to war," Yugoslavia called on the major powers to resume arms talks "as soon as possible" in "a negotiating body . . . constituted on a broader basis than the 10-nation committee on disarmament"; participants should be willing to accept "a partial agreement" that might lead to "disarmament in . . . entirety": although a partial arms pact "will fall short of perfection," the "risks involved are . . . incomparably smaller than those contained in the present completely uncontrolled" arms race.

Cuban Premier Castro (Sept. 26)— The U.S. hoped to destroy the Cuban revolution on the pretext that it was Communist-dominated; actually Cuba was being punished with "economic aggressions" for its land reform & nationalization measures against U.S. monopolies that had made Cuba a satellite of the U.S.

Cuba supported most major Soviet foreign policies, particularly its proposals for total disarmament. Cuba shared Soviet opposition to formation of an international peace force that could be used to halt revolutions in the smaller states. It "condemned" Hammarskjöld's policies in the Congo and supported Algeria's war for independence & Communist China's right to membership in the UN.

UAR Pres. Nasser (Sept. 27)—The UAR asked that Pres. Eisenhower & Khrushchev meet "without delay" in order to fix "guiding rules for a new attempt toward disarmament."

Polish CP First Secy. Gomulka (Sept. 27)—Poland agreed with the view that war would "leave civilization in a shambles"; Poland would support the Eisenhower proposal for a worldwide popular referendum on condition it was used to ascertain popular approval for general & nuclear disarmament.

Poland proposed that the UN call for (a) a pact halting nuclear weapons tests; (b) "the states possessing nuclear weapons not to transfer them to other states nor to help them in starting their own production of those weapons"; (c) states possessing "no installations for missile-launching" to "refrain from establishing them"; (d) a halt to "the establishment of new foreign military bases."

Danish Foreign Min. Jens O. Krag (Sept. 28)—Denmark, as a test of the effectiveness of the UN surveillance plan proposed by Pres. Eisenhower, "would be prepared to open up for inspection purposes the vast territory of Greenland" as part of a mutually balanced inspection arrangement designed eventually to remove the danger of surprise attack; the opening to inspection of the Western & Soviet military machines was a "necessary condition for . . . total disarmament."

Indonesian Pres. Sukarno (Sept. 30) —Indonesia and other neutralist nations asked UN approval of a draft appealing for a personal meeting between Pres. Eisenhower & Khrushchev; this "unique opportunity . . . for combining private & public diplomacy" must be grasped in spite of the fact that participants in a summit meeting "have the power to disrupt the peace but . . . no moral right . . . to settle the future of the world."

1961

The 3-year moratorium on nuclear weapons tests was broken by the Soviet Union in September after the mounting Berlin crisis had spurred both East and West to an intensified arms race. The Soviet tests included a detonation of 58 megatons in intensity—the largest ever staged by any nation. They brought a renewal of U.S. testing and wrecked the Geneva talks begun in 1958 to seek a treaty banning tests. They also brought East-West tensions to a new peak and lent immediacy to popular fears that the current crisis would result in a new world war.

Reopening of 3-power nuclear test ban conference in Geneva's Palais des Nations Mar. 21. USSR's Semyon K. Tsarapkin (at head of table) presides. U.S. delegation at left, British at right.   (Wide World photo)

Geneva Talks Reconvened

Negotiations on a treaty to prohibit nuclear weapons tests had been begun by the U.S., Britain and Soviet Union Oct. 31, 1958, simultaneously with the 3 powers' agreement to begin a voluntary moratorium on tests.

The moratorium remained in effect at the beginning of 1961 despite both (a) the apparent lack of progress toward an acceptable treaty and (b) France's successful detonation of its first nuclear device Feb. 13, 1960, in defiance of worldwide appeals for it to observe the moratorium. France detonated 2 more atomic devices in 1960, but the 3 other nuclear powers went on with their painstaking negotiations, centering on questions of an adequate international inspection system to prevent clandestine tests and on control of the international body to be created to supervise the treaty.

The Geneva talks were recessed at U.S. request Dec. 5, 1960 to permit a review of test-ban policy by the incoming Kennedy Administration.

USSR Demands 'Troika' Rule. The 3-power Geneva negotiations for a treaty to ban the testing of nuclear weapons reconvened Mar. 21 for its 274th session after a recess of 3½ months. Representing the 3 powers were chief negotiators Arthur H. Dean of the U.S., David Ormsby-Gore of Britain and Semyon K. Tsarapkin of the Soviet Union.

In an address reopening the conference, Tsarapkin, chairman for the day, withdrew the USSR's previous agreement to name a single administrator for a proposed test-ban control commission. He instead demanded that the proposed control commission be run by a 3-member executive chosen to represent the West, the Soviet bloc, and neutralist nations. The USSR had demanded similar "troika" rule of UN and other international bodies.

The "troika" proposal was unacceptable to the west because, coupled with Russian demands for unanimity on major decisions, it would assure the Soviet bloc veto power over all control commission actions.

41

(Pres. Kennedy said at his news conference Apr. 21 that he was "very discouraged" by Soviet insistence on a 3-member executive for the proposed nuclear test control system. He said that "it is quite obvious that the Senate would not accept such a treaty nor would I send it to the Senate, because the inspection system then would not provide any guarantees at all.")

Western Draft. A Western draft of a proposed nuclear test ban treaty, incorporating all major proposals made to the conference since it began in 1958, was presented to the conference Apr. 18 by Dean on behalf of the U.S. and Britain.

The Western draft contained these major provisions:

■ Cessation of all nuclear tests on the earth's surface, in the atmosphere, in space and under water; all underground detonations producing seismic shocks of 4.75 or higher on the Richter Magnitude Scale would be banned.

■ A voluntary moratorium on all underground tests beneath the 4.75 level, considered by the West to be undetectable with certainty and hence excluded from the treaty. The moratorium would extend for 3 years and would be renewable annually pending the perfection of techniques for detection of small underground tests.

■ A quota of up to 20 on-site inspections annually of suspected clandestine nuclear tests on the territory of each of the 3 powers. Inspection teams would not include nationals of the country inspected, but Soviet observers would be permitted to accompany teams operating in the USSR.

■ Direction of the international control commission to be created by the treaty by a single administrator acceptable to all 3 powers. The USSR would be given the right to name 2 of the control commission's deputy administrators.

Tsarapkin rejected the Western draft Apr. 19 as "unacceptable to the USSR." He reiterated past Soviet demands that on-site inspections be limited to 3 annually in each country and that inspection teams operating in the USSR include Russians.

Dean told the conferees Mar. 21 that the U.S. was willing to go to unprecedented lengths to allay Soviet mistrust of Western intentions. He said Pres. Kennedy was prepared to seek "the necessary Congressional action" to amend the Atomic Energy Act to let Soviet scientists inspect U.S. nuclear devices used for a proposed program to perfect the detection of small underground detonations. The West also had offered (a) to reduce the number of detection-control posts to 19 on Soviet territory, to 17 in the U.S., to one in Britain and to 13 elsewhere in Commonwealth nations and British dependencies; (b) to accept an 11-member treaty control commission, in which the Soviet and Western powers would have 4 seats each and in which 3 seats would go to uncommitted nations.

Warning on French Test. The Soviet delegation warned May 15 that the USSR would resume its nuclear test program unless the U.S. and Britain took steps to insure that France halted its atomic tests. Tsarapkin said that if France carried out any new nuclear tests in defiance of the Soviet warning, its action would "free the Soviet Union to resume testing of nuclear and hydrogen bombs." Tsarapkin accused the U.S. and Britain of having encouraged the continued French tests in order to obtain new weapons research data without resuming their own tests.

(France had detonated its 4th nuclear device Apr. 24 near Reggan, in the Sahara.)

West Offers 12-20 Inspections. The U.S. and Britain offered May 29 to abandon their demand for a minimum annual quota of 20 on-site inspections of suspected treaty violations and to accept instead a variable annual quota of 12 to 20 inspections.

Under the Western plan, a minimum of 12 on-site inspections annually of suspicious seismic events registering 4.75 or more on the Richter Magnitude Scale would be permitted on the territory of each of the 3 powers. One additional on-site inspection, up to a total of 20, would be added to the annual quota applied to each signatory for every 5 seismic events (of 4.75 or higher reading) above a quota of 60 for each country.

(Western scientists had estimated that at least 100 unverifiable seismic events that could be confused with nuclear detonations occurred each year on Soviet territory.)

Tsarapkin rejected the Western proposal May 31. He asserted that the inspection quota sought by the West was still "artificially high" and that an acceptable quota would have to be determined politically, rather than scientifically.

Summit Talks & Soviet Memo

Vienna Meeting. Pres. Kennedy and Soviet Premier Khrushchev met in Vienna June 3-4 to discuss East-West problems, among them the long-deadlocked negotiations on a nuclear test ban and on disarmament.

The 2 leaders were said to have repeated their governments' hardened views on both questions—Mr. Kennedy, that the West could accept no disarmament pact or nuclear-test ban treaty unless it provided for strict international control and inspection; Khrushchev, that the Soviet bloc could not permit the installation of international control agencies on its territory until its safety had been assured by substantial disarmament and ironbound pledges that no more nuclear tests would be held.

Mr. Kennedy, in a radio-TV report June 6 on the Vienna meeting, gave this impression of Khrushchev's views on disarmament and the Geneva talks:

"Mr. Khrushchev made it clear that there could not be a neutral administrator [heading a test-ban control organization] in his opinion because no one was truly neutral, that a Soviet veto would have to apply to acts of enforcement, that inspection was only a subterfuge for espionage in the absence of total disarmament, and that the present test-ban negotiations appeared futile.

"In short, our hopes for an end to nuclear tests, for an end to the spread of nuclear weapons, and for some slowdown of the arms race, have been struck a serious blow."

Reds Ask New Talks. A Soviet policy memo delivered to U.S. officials at the end of the Kennedy-Khrushchev meeting called on the West to accept Soviet terms for a nuclear test ban treaty or to join in entirely new negotiations dealing both with tests and disarmament.

The memo's text was made available by the Soviet Tass news agency June 11. Its major policy statements:

A-test moratorium — "The Soviet government agreed to the American proposal that the [nuclear test-ban] treaty should temporarily exclude from the ban underground tests of nuclear weapons below a definite [seismic] threshold value. Now we must reach agreement on a moratorium on underground nuclear explosions temporarily not covered by the treaty. . . . [The] moratorium must be of such a nature that no nation could violate it arbitrarily and resume test explosions of nuclear bombs. . . ."

3-member executive — The USSR proposed that the test ban be supervised by "an Administrative Council of 3 equal representatives, one each from the principal groups of states— the Socialist states, the countries belonging to the Western military blocs and the neutralist states." The Western proposal for entrusting a test-ban control commission to the administration of one man, a neutral, was unacceptable to the USSR because "it is well known that, while there are neutral states, there are not nor can there be neutral men."

Inspection quota—"Our proposal of 3 inspections each on the territory [of the U.S., USSR and Britain] . . . a year provides quite adequate guarantees against violations of the treaty on the cessation of nuclear weapons tests." The Western powers had demanded "an excessive number of inspections." The USSR could not "disregard the circumstances that while there are military alignments of states in the world, inspections can be used for intelligence purposes."

New talks—It was apparent "that the parties to the Geneva talks . . . now find it difficult to agree on the cessation of nuclear tests." "Would it then not be better for our countries to take up the main, cardinal question—the question of general and complete disarmament?" "Indeed, let us solve both problems in their interdependence, then the main obstacle will be eliminated which the Western powers now see in the Soviet proposal for . . . a 3-member Administrative Council."

Disarmament & control—"The Soviet government . . . is willing unconditionally to accept any Western control proposals if the Western powers accept the proposal for general and complete disarmament." It would "sign a document which will include the Western proposals on the cessation of nuclear tests." "If the armed forces of states are maintained, no control can be separated from intelligence. Control will not be associated with intelligence only when armed forces are abolished and armaments destroyed."

U.S. Rejects Red Terms. The Kennedy Administration formally warned the USSR June 17 that it would not indefinitely continue the U.S.' voluntary suspension of nuclear tests in the absence of progress toward a test-ban agreement. The warning was given in a U.S. note that was considered a reply to the Soviet summit memo and a rejection of its terms.

The U.S. note rejected as a delaying tactic the USSR's suggestion that the nuclear test talks be merged with general disarmament negotiations. It also refused to accept the Soviet view that no test ban administrator could be neutral. It declared: "The Soviet proposal for a tripartite administrative council involves a built-in veto over the operation of the control system."

The note contained these indications that the U.S. might find it necessary to resume testing:

■ It was evident that "the Soviet Union is attempting to continue a situation in which the United States accepts an unenforced commitment not to test. This would leave the Soviet Union, with its closed society . . . and its action shrouded in a veil of secrecy, free to conduct nuclear weapons tests without fear of exposure. For almost 3 years, the United States has been willing to assume . . . [this risk. The] defenses of the free world do not allow this risk to be assumed indefinitely."

■ "To throw away the progress made toward a test ban agreement . . . would mean the further proliferation of nuclear weapons and the testing of such weapons by an ever-greater number of countries. In view of the ease of clandestine nuclear testing under an unpoliced ban, it means that each government will face an increasing need to take whatever steps may be necessary in its own defense, including nuclear testing."

Red Ultimatum at Geneva. The USSR's memo was transmitted to the U.S.-British-Soviet nuclear test ban conference in Geneva June 12 as the only acceptable basis for continued negotiations.

Soviet delegate Tsarapkin gave the Western powers the choice of accepting the Soviet proposals for a 3-member Administrative Council and a small number of on-site inspections or of agreeing to merge the Geneva talks with a new East-West conference on disarmament. Tsarapkin declared that the USSR would not compromise on the memo's proposals.

U.S. delegate Dean rejected the Soviet document June 12 as an attempt to "dictate" to the conference. "Today, more blatantly than ever before," he charged, "the 2 Western delegations . . . have been presented with the Soviet position on a take-it-or-leave-it basis."

Dean was recalled to Washington June 20 as an expression of the U.S.' belief that the talks were hopelessly deadlocked. He was replaced by his deputy, Charles C. Stelle.

U.S. Tests Urged. A Congressional campaign for the resumption of U.S. nuclear tests was launched June 14 by Chrmn. Chet Holifield (D., Calif.) of the Joint Congressional Committee on Atomic Energy.

Rep. Holifield, who said his views were supported by a majority of his committee, appealed to Pres. Kennedy to announce "within a few weeks" that the U.S. would resume its test program and would continue to participate in the Geneva negotiations. Holifield's views, outlined in a House speech and a subsequent news conference, were described as a possible Administration "trial balloon" on abandoning the U.S. test moratorium.

Holifield said: "The time has come when we can no longer gamble with the destiny of the United States and the free world" through prolongation of the moratorium; the USSR, which had refused constructive negotiations at Geneva, might be conducting clandestine tests.

(U.S. Atomic Energy Commission spokesmen confirmed July 8 that work was progressing in the Cactus Mountains near Mercury, Nev. on 2 tunnel complexes designed for underground nuclear testing. The AEC July 19 denied reports that it had been ordered to prepare for a resumption of underground nuclear tests in December.)

Khrushchev Test Warning. Premier Khrushchev warned June 21 that the USSR would resume nuclear testing "immediately" if the U.S. resumed tests. Khrushchev, speaking at a Kremlin meeting marking the 20th anniversary of the Nazi invasion of Russia, replied specifically to the June 17 U.S. note.

He declared: "For close to 3 years . . . the Soviet Union has been making no nuclear weapons tests. . . . We can continue abstaining from nuclear tests and offer to the Western powers to reach agreement on the disarmament problem as a whole . . . including the question of nuclear weapons tests." "Some American leaders urge . . . [the U.S.] to resume nuclear weapons tests [if the USSR does not accept Western demands]. . . . We must warn these gentlemen: No sooner the United States resumes nuclear explosions, the Soviet Union . . . will start testing. . . . This testing . . . will increase the fighting power of our armed forces and enable us to develop even better . . . nuclear bombs, enable us to improve the technology of their manufacture."

U.S. Note Rejected. A Soviet note delivered to the U.S. July 5 (made public July 7) rejected the Western views outlined in the U.S.' June 17 warning on the Geneva talks.

The Soviet message charged that the U.S. note had betrayed the Kennedy Administration's concern "with only one thing, how to justify in the eyes of public opinion the resumption of nuclear tests which is being prepared in the United States, what pretext to find for burning the bridges to agreement on the prohibition of such tests." It asserted that "the United States is not interested in honest agreement on a treaty which would put an end to nuclear testing for all time and is seeking loopholes to circumvent the treaty and thus turn it into a scrap of paper."

The USSR renewed its demand that the Geneva talks be merged with general disarmament negotiations; it again insisted on a 3-member test-ban executive representing the Soviet, Western and neutralist blocs.

A U.S. note rebutting the Soviet charges and demands was delivered in Moscow July 15. It denounced the Soviet proposals as calculated to lead inevitably to "paralysis" of any international control and inspection organs that the Geneva negotiations might succeed in creating.

U.S. Checks for Red Tests. Pres. Kennedy disclosed Aug. 10 that a special panel of his Science Advisory Committee had made a study of the possibility that the USSR had been conducting secret nuclear tests.

Mr. Kennedy said that the committee, after assessing all available evidence, had found it "impossible to make a precise determination without inspection of whether [Soviet] nuclear testing is going on." (The President, in an announcement June 28 of the panel's formation, had disclosed that neither his nor the preceding Administration had "any knowledge which would state that the Soviet Union had been testing.") Mr. Kennedy added, however, that the panel's report had "made me feel more urgently than ever that without an inspection system . . . no country in the world can ever be sure that a nation with a closed society is not conducting secret nuclear tests."

'Final' U.S. Offer. Arthur H. Dean returned to Geneva Aug. 24 to present a "final" U.S. offer of a draft treaty to ban nuclear tests.

The U.S. draft, prepared with the personal participation of Pres. Kennedy, was submitted to the conference by Dean Aug. 28 with the support of Britain. It was immediately rejected by the Soviet delegation.

The plan accepted Soviet objections to the prior Western draft, presented Apr. 18, that would have provided for a treaty ban on all atmospheric tests and detectable underground tests but would have left small underground detonations to be covered only by a 3-year voluntary moratorium. The new proposal offered a treaty ban on all nuclear tests without exception, provided the USSR accepted a stronger inspection and control system than previously envisaged. It gave the USSR the alternative of accepting the Apr. 18 plan with the provision that a panel of scientists from 4 Western, 4 Soviet-bloc and 3 neutral countries would decide the question of controls for small underground tests after the 3-year moratorium.

Tsarapkin declared that it was senseless to talk of a test ban while international tensions mounted and "arms . . . are being increased throughout the world."

The conference was recessed Sept. 9, after the resumption of Soviet nuclear tests.

Russia Resumes Tests

The Soviet government announced Aug. 31 that it was breaking the 34-month-old voluntary moratorium on nuclear weapons tests. It said that it was forced to resume the testing of new nuclear weapons to defend the USSR against war threats from the U.S. and its Western allies.

The Soviet announcement said the USSR had designed "super-powerful nuclear bombs" with a yield equivalent to up to 100 million tons of TNT. It asserted that "powerful rockets similar to those" used in Soviet manned orbital flights could deliver such bombs "to any point on the globe."

Within 24 hours of its announcement the USSR detonated a nuclear device—the first it was known to have tested since Nov. 3, 1958. The test provoked widespread criticism, from Western and neutral nations alike. It was followed by the U.S.' announcement that it, too, now felt compelled to resume testing.

Soviet Announcement. A Soviet statement issued through the Tass news agency Aug. 31 (Aug. 30 U.S. time) said the USSR was "compelled" to resume nuclear testing "for the sole aim" of averting a world war.

The statement said it was "an open secret" that the U.S. was "at the threshold of carrying out underground nuclear explosions and only waits for the first suitable pretext to start them. . . . Since the U.S. government has the intention to resume nuclear weapons tests, it is only a matter of time."

The statement said: The USSR "has already taken a number of serious measures for strengthening" its security in the face of the West's military buildup and "threats . . . to unleash war as a countermeasure" to a peace treaty with East Germany; "those who are preparing a new world holocaust are sowing illusions that a new world war . . . would allegedly be waged without thermonuclear weapons; but this is a deceit of the peoples"; "any armed conflict . . . would inevitably grow into a universal rocket and nuclear war should the nuclear powers have been drawn into it"; "the harmful consequences of thermonuclear weapons tests for living organisms are well known in the Soviet Union," and

"every measure is being taken [in the tests] to minimize these effects."

Move Condemned. The Soviet announcement was condemned in statements issued by the U.S. and every other Western nation. It was protested by Japan, where public sentiment was unusually sensitive on the nuclear weapons question. It was criticized by Indian Prime Min. Jawaharlal Nehru and other neutralist leaders attending a conference in Belgrade. It was defended only by Communist nations.

A White House statement issued Aug. 30 predicted that the Soviet action "will be met with deepest concern and resentment throughout the world." It said: "The Soviet government's decision to resume nuclear testing presents a threat to the entire world by increasing the dangers of a thermonuclear holocaust . . . [and] indicates the complete hypocrisy of its professions about general and complete disarmament"; "the pretext offered by the [USSR] announcement for Soviet resumption of weapons testing is the very crisis which they themselves have created by threatening to disturb the peace which has existed in Germany and Berlin."

(Pres. Kennedy conferred Aug. 31 with National Security Council members and Congressional leaders of both parties. A 2d White House statement issued later Aug. 31 said: "The President is entirely confident that . . . [the U.S.] nuclear weapons stockpile and the capabilities of individual weapons and delivery systems are wholly adequate" for U.S. and free-world defense.)

Japanese Amb.-to-USSR Hisanori Yamada delivered to Soviet Deputy Foreign Min. Vasily V. Kuznetsov a Japanese government protest asserting that the Soviet decision "mercilessly tramples on the prayerful hopes for peace of all peoples who fear war and love peace."

The Earl of Home, British foreign secretary, asserted in an Aug. 31 statement that the Soviet decision "contemptuously ignores the desires of ordinary people everywhere . . . to see an end of nuclear tests."

A French statement through the Agence France-Presse Aug. 31 called the Soviet decision "a deliberate menace designed to bring the free world around to its way of thinking."

West German Chancellor Konrad Adenauer said in Goettingen Aug. 31 that the Soviet action proved West Germany's need for A-weapons.

Dr. Linus Pauling, Nobel Prize-winning biochemist and opponent of A-tests, cabled Khrushchev Sept. 2 an appeal to "cancel the new . . . tests and announced expansion of the Soviet nuclear arsenal."

5,000 persons marched in London in a protest organized by the Campaign for Nuclear Disarmament against the Soviet decision.

Soviet Tests Begin. The opening of the Soviet atomic test series was disclosed by the White House Sept. 1 with the release of a 35-word announcement that said: "The Soviet Union today has conducted a nuclear test in the general area of Semipalatinsk in Central Asia [in Siberia, about 350 miles south of Novosibirsk]. The device tested had a substantial yield in the intermediate range. It was detonated in the atmosphere." Andrew Hatcher, assistant White House press secretary, said the test had been detected "early this morning, Western time," by means of "long-range detecting equipment."

The 2d Soviet test after the ending of the moratorium took place Sept. 4 and was announced the same day by the U.S. Atomic Energy Commission, which said the device was detonated in the atmosphere in the Semipalatinsk area. The AEC said its yield was in the "low kiloton range"—probably the equivalent of 20 kilotons

(20,000 tons) of TNT. The 3d and 4th Soviet tests were carried out Sept. 5 and 6 and also were announced by the AEC. Both were described as in the "low-to-intermediate range." The 4th was said to have been carried out "east of Stalingrad," in European Russia.

Anglo-U.S. Proposal. Pres. Kennedy and Prime Min. Macmillan proposed in a joint message to Khrushchev Sept. 3 "that their 3 governments agree, effective immediately, not to conduct nuclear tests which take place in the atmosphere and produce radioactive fallout."

The note, delivered to the Soviet embassies in Washington and London, urged Khrushchev "to cable his immediate acceptance of this offer and his cessation of further atmospheric tests." It proposed that the 3 nations' "representatives at Geneva meet not later than Sept. 9 to record this agreement" and report it to the UN. The note declared that the U.S. and Britain "are prepared to rely upon existing means of detection, which they believe to be adequate," for atmospheric tests. It added that they "reaffirm their serious desire to conclude a nuclear test ban treaty, applicable to other forms of testing [underground] as well."

The U.S.-British offer was rejected by Khrushchev Sept. 9 in a note that said "nuclear tests can now be ended . . . only on the basis of general and complete disarmament."

U.S. to Resume Tests. Pres. Kennedy announced Sept. 5, after the 3d Soviet test, that "in view of the continued [Soviet] testing . . . I have today ordered the resumption of nuclear tests in the laboratory and underground, with no fallout."

The President's statement said: "In our efforts to achieve an end to nuclear testing, we have taken every step that reasonable men could justify. In view of the acts of the Soviet government, we must now take those steps which prudent men find essential. We have no other choice in fulfillment of the [U.S. government's] responsibilities . . . to its own citizens and to the security of other free nations. Our offer to make an agreement to end all fallout tests remains open until Sept. 9."

Neutralists Urge Summit. The Soviet decision to resume atomic tests was received with expressions ranging from severe criticism to broadminded understanding at a conference

Nobel Peace Prize Winners

The Nobel Peace Prize Committee announced in Oslo Oct. 23 that it had awarded the 1961 Peace Prize to the late UN Secy. Gen. Dag Hammarskjöld (left) and the 1960 Peace Prize, withheld the previous year, to Albert John Luthuli, 61 (right), a deposed Zulu chief and a leader in the campaign against South Africa's apartheid policies.

The prizes were accepted in Oslo ceremonies Dec. 10 by Luthuli and, on the behalf of Hammarskjöld, by Swedish Amb.-to-Norway Rolf Edberg. Luthuli had been granted a South African passport to go to Oslo for the award but was forbidden to prolong his stay or to make a requested visit to the U.S.

The 1960 prize carried a cash award of $43,615; the 1961 prize $49,294.

of 25 "non-aligned" nations held in Belgrade, Yugoslavia Sept. 1-5.

The conferees compromised Sept. 5 on an appeal to Mr. Kennedy and Khrushchev to make "immediate and direct approaches to each other to avert the danger of war." Their declaration said the U.S. and USSR "should immediately suspend their war preparations, take no steps which might aggravate the situation, and take steps toward negotiations until they . . . achieve total disarmament and world peace."

The conferees chose Indian Prime Min. Jawaharlal Nehru and Ghanaian Pres. Kwame Nkrumah Sept. 5 to present the appeal to Khrushchev. Presidents Sukarno of Indonesia and Modibo Keita of Mali were delegated to deliver the appeal to Pres. Kennedy.

At the conference, the sharpest criticism of the Soviet decision was voiced by Nehru, who declared Sept. 2 that "the danger of war has been enhanced" by the Soviet action. "This decision makes the [troubled world] situation much more dangerous," he declared. "It may lead other countries to start tests."

Yugoslav Pres. Tito, who had proposed the conference, treated the Soviet decision tolerantly. He told the conferees Sept. 3 that "we were not surprised so much by the communiqué on the resumption of . . . tests because we could understand the [USSR's] reasons. . . . We were surprised more by the fact that this was done on the opening of this conference of peace."

UAR Pres. Gamal Abdel Nasser said Sept. 1 that the Soviet "decision shocked me just as it shocked world public opinion." Ghanaian Pres. Nkrumah declared Sept. 2 that it was "a shock" that "shows what a big danger humanity is facing." Burmese Premier U Nu said Sept. 2: "Today the situation is closer to war than to coexistence."

Khrushchev Scorns Accord. The Soviet government's refusal to consider a renewal of the moratorium on testing or a formal test ban on Anglo-U.S. terms was made clear by Premier Khrushchev in a lengthy interview granted Cyrus L. Sulzberger of the N.Y. Times Sept. 5.

In an additional statement given Sulzberger Sept. 7 to clarify his position on proposals for a summit meeting, Khrushchev said that he was willing to meet with Pres. Kennedy to settle world problems but that such a meeting would be "fruitful" only if the President accepted Soviet terms for settlement of the current tension.

The Khrushchev interview, published by the Times Sept. 8, contained these views:

■ A "cessation of thermonuclear tests without a solution of the disarmament problem" would be useless "if the arms race continued and war industry went on . . . creating nuclear weapons. . . . The chief danger now facing mankind is the danger of thermonuclear war, and it would not be lifted as a result of a moratorium." "The Kennedy-Macmillan proposal says nothing on a cessation of underground test explosions." The USSR was "lagging far behind" the West in the number of tests. "We . . . have a moral right to equal conditions as regards . . . our security."

■ The USSR would not promise that it would not be the first to use nuclear weapons in a war. "Anyone who made such a statement could turn out to be untruthful even though, when making such a pledge, he would be sincere." Even if both sides in a war promised "not to employ nuclear weapons while retaining their stockpiles," the side that thought it was losing "would undoubtedly use its nuclear bombs." "If atomic weapons are preserved and if war is unleashed, it will be a thermonuclear war."

■ "We already have" a bomb "equal in capacity to 100 million tons of TNT . . . and shall test the explosive device for it." "We will stop short of nothing if aggressors attack us. . . . Several such super bombs at our disposal will considerably increase the [USSR's] defensive capability. . . . The aggressors will think twice before attacking us. . . . [We] have repeatedly declared we have no intention of attacking anyone."

Neutralist Missions Fail. The neutralist leaders sent by the Belgrade conference to Khrushchev and Pres. Kennedy failed to persuade either to restore the moratorium on testing or to agree to a summit meeting.

Indian Prime Min. Nehru arrived in Moscow Sept. 6 to begin his talks with Khrushchev. Speaking at an Indian embassy luncheon given by Nehru Sept. 7, Khrushchev said the USSR could not "watch passively while . . . unprecedented war preparations are being carried out against the Soviet Union." Nehru repeated his plea publicly at a Kremlin meeting Sept. 8. "Whatever the military justification of these tests," he said, "they expose the whole human race to peril." Khrushchev, in a joint com-

Lenin Peace Prizes

The Soviet Union Apr. 30 awarded Cuban Premier Fidel Castro a 1960 Lenin Peace Prize as a "statesman . . . whose entire life is dedicated to the . . . struggle . . . for freedom and independence."

Other 1960 Lenin prize recipients: Pres. Sékou Touré of Guinea; Mrs. Rameshwari Nehru, an Indian peace movement leader; Mikhail Sadoveanu, Rumanian writer; Antoine Georges Tabet, Lebanese architect; Polish Communist Ostap Dluski, one of the founders of the World Peace Council; William Morrow, Australian labor leader.

muniqué issued with Nehru Sept. 10, refused to resume the moratorium. He wrote Nehru Sept. 16 to assert that he was willing to meet Mr. Kennedy but had little hope such talks would succeed.

Presidents Sukarno of Indonesia and Modibo Keita of Mali delivered the neutralist appeal to Pres. Kennedy in Washington Sept. 12-13. Mr. Kennedy refused to commit himself to a hasty summit meeting on the ground that an ill-prepared meeting would fail and increase, rather than decrease, world tensions. In a letter given the 2 neutralist leaders Sept. 13, Mr. Kennedy said: "We see no reason why eventual negotiations should not be successful in coping with the present crisis. However, we do not intend to enter into negotiations under ultimata or threats. . . . We are determined to honor our commitments [in Berlin] and are prepared to meet force with force if it is used against us."

U.S. Resumes Tests. The U.S. ended its 3-year self-imposed ban on atomic tests by detonating 2 "low-yield" nuclear weapon devices Sept. 15 and 16 in tunnels at the mountainous Nevada test site 65 miles northwest of Las Vegas. Both tests were announced by the U.S. immediately. Neither produced radioactive fall-out.

Pres. Kennedy, disclosing Sept. 15 that the first test had taken place minutes earlier at 1 p.m. EDT, pointed out that the USSR already had conducted 10 post-moratorium tests, "3 of them in the megaton range." The lack of fallout from the underground U.S. tests was "in marked contrast to the Soviet nuclear tests in the atmosphere," the President said. Mr. Kennedy asserted that the "extensive Soviet testing" had made the U.S. action necessary for free-world security. He reiterated that the U.S. was ready "to negotiate a controlled test-ban agreement of the widest possible scope." (The Moscow newspaper Pravda

U.S. & European "peace marchers" parade in Moscow's Red Square Oct. 3 but are forbidden to make speeches. Sign at left says: "We appeal to all peoples to reject hydrogen weapons at once." Other signs carry similar pacifist messages. (Wide World photo)

Sept. 16 reported the first test in the new U.S. series. No Soviet newspaper or official so far had done more than indicate obliquely that the postmoratorium Soviet tests had started. The only reported public disclosure by the USSR of its tests was made in brief phrases buried in Pravda and Izvestia Sept. 9-10 in reports of Premier Khrushchev's interview with C. L. Sulzberger of the N.Y. Times.)

U.S. Pacifists in USSR. 31 "peace marchers" from the U.S. and 8 other countries arrived by foot in Moscow Oct. 3 to argue for unilateral disarmament and an end to nuclear tests. The 13 Americans among them included 8 who had started the 10-month walk in San Francisco Dec. 1, 1960. The group, organized by the Committee for Non-Violent Action, headed by the Rev. A. J. Muste, 77, walked across the U.S. and then from Western Europe into the USSR. Some members dropped out but new ones joined during the march.

On arriving at Red Square in Moscow Oct. 3, the walkers were forbidden to make speeches but were permitted to talk to individual Russians and to hand out pamphlets. Members of the group debated with Moscow University students in a university auditorium Oct. 5, and the Soviet students angrily shouted down professors who tried to break up the meeting after about 2 hours. Some of the students learned only from the peace marchers that the USSR had resumed nuclear testing.

Mrs. Nina Petrovna Khrushchev, wife of Premier Khrushchev, met at tea Oct. 6 with 9 of the women and one man who had made the march. She learned from them how many nuclear tests the USSR had conducted since the moratorium had been ended (17 reported by the U.S. AEC at that time), but she had known that testing had started. Mrs. Khrushchev defended the Soviet tests and denied that they were harmful to health.

Most of the marchers left Moscow for home by Oct. 9.

French A-Tests End. The French Atomic Energy Commission announced Oct. 7 that its series of nuclear tests had been completed and no more currently were planned.

Red 'Superbombs' Tested

The 2 most powerful nuclear bombs ever tested—of 25 and of 58 megatons intensity, respectively—were detonated by Soviet scientists at the end of October at the USSR's Novaya Zemlya proving area in the Arctic.

Plans for the tests had been announced in advance by Khrushchev; the plans were carried out despite worldwide protests and an appeal for their cancellation from a majority of UN member states.

The Soviet action brought wide condemnation of the USSR. It did not, as Khrushchev had suggested in his initial announcement, bring an end to the Russian test series.

Khrushchev Announcement. The Soviet plan to detonate a hydrogen bomb with an explosive force of 50 megatons was announced by Khrushchev Oct. 17 in an address at the opening session of the 22d Soviet Communist Party Congress in Moscow.

The 50-megaton bomb—more than 2½ times more powerful than any nuclear device yet tested—was to be detonated to proof-test the mechanism of a 100-megaton bomb said to be in the Soviet arsenal.

Khrushchev's announcement was made in the course of a 6½-hour speech reporting on Soviet achievements since the previous party congress. His remarks, as translated by the USSR's Novosti Press Agency:

"We're . . . having very successful tests of new nuclear weapons. . . . It's most likely that to wind up the series we shall detonate an H-bomb with an explosive power of 50 million tons of TNT. We said that we had a bomb with an explosive power of 100 million tons of TNT. That's quite true. But we shan't explode it because . . . even if we do that in the most faraway places, our window panes might fly out. . . . However, by detonating a bomb with an explosive power of 50 million tons of TNT we shall thereby be able to try out the arrangement also for exploding the bigger bomb."

"But, as they used to say, God save us from ever exploding these bombs over any territory. That is the most desired dream of our life!"

(Khrushchev's statement was the first official announcement to the Russian people that the USSR actually had resumed nuclear tests.)

U.S. Appeals Against Test. The U.S. government called on the USSR Oct. 17 to cancel its 50-megaton test. The U.S. appeal was made in a White House statement that said:

"It is reported that the Soviet Union plans to explode a giant nuclear bomb—the equivalent to 50 million tons of TNT. We call upon the Soviet Union to reconsider. . . . We know about high-yield weapons. Since 1957 the United States has had the technical know-how and materials to produce bombs in the 50-100 megaton range and higher. But we also know that such weapons are not essential to our military needs. Furthermore, full-scale tests are not necessary to develop 50-megaton bombs. . . . We believe the peoples throughout the world will join us in asking the Soviet Union not to proceed with a test which can serve no legitimate purpose and which adds a mass of additional radioactive fallout."*

Similar appeals were issued by nearly every major non-Communist government and by many other groups throughout the world.

25-Megaton Blast. Soviet scientists Oct. 23 detonated a nuclear bomb with a force of 25 megatons—equivalent in explosive power to 25 million tons of TNT.

The blast was reported first by the Uppsala (Sweden) University Seismological Institute. Similar reports followed from the French Atomic Energy Commission, the Japanese Meteorological Agency and the U.S. Atomic Energy Commission.

The U.S. announcement: ". . . The Soviet Union today has carried out 2 nuclear test explosions in the Novaya Zemlya area. The first of these was detonated in the atmosphere. The yield of this test was very high, possibly . . . 50 megatons. Preliminary analysis indicates it was more probably on the order of 30 megatons. The 2d was detonated . . . later under water south of . . . Novaya Zemlya. It was in the low-yield range."

It was reported Oct. 30 that AEC scientists, using revised calculations, had rated the blast at 25 megatons.

Worldwide Protests. Political leaders and private citizens in nearly every non-Communist country denounced the detonation and the USSR's apparent lack of concern for world peace and health.

Among reactions reported Oct. 24:

Queen Elizabeth II, in a message from the throne read at the closing of the British Parliament, said Britain deeply regretted Soviet testing in the face of world efforts to reach a test-ban agreement.

U.S. Amb.-to-UN Adlai E. Stevenson said the Soviet test "expressed contempt of the peaceful sensibility of all mankind."

Indian Prime Min. Jawaharlal Nehru said the "horrible" test left him "deeply pained and shocked."

Lord Russell, leader of Britain's Committee-of-100 movement against nuclear weapons, protested the blast at the Soviet embassy in London but walked out because he could not "swallow comments about the innocence of the Soviet Union."†

Japanese Foreign Min. Zentaro Kosaka said Japan would protest the Soviet test, and Japanese Socialist Party members filed protests at the USSR's Tokyo embassy.

Delegates from 43 Socialist parties, attending the 7th Congress of the Socialist International in Rome, approved a resolution condemning the blast as a "monstrous crime against humanity."

Students staged protest marches in Rome, Copenhagen and other European cities.

UN Votes Appeal. The UN General Assembly appealed to the USSR Oct. 27 to cancel its planned 50-megaton test.

The UN appeal was voiced in a resolution adopted by the Assembly that day by a vote of 87 to 11. The resolution was opposed only by the

*Washington officials, basing their estimates on the known power of the 15-20 megaton bomb detonated by the U.S. in the Pacific Mar. 1, 1954, said that a 50-megaton bomb could: (1) kindle fires and cause severe burns to exposed persons within a 40- to 50-mile radius of ground zero; (2) kill all persons within 2¾ miles nearly instantly with radiation; (3) destroy all heavy industrial buildings within 2¾ miles and residential structures within 14 miles of the impact point.
†513 members of the Committee of 100 had been arrested Oct. 21 as they marched to the Soviet embassy in London to protest Russian plans to detonate the superbomb. The marchers staged a sit-down in a street near the embassy when ordered to disperse by the police.

USSR, Outer Mongolia, other Soviet-bloc nations and Cuba; Mali abstained, and 4 countries were absent (Dahomey, Morocco, Nicaragua and Somalia.) The resolution called on Soviet leaders "solemnly . . . to refrain from carrying out their intention to explode in the atmosphere a 50-megaton bomb before the end of this month." The plea was rejected Oct. 27 by Soviet delegate Semyon K. Tsarapkin, who told the Assembly that the West need have "no illusions" about the USSR continuing its nuclear tests as long as it considered them militarily necessary.

The resolution had been introduced Oct. 20 by 6 nations lying directly in the belt of radioactive fallout produced by the Soviet tests—Canada, Denmark, Iceland, Japan, Norway and Sweden.

58-Megaton Bomb Exploded. The largest known man-made explosion in history was set off Oct. 30 by Russian scientists who detonated a hydrogen bomb with a force later said by U.S. sources to equal 58 megatons.

The bomb was exploded at 8:30 a.m. GMT at the USSR's Novaya Zemlya atomic proving grounds in the Arctic. It exceeded the power planned by its designers.

The White House, announcing the explosion on the basis of "preliminary" AEC data, said it appeared to be "on the order of 50 megatons."

The angry White House statement pointed out that "the explosion took place in the atmosphere" and "will produce more radioactive fall-out than any previous explosion." It said:

"The Soviet explosion was a political rather than a military act. The device exploded does not add in effectiveness against military targets to nuclear weapons now available" to both the USSR and the U.S. "Any such weapon would be primarily a mass killer of people . . . — and the testing of this device primarily an incitement

to fright and panic in the cold war." The USSR "intends through this display to spread such fear . . . that peace-loving men will accept any Soviet demand. . . . There is no mystery about producing a 50-megaton bomb, nor is there any technical need for testing such a weapon at full-scale detonation."

It was reported that the bomb had been set off at an altitude of 12,000 feet; its fireball, 25,000 feet in diameter, was believed to have touched the ground, creating vast quantities of radioactive debris.

Khrushchev, joking about the test at the Soviet Communist Party Congress in the Kremlin, said Oct. 31: "Our scientists miscalculated"; the explosion "proved somewhat bigger than 50 megatons," but "we shall not punish them for it."

U.S. Readies Air Tests. Pres. Kennedy announced Nov. 2 that he had ordered U.S. scientists to prepare to resume nuclear tests in the atmosphere if "it becomes necessary."

The President's decision was reached—or confirmed—at a White House meeting earlier that day of the National Security Council. Newsmen reported that the meeting was attended by an unusual number of advisers, among them ex-Pres. Truman.

Mr. Kennedy's announcement was read to newsmen immediately after the NSC session. It said:

"The United States is carefully assessing the current series of nuclear tests being conducted by the Soviet Union"; "I do not suggest that we can dismiss these Soviet nuclear tests as mere bluff and bluster"; "these tests are no doubt of importance to Soviet leaders and scientists in developing new weapons"; the U.S. had "many times more nuclear power than any other nation on earth"; "in view of the Soviet action, it will be the policy of the United States to proceed in developing nuclear weapons

Path of radioactive cloud from 58-megaton Soviet nuclear explosion Oct. 30. Radioactive fallout dropped on Siberia, Alaska, Canada, northern U.S., North Atlantic and Scandinavian countries as radioactive cloud circled Northern Hemisphere.   (Wide World map)

to maintain this superior capability"; "we shall make necessary preparations for such [atmospheric] tests . . . in case it becomes necessary to conduct them."

(British Prime Min. Macmillan told Parliament Oct. 31 that Britain was prepared to join the U.S. in nuclear tests necessary to develop an anti-missile missile and other weapons if the USSR showed signs of surpassing Western weapons technology.)

Radioactive Fallout Spreads. Among reports on fallout from the first test in the new Soviet series Oct. 23 and 30 and the superbombs detonated Oct. 23 and 30:

The U.S. Weather Bureau reported Sept. 8 that a 500-mile-wide cloud of radioactive debris from the first test in the series had reached the Great Lakes area and was following the usual west-to-east path taken by fallout from atmospheric tests in the Northern Hemisphere.

U.S. Health - Education-&-Welfare Secy. Abraham A. Ribicoff announced Sept. 18 that test-caused radioactivity had increased sharply in 12 eastern and northern states Sept. 11-17 but had not reached even a fraction of the levels considered dangerous to health. Much higher readings were cited in a Public Health Service report issued Sept. 19 for 6 southern states; the highest readings were recorded in Montgomery, Ala. (500 micro-microcuries) and Pascagoula, Miss. (472.6 mmc.). (Human health was not believed to be affected by air contamination unless exposure reached 100 mmc. or more continuously for a year.)

The Canadian government announced Sept. 28 that the average weekly readings taken by a nation-wide fallout sampling network had shown an increase from .77 to 35.3 in its rating scale. Similar increases were reported during the latter half of September from nearly every country in the Northern Hemisphere.

The Public Health Service reported Oct. 12 that fallout-produced iodine-131 had increased in milk samples tested in 6 major U.S. cities (to a high of 530 mmc. per liter in New Orleans) but that it posed no danger due to the brief half-life (8 days) of the radio-isotope.

British Defense Min. Harold Watkinson informed Parliament Oct. 24 that Britain would supply powdered milk for infants if radioactive iodine-131, particularly harmful to the thyroid glands of children, reached dangerous levels in whole milk supplies.

The U.S. Public Health Service briefed health officials from the 50 states on the fallout situation at a Washington meeting Oct. 26 but denied any current danger from test-produced radiation. A PHS background report issued the same day conceded, however, that the "extra radiation caused by the Soviet tests will add to the risk of genetic effects in succeeding generations and possibly to the risk of health damage to some people in the United States."

A Peiping radio broadcast Oct. 27 warned that heavy radioactive fallout had occurred in "vast areas of north-east China." The broadcast, reported by the London Times and Reuters, called on the Chinese people to "maintain a vigilant alert against a general radioactive fallout from all directions." The Communist Chinese Foreign Ministry denied Oct. 28 that such a warning had been broadcast, but Hong Kong newsmen reported that re-examination of monitoring tapes had confirmed the radio text.

Clouds of radioactive debris from the USSR's 2 large detonations—of 25 megatons Oct. 23 and 58 megatons Oct. 30—followed the west-to-east path over the Northern Hemisphere. The 200-mile-wide fallout cloud caused by the first of the big tests crossed the U.S.' west coast Oct. 28. A 200-to-300-mile-wide cloud generated by the 2d large blast crossed Alaska Nov. 2, western Canada and the Great Lakes region Nov. 3. Japan's Central Meteorological Agency reported Nov. 5 that a heavily radioactive rain had fallen in Fukuoka, southern Japan, earlier that day. Japanese radiation levels reached a height at which it was deemed necessary to disseminate instructions for the special treatment of food and water.

Khrushchev Warning. Khrushchev was reported Nov. 4 to have warned that the USSR would continue its tests if the U.S. resumed tests in the atmosphere. He was said to have voiced the warning Nov. 3 in reply to an Interparliamentary Union resolution against nuclear tests given him Nov. 3 by Giuseppe Codacci Pisanelli, IPU Council chairman.

The warning was made explicit by an authorized statement issued by the Tass news agency Nov. 5. Tass said that if the U.S. resumed tests in the atmosphere, the USSR would "watch these military preparations, primarily the steps in improving the nuclear weapons, because it cannot permit [that] . . . its security would not be reliably insured."

Khrushchev, talking to Western reporters at a Kremlin reception Nov. 7, said bluntly that "if the West carries out tests, our tests will continue."

Path to New Negotiations

UN Asks Moratorium, Talks. The UN General Assembly voted by huge majorities Nov. 6 and 8 to call for renewal of the voluntary moratorium on nuclear tests and for resumption of the 3-power Geneva talks.

The appeal for renewal of the moratorium was made in an Indian-sponsored resolution adopted Nov. 6 by a 71-20 vote (8 abstentions, 4 absent). The resolution, opposed both by the Soviet bloc (10 negative votes) and by the U.S. and other Western nations (10 negative votes), called on the nuclear powers to halt all testing "pending the conclusion of the necessary international binding agreement" on a test ban. During debate Oct. 30-Nov. 2 by the Assembly's Political Committee, the U.S. and Britain had declared that no unsupervised moratorium could be effective, and the USSR had rejected any treaty ban except as part of a general disarmament agreement.

The call for resumption of the Geneva conference was made in a U.S.-British resolution approved by the Assembly Nov. 8 by a 71-11 vote (15 abstentions, including France; 6 nations absent). The resolution, opposed only by the USSR, other Soviet-bloc countries and Cuba, urged the U.S., Britain and Soviet Union to resume immediately their talks on a treaty banning tests under "effective international control." India, which had opposed the draft to win priority for its own proposal, supported it in the final vote.

Nehru & JFK Confer. Prime Min. Jawaharlal Nehru of India visited the U.S. Nov. 5-14 for a series of talks with Pres. Kennedy at a time when India was coming under increasing criticism for refusing to differentiate between the motives for and the dangers posed by American and Soviet nuclear tests.

Nehru, interviewed by CBS-TV's "Meet the Press" in New York Nov. 5, said: All nuclear tests were "evil things," but it was "obvious that the Soviet Union broke the moratorium . . . and therefore they were responsible for this new phase"; India favored an immediate test moratorium as the only way to halt tests, but "I would not presume" to advise the U.S. on what it should do.

Nehru flew from New York to Newport, R.I. Nov. 6 to begin his talks with Mr. Kennedy. They flew to Washington together the same day, continued their discussions Nov. 7-9 and outlined their views in a joint communiqué Nov. 9.

Nehru returned to New York Nov. 10 to appeal to the UN General Assembly for a nuclear test ban and general disarmament. He warned: The choice no longer was "war or peace"; it was "cooperate or perish; coexistence or no existence at all." In a TV appearance with U.S. Amb.-to-UN Stevenson, Nehru acknowledged that the USSR's resumption of tests was "evil" and its suppression of the 1956 Hungarian revolt "brutal."

USSR Accepts Western Bid. The Soviet Union announced Nov. 21 its acceptance of an Anglo-U.S. proposal to renew the 3-power Geneva negotiations on a treaty to prohibit nuclear weapons tests.

The USSR, however, made it clear that it would resume the tests it had ended Nov. 4 if Western tests were continued. The U.S. the same day rejected a new voluntary moratorium.

The Western proposal was made in separate but similar U.S. and British notes delivered in Moscow and made public Nov. 13. The U.S. note suggested that the 3 powers comply with UN requests for renewal of the talks and hold their first meeting in Geneva Nov. 28. The USSR accepted the Western proposal in parallel notes

Pres. Kennedy and Nehru at White House Nov. 8. (Wide World photo)

sent to the U.S. and Britain Nov. 24. The Soviet notes warned that "if during the talks any power starts to test nuclear weapons, then . . . the other side would be compelled to draw appropriate conclusions."

A statement issued by the State Department after the receipt of the Soviet note gave notification that the U.S. would not participate in a voluntary moratorium on tests and would continue to stage weapons tests "as it deems necessary to safeguard its national security until a controlled test-ban agreement is achieved."

Geneva Talks Resumed. The 3-power negotiations on a treaty to ban nuclear weapons tests were resumed in Geneva Nov. 28.

The conference was reconvened by Joseph B. Godber, British delegate, under the rotating chairmanship system in use at the talks since 1958. The U.S. was represented by Arthur H. Dean and the USSR by Semyon K. Tsarapkin.

A new Soviet draft proposal for an unsupervised test ban was submitted at the conference's first session and immediately was rejected by the West. The Soviet draft, made public through Tass Nov. 27, sought to pledge the world's 4 nuclear powers to refrain from all nuclear tests and to rely on their nationally-controlled test detection systems for supervision.

A Soviet government statement published Nov. 27 by Tass with the draft said that the proposal for nationally-controlled supervision was an extension of the plan advanced by Pres. Kennedy and Prime Min. Macmillan in their Sept. 3 appeal against nuclear tests in the atmosphere. It said that the USSR would be willing to replace nationally-controlled detection with an internationally controlled system only under a treaty for general disarmament.

Speaking for the West Nov. 28, Dean rejected the Soviet draft. He said there was "no chance whatsoever" for U.S. acceptance of any draft that failed to provide effective international supervision of the test ban.

Tsarapkin replied the same day that the USSR could not permit the presence of international inspection machinery on its territory because, under current world conditions, an international inspectorate would be used for "espionage and intelligence."

(The Geneva negotiations continued, without result, until Dec. 21, when they were recessed until Jan. 16, 1962. The U.S. and Britain reported to the UN Disarmament Commission Dec. 19 that the Soviet test-ban proposal had withdrawn even the insignificant control provisions offered in the Soviet draft given the conference at its first session in 1958.)

UN Opposes Weapons, Tests. UN efforts to prohibit the development and use of nuclear weapons were continued by the General Assembly in a series of resolutions adopted Nov. 24-Dec. 4.

A declaration condemning any use of nuclear weapons as a "violation of the [UN] Charter" "contrary to the rules of international law and to the laws of humanity" was adopted Nov. 24 by a 55-20 vote (U.S. and most NATO states opposed; 26 abstentions, including most Latin and SEATO states; 2 absent). The declaration

called on U Thant to begin consultations for the convening of "a special conference for signing a convention on the prohibition of the use of nuclear and thermonuclear weapons for war purposes." The declaration was sponsored by 12 Asian-African states.

A resolution calling for the setting aside of Africa as a "denuclearized zone" was approved Nov. 24 by a 55-0 vote (44 abstentions, including most NATO, Latin and French African states, 4 absent). The resolution asked all states to refrain from nuclear tests in Africa or from storing or transporting A-weapons there.

2 resolutions urging international action to prevent the spread of nuclear weapons were adopted by the Assembly Dec. 4. The first, adopted unanimously, called on all states to seek "an international agreement . . . under which the nuclear states would undertake to refrain from relinquishing control of nuclear weapons and from transmitting the information necessary for their manufacture to states not possessing such weapons." The 2d, approved by a 58-10 vote (23 abstentions), called on Thant to investigate "the conditions under which countries not possessing nuclear weapons might be willing to enter into specific undertakings to refrain from . . . acquiring such weapons."

Khrushchev on Huge Bomb. Soviet Premier Khrushchev declared Dec. 9 that the USSR had nuclear bombs more powerful than 100 megatons and would use them "against our enemies whenever they unleash war against the Socialist countries."

Addressing a Moscow congress of the World Federation of Trade Unions, Khrushchev warned the West against pursuing what he termed its "policy of positions of strength." "You do not have 50 and 100-megaton bombs and we have them already and even more." He warned that the U.S.' continuation of nuclear tests "gives us the right . . . to continue our tests in order to increase further the power of the Socialist camp." Noting that "many honest people" had expressed concern at fallout from Soviet nuclear tests, he said that "the countries of socialism have to think first . . . about the fact that nuclear bombs might begin to destroy whole cities and millions of people."

Soviet Tests Analyzed. The U.S. Atomic Energy Commission said Dec. 9 that the USSR's recent tests probably had advanced Soviet nuclear weapons technology but had not enabled it to overtake the U.S.' lead in this field. The USSR was said to have carried out "approximately 50 atmospheric tests" in its series.

The AEC, in a statement issued in Washington, said: "Preliminary analysis of the recent Soviet nuclear test series . . . indicates that the Soviet Union has made advances in certain areas, especially in improving the yield-to-weight ratios of weapons in the megaton range. . . . Of special interest is the small fission yield of the 55 to 60-megaton test conducted on Oct. 30." "Although substantial progress had been made and much useful information obtained by the Soviet Union, there is no reason to believe that the balance of nuclear power has been changed to favor the Soviet Union."

AEC officials reported Dec. 11 that U.S. scientists had revised downward their estimates of the amount of radioactive fallout produced by the recent Soviet tests. The revised estimates held that the Soviet tests would increase by 50%, rather than double, the amount of radioactive debris on the ground from nuclear tests.

First U.S. 'Peace' Test. The U.S.' first atoms-for-peace test was carried out Dec. 10 with the detonation of a 5-kiloton nuclear device 1,216 feet underground at a test site 25 miles southeast of Carlsbad, N.M.

The test—dubbed Project Gnome—was not an unqualified success. The nuclear device, exploded in an 8-by-10-foot chamber cut into a strata of rock salt, produced pressures greater than expected. It rocked the surrounding desert floor and caused clouds of intensely radioactive steam to escape from the mouth of a vertical shaft connected with the detonation chamber by a 1,000-foot tunnel. Radioactivity reached 10,000 roentgens an hour (maximum safe exposure: ½ roentgen yearly) at the shaft's mouth. The AEC closed nearby highways and took other local precautions.

Project Gnome was the first nuclear explosion planned under the AEC's Project Plowshare program for the development of such explosions for peaceful purposes. Its aims: (a) to test whether heat from an underground explosion could be stored and tapped for steam to power electric generators (a 750-foot shaft was sunk into the desert floor over the detonation chamber to see whether, when filled with water, it would yield usable steam); (b) the production of radioactive isotopes; (c) to measure the characteristics of nuclear detonations in salt formations; (d) to obtain neutrons for laboratory analysis; (e) to test the design of nuclear devices for peaceful detonations.

(Chief seismologist Leonard H. Murphy of the U.S. Coast & Geodetic Survey disclosed Dec. 18 that the Gnome test had been detected by seismological observatories as far as 7,200 miles away in Tokyo and 5,500 miles away in Uppsala, Sweden.)

Kennedy-Macmillan Talks. Pres. Kennedy and British Prime Min. Macmillan met Dec. 21-22 in Bermuda to confer on the problems facing the West, particularly that of the continuing East-West nuclear race.

The talks were held in Government House in Hamilton. Mr. Kennedy and Macmillan were accompanied by State Secy. Rusk and Foreign Secy. Lord Home; their discussions of the nuclear threat were attended by AEC Chrmn. Glenn T. Seaborg and Sir William Penny, research member of the British Atomic Energy Authority.

A final communiqué issued by the 2 leaders Dec. 22 affirmed that their talks would form "the basis of continued United States-United Kingdom cooperation during the coming months on a great variety of questions." It specifically cited their agreement on the need to press forward with preparations "for atmospheric [nuclear] testing to maintain the effectiveness of the deterrent." It said these preparations should be completed in view of "the new situation created by the massive series of atmospheric tests" recently held by the USSR. It made no mention of a final decision on whether or not such tests would be resumed by the West.

UN Votes New Arms Talks

U.S.-Soviet Draft Adopted. A joint U.S.-Soviet resolution calling for the resumption of general disarmament negotiations early in 1962 was adopted unanimously Dec. 20 by the UN General Assembly.

The joint resolution created a new 18-nation Disarmament Committee charged with renewing negotiations toward an "agreement on general and complete disarmament under effective international control." It was to convene as quickly as possible and report to the UN Disarmament Commission no later than June 1, 1962. Membership in the new committee: Brazil, Britain, Bulgaria, Burma, Canada, Czechoslovakia, Ethiopia, France, India, Italy, Mexico, Nigeria, Poland, Rumania, Sweden, the USSR, UAR and U.S.

The new talks would be the first general disarmament negotiations held since a 10-nation committee, composed exclusively of Western and Soviet-bloc nations, had met in Geneva Mar. 15-June 27, 1960. The 1960 talks had been broken off when Soviet Deputy Foreign Min. Valerian A. Zorin led the 5 Communist delegations in a walkout from the conference's 47th session.

The U.S.-Soviet agreement to cooperate in the launching of new negotiations was the product of contacts begun by U.S. Amb.-to-UN Adlai E. Stevenson and Soviet Foreign Min. Andrei A. Gromyko during the 2d session of the 15th UN General Assembly in New York early in 1961. A suggestion that more formal discussions be begun by U.S. and Soviet representatives was said to have been made by Pres. Kennedy in a personal message conveyed to Khrushchev Mar. 9. The first formal talks were begun in Washington in June by Soviet Deputy Foreign Min. Zorin and John J. McCloy, Pres. Kennedy's special adviser on disarmament; the talks were transferred to Moscow in July and to New York in September.

The U.S. and USSR marked their agreement on the convening of new talks with the submission to the General Assembly of a joint declaration of principles to govern future East-West arms negotiations. The 8-point declaration, presented to the Assembly Sept. 20, called for balanced and phased disarmament, "general and complete," down to the level of non-nuclear forces necessary for maintaining each nation's internal security. It said all disarmament measures should be subject to "strict and effective international control" and should be supervised by a UN organization having "unrestricted access without veto to all places as necessary for . . . effective verification."

U.S. Developments

'Ike' Regrets Peace Failure. Dwight D. Eisenhower said at his farewell Presidential news conference Jan. 18 that his greatest disappointment in office had been "the fact that we could not in these 8 years get to . . . where we could say it now looks as if permanent peace with justice is in sight." Mr. Eisenhower said, however, that he drew consolation from the fact that the U.S., during his Administration, had been able to avoid a large-scale war.

Disarmament Agency. A compromise bill (HR9118) establishing a U.S. Arms Control & Disarmament Agency was passed Sept. 23 by Senate voice vote and 253-50 House vote (178 D. & 75 R. vs. 34 R. & 16 D.). It was signed by Pres. Kennedy Sept. 26 as Public Law 87-297.

The bill provided for an agency director who would be principal arms control and disarmament adviser to the President and State Secretary. The director would be under the direction of the State Secretary. The agency itself was made a separate one. The bill stated that U.S. disarmament or reduction of armed forces or armaments could not be effected without legislation or use of the President's treaty-making power. The agency was to conduct research on methods and results of arms limitation.

The bill conformed in large part to Pres. Kennedy's proposals, which he had submitted to Congress June 29. It differed from the President's draft and from an early bill (S2180) passed by the Senate Sept. 8 in that it made the agency semi-autonomous. In this respect, it adhered to the version passed by the House Sept. 19.

Pres. Kennedy Sept. 26 appointed William Chapman Foster, 64, a Republican, as the agency's director. Mr. Kennedy said Foster would have State Undersecretary rank (salary: $22,500 a year). Foster, president and board chairman of United Nuclear Corp., had been Commerce Undersecretary 1946-48, representative to the Economic Cooperation Administration 1948, deputy administrator and later administrator of ECA 1949-51, Deputy Defense Secretary 1951-53, an Olin Mathieson Chemical Corp. vice president since 1958. In 1958 Foster headed the U.S. delegation to an abortive disarmament conference with the Soviet Union. Foster had been working for months with the President's previous principal disarmament adviser, John J. McCloy, whose resignation was accepted Oct. 6.

1961's Nuclear Explosions

From 60 to 70 nuclear devices were probably detonated during 1961.

The principal authoritative information made public on both U.S. and Soviet tests was supplied by the U.S. Atomic Energy Commission. The AEC announced 31 Soviet and 9 U.S. tests as they took place but conceded that unannounced ones had also occurred. According to the AEC, "approximately 50 atmospheric tests" were carried out by the USSR in 1961. U.S. Congressional sources estimated that the number of U.S. nuclear tests in 1961 was probably about twice the 9 announced. France exploded one nuclear device in 1961.

The following tests were announced during 1961. (A kiloton indicates a force yield equivalent to 1,000 tons of TNT. A megaton indicates a yield equivalent to 1,000,000 tons of TNT. Low-yield or low-range explosions are those of less than 20 kilotons. Intermediate-yield explosions produce 20 to 500 kilotons.)

Soviet Explosions

Date	Force	Site
Sept. 1*	Intermediate yield	Semipalatinsk area (Siberia)
Sept. 4*	About 20 kilotons	Semipalatinsk
Sept. 5*	Low to intermediate range	Semipalatinsk
Sept. 6*	Low to intermediate range	Southeast European Russia (east of Stalingrad)
Sept. 10*	Several megaton yield	Novaya Zemlya area (Arctic islands between Barents and Kara Seas)
Sept. 10*	Kiloton range	Novaya Zemlya
Sept. 12*	Several megatons	Novaya Zemlya
Sept. 13*	Low to intermediate range	Semipalatinsk
Sept. 13*	Low to intermediate range	Novaya Zemlya
Sept. 14*	Several megatons	Novaya Zemlya
Sept. 16*	"On the order of a megaton"	Novaya Zemlya
Sept. 17*	Intermediate yield	Semipalatinsk
Sept. 18*	"On the order of a megaton"	Novaya Zemlya
Sept. 20*	"On the order of a megaton"	Novaya Zemlya
Sept. 22*	"On the order of a megaton"	Novaya Zemlya
Oct. 2*	"On the order of a megaton"	Novaya Zemlya
Oct. 4*	"On the order of several megatons"	Novaya Zemlya
Oct. 6*	10 megatons	Novaya Zemlya
Oct. 8*	Low yield	Novaya Zemlya
Oct. 12*	Low to intermediate range	Semipalatinsk
Oca. 20*	Several megatons	Novaya Zemlya
Oct. 23*	25 megatons	Novaya Zemlya
Oct. 23†	Low yield	South of Novaya Zemlya
Oct. 25*	"Probably less than a megaton"	Novaya Zemlya
Oct. 27*	Low to intermediate range	Novaya Zemlya
Oct. 30*	58 megatons	Novaya Zemlya
Oct. 31*	Several megatons	Novaya Zemlya
Oct. 31*	Intermediate to high range	Novaya Zemlya
Nov. 2*	Low to intermediate range	Novaya Zemlya
Nov. 2*	Low to intermediate range	Novaya Zemlya
Nov. 4*	Several megatons	Novaya Zemlya

U.S. Explosions

Date	Force	Site
Sept. 15‡	Low yield	Nevada test site, 65 miles northwest of Las Vegas
Sept. 16‡	Low yield	Nevada test site
Oct. 10‡	Low yield	Nevada test site
Oct. 29‡	Low yield	Nevada test site
Dec. 3‡	Low yield	Nevada test site
Dec. 10§	5-kiloton peaceful-use test	25 miles southeast of Carlsbad, N.M.
Dec. 13‡	Low yield	Nevada test site
Dec. 17‡	Low yield	Nevada test site
Dec. 22‡	Low yield	Nevada test site

French Explosion

Date	Force	Site
Apr. 25*	Low yield	Near Reggan in Sahara

*—Atmosphere
†—Underwater
‡—Underground
§—Underground (1,216 feet)

A new general disarmament conference opened in Geneva early in 1962 for a fresh attempt to end both the East-West arms race and nuclear weapons tests. The new conference had been called by the UN in 1961 after the USSR, in violation of a 3-year 'gentlemen's agreement' against testing, had carried out a series of the largest nuclear detonations ever known to have taken place. Despite its hopeful participation in the new Geneva talks, the U.S., which had resumed underground testing in response to the USSR's 1961 series, considered itself forced by the threat of Soviet weapons advances to begin a new series of air and missile-borne tests in the atmosphere over the Pacific. The USSR, prefacing its action with a denunciation of the U.S.' threat to its security, again began a series of atmospheric tests of enormous power. Faced with these actions by the 2 nuclear superpowers, the Geneva conference faltered through more than 100 sessions with no substantive agreement on the major issues dividing the opposing sides—the terms for inspection and control of the proposed pacts on disarmament and a nuclear test ban. Despite the conference's inability to halt the nuclear arms race, it was apparent by the year's end that the U.S. and USSR had narrowed their differences on control and inspection and would heed a new UN appeal for the cessation of nuclear weapons tests by Jan. 1, 1963.

Road to New Negotiations

The UN General Assembly had voted unanimously Dec. 20, 1961 to adopt a joint U.S.-Soviet resolution establishing a special 18-nation UN Disarmament Committee to renew negotiations toward an "agreement on general and complete disarmament under effective international control."

The new disarmament talks had been agreed on by the U.S. and Soviet Union in response to worldwide fears that the nuclear arms race resumed by the 2 great powers in 1961 was leading them inexorably toward a new world war fought with weapons of unprecedented destructive power.

The Geneva conference was to be the first full-scale international arms meeting held since 1960, when the USSR had broken off negotiations then under way, also in Geneva, in a 10-nation conference of Western and Soviet-bloc nations. The new conference, scheduled to begin early in 1962, originally had been intended to be devoted to disarmament alone. But the pressing problem of nuclear weapons tests and the collapse of the 3-year-old U.S.-British-Soviet talks on banning such tests led to the inclusion of this question on the Geneva meeting's agenda. It eventually dominated the conference's work.

The stage for the new conference was set at the beginning of 1962 with the collapse of the 3-power Geneva talks on a nuclear test ban and in exchanges of notes between Western and Soviet leaders on Soviet proposals (opposed by the West) that the new conference be convened at the "summit" level by the heads of the participating governments.

Geneva A-Talks Collapse. The U.S.-British-Soviet conference in Geneva on a treaty to ban nuclear weapons tests adjourned in failure Jan. 29 after its 353d session since Oct. 1958.

The adjournment, said to be final, came after the USSR had reversed itself and had refused to accept its own proposal that the test question be transferred to forthcoming Geneva arms talks.*

The USSR's final position was delivered to the Western powers Jan. 26 by Soviet delegate Semyon K. Tsarapkin. Replying to the West's acceptance of the prior Soviet suggestion that the test problem be taken up by the new 18-nation disarmament committee created by the UN, the USSR demanded that the 3-power talks be continued, and that they be devoted to the Soviet plan for self-inspection of nuclear ban violations. The Soviet Union ignored the fact that it repeatedly had urged the transfer of the talks; it charged that the West sought this action to divert the disarmament conference from its principal task of an accord on "general and complete disarmament."

The Soviet demands were rejected by Charles C. Stelle of the U.S. and Sir Michael Wright of Britain when the conference met again Jan. 29. Stelle told Tsarapkin that the U.S. was prepared to resume meaningful negotiations on an internationally-inspected test ban at any time or place. But he made clear that the West could not accept the USSR's self-inspection plan and no longer could ignore the fact that the conference "has now reached the stage of total deadlock." The U.S. therefore proposed that "this conference recess immediately until a

common basis for negotiatons can be re-established."

The conference adjourned later Jan. 29. Statements made by all 3 delegates after the meeting stressed that the break was final. It was generally accepted that the dispute over transfer of the test ban problem to the planned disarmament conference had been used by both sides as an excuse for adjourning the 3-power negotiations.

West Rejects 'Summit.' Soviet proposals for convening the planned disarmament conference at the "summit" level were rejected by the U.S. and Britain in an exchange of notes in February.

The proposal for a heads-of-government meeting was advanced by Soviet Premier Nikita S. Khrushchev Feb. 10 in a letter in which he replied to a joint message in which Pres. John F. Kennedy and Prime Min. Harold Macmillan had suggested Feb. 7 that the conference be opened by the foreign ministers of the 18 participating nations. Mr. Kennedy rejected the Khrushchev proposal in a new message written to Khrushchev Feb. 13. The President did not explicitly rule out the prospect of raising the conference to the summit level if the initial meetings gave promise of success.

The proposal was re-examined and rejected anew in a 2d series of messages exchanged by the 3 leaders Feb. 21-26. This was the last display of official Soviet pressure for a summit meeting in 1962.

Excerpts from the 3 messages:

Khrushchev, in his Feb. 21 letter to Pres. Kennedy—"I must say frankly that I am grieved at your negative attitude to this [summit] proposal. . . . If the experience of the previous disarmament talks is of any use, it is . . . because they showed how little practical progress on disarmament can be expected without the most direct

---

* The Soviet proposal to merge the test-ban and disarmament talks had been accepted reluctantly by the U.S. and Britain in statements by their delegates Jan. 16 at the first 1962 session of the test-ban conference. The USSR's acceptance of the Western offer was announced Feb. 22; it was rejected the same day by the U.S. State Department on the ground that it was predicated on the use of Soviet inspection and control proposals as a basis for the new test-ban agenda. Despite the great powers' differences on the terms for inclusion of the test-ban question in the disarmament talks, the conference took up the matter and averted further disagreements by confiding it to a 3-power subcommittee made up of the same nations that had conduced the 3-year Geneva talks—the U.S., Britain and USSR.

and businesslike participation . . . of leaders of the highest standing. . . . [Your refusal] can only mean that you do not yet have the determination to reach agreement on questions of disarmament. . . . The United States and its allies would apparently like the Soviet Union to put all its armed forces under control and reveal the entire system of its defense even before disarmament properly begins. I must tell you frankly: . . . We will not agree to this. . . ."

Pres. Kennedy, in his reply to Khrushchev, dated Feb. 24—"As I have said, . . . I think it is of the utmost importance that the heads of government of the major nuclear powers assume a personal responsibility for directing their countries' participation . . . in these negotiations. I can assure you that the Secretary of State would present my views with complete authority. . . . I hope developments in the conference and internationally would make it useful to arrange for the participation of the heads of government before June 1. . . . The heads of government should meet to resolve explicit points of disagreement which might remain after . . . the largest possible measure of agreement has been worked out at the diplomatic level."

*Macmillan, in his reply delivered Feb. 26—*Britain saw "2 situations" in which a summit meeting "might be fruitful." "The first is if the conference is making satisfactory and definite progress; in such a case a meeting of the heads of government might well serve to consolidate what had been achieved and to make a further step towards an actual agreement. The 2d situation is one in which certain major and clear points of disagreement have emerged. . . . In that case, the heads of government should perhaps meet in order to try to break the deadlock. It seems to me that either of these situations may arise fairly soon after the work of the committee begins."

French Boycott Talks. The French government announced Mar. 5 that it would not be represented at the Geneva disarmament conference.

A Foreign Ministry statement declared that France saw no point in sending representatives to disarmament discussions that "offer no hope of solutions." The statement said France would be ready to join later in negotiations if they were held "in an atmosphere free of any spirit of polemics and propaganda" and gave some promise of success.

The French action apparently was taken in response to the USSR's rejection of proposals of Pres. Charles de Gaulle for a radical reshaping of the Geneva conference. De Gaulle, in a note replying Feb. 19 to Khrushchev's call for a summit-level meeting, had suggested that the negotiations be held by and be limited to "powers that possess nuclear weapons or will possess them in the near future." De Gaulle, who rejected the idea of a summit-level conference, declared that the essential question faced by the negotiators was "the destruction of existing [nuclear] weapons and the banning of the manufacture of new ones." Since it was "easy to conceal" nuclear weapons, "no one could . . . be certain that they would be destroyed, even if all conceivable methods of control were employed." For this reason, de Gaulle said, France proposed that "the destruction, the banning and the control should first be applied to the means of delivery of nuclear weapons—launching pads, planes, submarines, etc."

De Gaulle's suggestions were rebuffed by Khrushchev in a note delivered to France Feb. 28.

U.S. To Resume Air Tests

2 weeks before the planned convening of the Geneva conference, amid the last-minute diplomatic and propa-

ganda preparations for the meeting, the U.S. announced its decision to resume nuclear weapons tests in the earth's atmosphere. The U.S. had resumed its underground testing at the AEC's Nevada proving grounds in 1961, but it had refrained from atmospheric tests in the hope that they would prove to be unnecessary. In deciding to resume atmospheric tests, the U.S. conceded that the USSR might have made substantial progress in weaponry in its 1961 atmospheric tests.

In its announcement, the U.S. again offered to sign an inspected ban on further weapons tests, and to seal the accord with a personal meeting of Pres. Kennedy and Premier Khrushchev.

JFK Announcement. The U.S. decision to resume nuclear tests in the atmosphere was announced by Pres. Kennedy Mar. 2 in a nationwide radio-TV address from the White House.

The President made clear his regret that international events—particularly the USSR's resumption of atmospheric tests in Sept. 1961—had made necessary this development. But, he declared: "In the absence of a major shift in Soviet policies, no American President—responsible for the freedom and safety of so many people—could in good faith make any other decision."

Mr. Kennedy said the U.S. tests would begin late in April "in the atmosphere over the Pacific Ocean" and would last for 2 to 3 months.

The announcement was coupled with an offer by Mr. Kennedy to meet with Soviet Premier Khrushchev to sign an agreement for an internationally-inspected and supervised ban on all nuclear weapons tests. Mr. Kennedy said that the U.S.' draft of such an agreement would be ready for transmission to Soviet authorities be-

fore the 18-nation disarmament conference due to convene in Geneva Mar. 14.

Mr. Kennedy added: "If the Soviet Union should now be willing to accept such a treaty, sign it before the latter part of April, and apply it immediately—if all testing can thus be actually halted—then the nuclear arms race would be slowed down at last, the security of the United States . . . would be safeguarded and there would be no need for our tests. . . ."

The President sketched the following reasons for his decision:

"Had the Soviet tests of last fall merely reflected a new effort in intimidation and bluff, our security would not have been affected. But in fact they also reflected a highly sophisticated technology, the trial of novel designs and techniques, and some substantial gains in weaponry.

"Many of these tests were aimed at improving their defenses against missiles—others were proof tests, trying out existing weapons systems—but over ½ emphasized the development of new weapons, particularly those of greater explosive power.

"A primary purpose of these tests was the development of warheads which weigh very little compared to the destructive efficiency of their thermonuclear yield. One . . . exploded with the force of 58 megatons. . . .

"Today, Soviet missiles do not appear able to carry so heavy a warhead. But there is no avoiding the fact that other Soviet tests, in the one-to-5-megaton range and up, were . . . [of] warheads actually capable of delivery by existing missiles.

"Much has been also said about Soviet claims for an anti-missile missile. . . . While apparently seeking information on the effects of nuclear blasts on radar and communication, which is important in developing an anti-missile defense system, these tests did not, in our judgment, reflect a developed system."

"In short, last fall's tests, in and by themselves, did not give the Soviet Union superiority in nuclear power. They did, however, provide the Soviet laboratories with a mass of . . . experience on which, over the next 2 or 3 years, they can base significant analyses . . . preparing for the next test series, which would confirm and advance their findings.

"And I must report to you in all candor that further Soviet series, in the absence of further Western progress, could well provide the Soviet Union with a nuclear attack and defense capability so powerful as to encourage aggressive designs. Were we to stand still while the Soviets surpassed us—or even appeared to surpass us—the free world's ability to deter, to survive and to respond to an all-out attack would be seriously weakened."

"We cannot make similar strides without testing in the atmosphere as well as underground," particularly in the vital areas of "missile penetration and missile defense" that apparently were the object of the Soviet tests. The U.S. had spent great sums to perfect these same aspects of its nuclear deterrent and defense systems. "But we cannot be certain how much of this preparation will turn out to be useless; blacked out, paralyzed or destroyed by the complex effects of nuclear explosion. We know enough

from earlier tests to be concerned about such phenomena. We know that the Soviets conducted such tests last fall. . . ."[*]

Decision Defended. The President said in his Mar. 2 speech that the decision to resume atmospheric tests had been given "the unanimous recommendations of the pertinent department and agency heads." The decision was supported in formal statements issued Mar. 3 by Defense Secy. Robert S. McNamara and by Gen. Lyman L. Lemnitzer, chairman of the Joint Chiefs of Staff.

McNamara's statement said that "while the weapons in the arsenal of the free world are adequate to meet the strategic objectives of the present, every effort must be made to insure that they do not . . . become obsolete in their relationship to capabilities of a potential enemy." It warned that "in the light of present and past Soviet actions" the U.S. could not accept the renewal of an uninspected test moratorium. "It would only be a matter of time before the present powerful United States nuclear strategic advantages would begin to diminish in relation to Soviet . . . capabilities and might ultimately shift in favor of the USSR."

The U.S. announcement was welcomed Mar. 2-3 by approving statements from the governments of Britain, France, West Germany, Canada, Australia, Italy and many other Western countries. It was deplored by the Indian Foreign Ministry Mar. 3 and was protested formally by Japan Mar. 5, despite a U.S. explanation delivered to Premier Hayato Ikeda's government before the decision was made public.

Khrushchev's Reply. Soviet Premier Khrushchev replied Mar. 4 to the President's announcement of the forthcoming U.S. atmospheric tests. He denounced Mr. Kennedy's offer to

* Director John A. McCone of the Central Intelligence Agency was reported to have told the Joint Congressional Atomic Energy Committee Jan. 19 that the USSR had made substantial weapons progress during its latest nuclear test series, possibly in the field of the anti-missile missile. Rep. Chet Holifield (D., Calif.), committee chairman, reported that McCone's information had shown the USSR to have "certain advantages" over the U.S. Marshal Rodion Y. Malinovsky, Soviet defense minister, declared in an interview for Pravda and Izvestia Jan. 24 that the USSR had the power "to wipe off the face of the earth with a single nuclear-rocket attack . . . all industrial and administrative centers of the United States." Malinovsky added that under modern warfare conditions, "shelters against atomic and hydrogen bombs are nothing but coffins and tombs prepared in advance."

cancel the tests and sign an inspected test-ban accord as an attempt at "atomic blackmail."

In his note to the President, however, Khrushchev agreed to send Foreign Min. Andrei A. Gromyko to Geneva to meet with Western foreign ministers on the nuclear test question and then to particpate in the opening of the 18-nation disarmament conference Mar. 14.

Mr. Kennedy informed Khrushchev Mar. 6 of his acceptance of the planned foreign ministers' talks.

Excerpts from the Khrushchev-Kennedy exchange:

Khrushchev, in his Mar. 4 message to Pres. Kennedy—"You declare that the United States must . . . hold nuclear weapons tests in order not to lag behind the Soviet Union. But you do not utter a single word to the effect that the United States and its NATO allies have held many more nuclear test explosions than the Soviet Union. And this is a fact . . . that if the United States and its allied add another series of tests . . . to improve their nuclear weapons, the Soviet Union will be faced with the need to hold . . . tests of new types of its nuclear weapons . . . to strengthen its security and maintain world peace."

". . . On the one hand, you in your speeches more than once asserted that the United States surpassed the Soviet Union for the might of stockpiled nuclear weapons and your military men can raze from the face of the earth the Soviet Union. . . ."

"On the other hand, you now say that the United States must hold nuclear weapons tests supposedly in order not to lag behind the Soviet Union in armament. There is obviously no logic here."

Pres. Kennedy's reply to Khrushchev Mar. 6—"I shall not undertake at this time to comment on the many sentiments in your letter with which . . .

the United States cannot agree. Let us, instead, join in giving our close personal . . . direction to the work of our representatives and . . . in working for their success."

Soviet Proposals to UN. Soviet notes delivered to Acting UN Secy. Gen. U Thant Mar. 12 called for an international convention against the use of nuclear weapons and for the creation of zones free from atomic weapons. The proposals were made in 2 letters from Foreign Min. Gromyko.

The first letter expressed Russia's unconditional support of a UN General Assembly resolution (adopted Nov. 24, 1961) urging prohibition of any use of nuclear weapons. The letter said: "The Soviet government attaches a great importance to the proposal . . . to summon a special conference to sign a convention banning the use of nuclear weapons. The conclusion of the . . . convention should be an important step toward the complete prohibition of nuclear weapons, with their removal from national armaments and the liquidation of all stockpiles of these weapons."

The 2d letter welcomed the Assembly's appeal (Dec. 4, 1961) for measures to prevent the spread of nuclear weapons, and its resolution (Nov. 24, 1961) urging that Africa be set aside as a zone free from atomic weapons. The letter said the USSR was "prepared to assume an obligation not to turn over nuclear weapons or information . . . to other countries, provided the United States, Britain and France assume identical obligations."

A U.S. note to the UN declared Mar. 13 that the U.S. supported efforts to prevent the spread of nuclear weapons but could not accept limitations on its right to base such weapons on the territory of its allies. The note said: "Both the United States and its allies have chosen these arrangements recognizing that nuclear weapons are a necessary deterrent to a potential aggressor who is armed with such weapons and openly threatens the free world."

Geneva Talks Begun

Foreign Ministers Meet. The foreign ministers of the U.S., Britain and the USSR conferred in Geneva Mar. 11-14 before joining with the representatives of 14 other countries to open the new disarmament conference. The 3 ministers—State Secy. Dean Rusk of the U.S., Foreign Secy. Lord Home of Britain and Foreign Min. Andrei A. Gromyko of the USSR —then continued their talks until Mar. 27 in a series of meetings held apart from but in conjunction with the conference.

The ministers' talks were devoted primarily to the question of possible agreements on terms for disarmament and the banning of nuclear tests. It was reported following their 2d meeting Mar. 14, however, that Gromyko had made it clear that the USSR would not accept either of the West's key inspection demands—for verification of arms destroyed and arms remaining in service at each stage of a general disarmament agreement and for on-site international inspection of any seismic events suspected to be clandestine nuclear tests. This position apparently was maintained by Gromyko throughout the remaining 2 weeks of ministerial talks. It was rejected as unacceptable by the U.S. and by Britain, which reportedly had been willing to compromise with Soviet demands for a self-inspected nuclear test ban but had agreed to support the U.S.' requirement for positive, on-site inspection.

The 3 ministers ended their talks Mar. 27 without having achieved the significant progress demanded by the West as a condition for meetings at the summit level.

(Rusk, Home and Gromyko took advantage of their meetings to discuss measures for easing East-West tensions in Berlin.)

Arms Conference Opens. The UN Disarmament Committee was convened in Geneva Mar. 14 by UN Undersecy. Omar Loutfi.

The conference, originally planned as an 18-nation meeting, was opened with the participation of the following 17 delegations, France having carried out its intention to boycott the meeting: West—U.S., Britain, Italy and Canada; Soviet bloc—USSR, Poland, Czechoslovakia, Rumania and Bulgaria; neutrals—Brazil, Burma, Ethiopia, India, Mexico, Nigeria, Sweden, and the UAR.

Heads of the 17 delegations: Brazil, Francisco San Tiago Dantas; Britain, Lord Home; Bulgaria, Carlo Loucanov; Burma, U Thi Han; Canada, Howard C. Green, Gen. E. L. M. Burns; Czechoslovakia, Vaclav David, Jiri Hajek; Ethiopia, Ketema Yifru, T. Gebr-Egzy; India, V. K. Krishna Menon, Morarji J. Desai; Italy, Antonio Segni, Carlo Russo; Mexico, Manuel Tello, Luis Padilla Nervo; Nigeria, Jaja Wachuku; Poland, Adam Rapacki; Rumania, Corneliu Manescu, George Macovescu; Sweden, Osten Unden, Mrs. Alva Myrdal; UAR, Mahmoud Fawzi; U.S., Dean Rusk, Charles E. Bohlen, Arthur H. Dean.

Basic Proposals Made. The U.S.' and USSR's basic proposals for general disarmament were submitted to the conference by State Secy. Rusk and Foreign Min. Gromyko at its first working session Mar. 15. The proposals were described as basically the same as the disarmament plans presented to the UN General Assembly by Soviet Premier Khrushchev in Sept. 1960 and by Pres. Kennedy in Sept. 1961.

The Soviet proposals were embodied in a formal 48-article draft treaty providing for the total disbanding of national armed forces within a period of 4 years. The U.S. plan was an elaboration of the draft given the UN by Mr. Kennedy; in addition to the basic draft, it proposed that (1) a 30% reduction be imposed on nuclear weapons delivery systems within 3 years; (2) the U.S. and USSR each transfer 50,000 kilograms of high-grade fission materials to nonmilitary uses; (3) measures be taken to "reduce the risk of war by accident, miscalculation, failure of communications or surprise attack"; (4) acceptable inspection procedures be sought to insure against violation of any disarmament agreement.

A UPI Geneva dispatch Mar. 15 gave the following comparison of the major points in the U.S. and Soviet plans:

Verification—"The United States calls for verification of arms destruction measures and troop cuts in each stage and of armed forces and armaments retained. The Soviet Union refuses to permit verification of what is retained."

Nuclear test ban—"The U.ited States wants an international controlled nuclear test ban in the first stage. The Soviet Union proposes an uncontrolled moratorium on underground nuclear explosions . . . and a ban on other tests checked only by national detection systems."

International supervision—The U.S. proposed that disarmament be supervised by an international organization controlled by a multi-nation commission but administered by a single executive. The USSR wanted a multi-nation commission composed on the "troika" principle to make decisions by ⅔ vote; its decisions would be transmitted to the UN Security Council, which would be responsible for ordering their execution unless stopped by a big-power veto.

Force levels—U.S. plan: all armed forces reduced to maximum levels of 2,100,000 men in the first stage. Soviet plan: U.S. and Soviet forces reduced to 1,700,000 men each in the first stage, other nations to specific agreed levels.

Missiles and nuclear delivery vehicles—"The United States plan provides for the discard of 30% of each nation's nuclear delivery vehicles . . . in the first stage. The Russians want to abol:sh all delivery vehicles and bases from which they would operate in the first stage."

Fission materials—"The United States calls for a complete cut-off of production of fissionable materials for weapons purposes in the first stage." The Soviet plan provided for similar measures in the 2d stage.

International force—Both plans called for the creation of an international peace-keeping force on the attainment of general disarmament; the U.S. proposed establishment of a permanent force under the UN; the USSR suggested that national contingents be earmarked for international erv:ce at the orders of the UN Security Council.

A-Ban Talks Resumed. The 3-power negotiations on a treaty to ban nuclear weapons tests were resumed informally outside the arms conference Mar. 15 to examine the U.S.' latest proposals for an inspected prohibition on future tests.

The 3 negotiators—Arthur H. Dean of the U.S., Joseph Godber of Britain, and Semyon K. Tsarapkin of the USSR—met at the order of their governments to see if there was any basis for a test-ban agreement that could be presented to the concurrent Geneva arms conference.

The U.S. proposals were made in the form of amendments to the final Western test-ban draft under consideration by the 3-power talks when they recessed in January. The proposals called for (a) use of mobile detection units to create, within 6 to 9 months, a temporary detection system that would function until establishment of the 180-post network of detection stations originally envisaged at Geneva; (b) certification by heads of participant states that no preparations were under way for secret tests; (c) a listing and inspection of all potential test sites in the 3 countries; (d) extension of the treaty prohibition on testing to all detonations, both above and below ground; (e) limitation of on-site inspections to zones of light natural seismic activity (in the case of the USSR, to 1/7 of its territory).

The proposals were rejected by the USSR. Tsarapkin said at a Geneva news conference Mar. 16 that the USSR had detected all U.S. nuclear tests since 1958 and that the U.S. apparently had detected all Soviet tests since that date. He asserted that the 2 countries' national detection systems were adequate to police a test ban and that this was the basis for the USSR's demand that it be self-inspected.

The formal resumption of test-ban negotiations was agreed on Mar. 20 by the 3 powers. The negotiators met Mar. 21 for their first official session since their recess Jan. 29. Tsarapkin told newsmen after the session that there was "a complete stalemate, no advance of any kind." He said "any sort of international inspection is out of the question" for the USSR.

The 3 nuclear powers reported to the conference Mar. 23 that the negotiators had been unable to agree on any plan for an inspected halt of nuclear weapons tests. Their disagreement was made clear in angry speeches by Rusk, Home and Gromyko. Rusk reminded the conference that only a few weeks remained in which to find a test-ban formula before the U.S. resumed its atmospheric tests. Gromyko retorted that Pres. Kennedy's time limit for an agreement was an ultimatum and an "aggressive act."

Neutrals Seek Test Ban. Brazilian Foreign Min. Dantas, the first delegate of a technically "neutral" country to address the conference, called Mar. 16 for an immediate halt to all nuclear tests, both in the atmosphere and underground. Dantas expressed the hope that the U.S. would cancel the atmospheric tests it had scheduled for April. He urged efforts to find a minimal test detection system acceptable to both the U.S. and USSR. At an informal meeting of all 17 delegations Mar. 19, neutral delegates pressed both sides to compromise on the question of test detection.

Lord Home reportedly acknowledged to the neutrals that current detection devices could detect atmospheric tests anywhere in the world without on-site inspection. Rusk, however, was said to have insisted that the West needed the extra assurance that could be provided only by on-site international inspection.

Indian Defense Min. V. K. Krishna Menon suggested at the conference Mar. 20 that it seek a nuclear test compromise on the basis of self-inspection by the existing U.S. and Soviet detection networks, with an additional monitoring system on the territory of the neutral states to check the operations and findings of the existing networks. The neutrals' campaign for U.S.-Soviet compromise on a test ban, and for the creation of atom-free zones in Africa and Asia, was continued in addresses Mar. 21 by U Thi Han of Burma, Mahmoud

Fawzi of the UAR and Ketema Yifru of Ethiopia.

Rusk and Home addressed the conference Mar. 27 before leaving Geneva at the end of their parallel talks with Gromyko. Rusk told the conferees that a "tolerable" balance of military power existed and could be made the basis for genuine efforts to halt the arms race, even short of the goal of general and complete disarmament. Rusk asserted that compromise was possible in many areas; he noted, for example, that "considerably less than total access to a nation's territory" might be adequate for a nuclear test inspection system if adequate detection techniques were accepted by both sides.

(Arthur Dean and Joseph Godber replaced Rusk and Home as heads of the U.S. and British delegations; respectively. Valerian Zorin replaced Gromyko as the USSR's chief delegate.)

Zorin submitted Mar. 28 a full range of Soviet proposals for priority on the conference's agenda: (1) the establishment of atom-free zones in central Europe and Africa, (2) a nonaggression pact between NATO and Warsaw Treaty countries and (3) an agreement to ban the spread of nuclear weapons. Dean proposed instead that the conference study (a) a nuclear test ban controlling and curbing fission materials production and (b) measures to prevent surprise attack and accidental war.

4 of the 8 neutral delegations—India, Burma, Ethiopia and Sweden—voiced their concern Apr. 2 at what they felt was the refusal of the U.S. and USSR to begin real negotiations on a test ban or any other question thus far discussed by the conference. Indian Foreign Secy. Morarji J. Desai asserted that agreement was possible only if the USSR accepted a broadening of its plan for "national control" of a test ban and the West reduced

its requirements for "international controls" on the ban.

The conference returned to the disarmament problem Apr. 4 after 3 days of fruitless discussion of the nuclear-test question. The U.S.-British-Soviet negotiations on a test ban were to be continued as a 3-power subcommittee of the larger conference. The test-ban subcommittee was to report to the conference periodically on its progress.

The conference met Apr. 5 as a committee of the whole to study measures for reducing tensions as a prelude to world disarmament. Soviet delegate Zorin charged that the principal cause of most world tension was the West's "war propaganda" against the Soviet bloc; he called on the conference to adopt a declaration banning all such propaganda. Replying to the Soviet demand Apr. 9, Dean presented a 7-point U.S. draft to counter war propaganda by the free international flow of information. He challenged the USSR to demonstrate its opposition to war propaganda by banning all works of Marx, Lenin and Stalin containing assertions of the inevitability of war.

'Final' JFK-Macmillan Plea. Pres. Kennedy and Macmillan addressed a joint appeal to Khrushchev Apr. 9 to abandon his opposition to an internationally supervised ban on nuclear tests. Kennedy Administration officials said the message represented the West's "final" attempt to win Russian acceptance of a viable test-ban accord before the U.S. resumed tests in the atmosphere.

The Kennedy-Macmillan message expressed disappointment that the USSR had rejected the test-ban verification proposals submitted by the West in Geneva. It said: "The ground given [by the USSR] seems to be that existing national detection systems can give adequate protection against clandestine tests. In the present state of scientific instrumentation, there are a great many cases in which we cannot distinguish between natural and artificial [test-caused] seismic disturbances. . . . A treaty, therefore, cannot be made effective unless adequate verification is included in it."

The message concluded with the warning that "if there is no change in the Soviet position," the West "must conclude that their efforts to obtain a workable treaty to ban nuclear tests are not now successful, and the test series scheduled for the latter part of this month will have to go forward."

Khrushchev rejected the appeal in a message to Macmillan Apr. 13. He asserted that the U.S. and Britain already had decided to resume their atmospheric tests and had made the appeal only "to make a show before public opinion." Khrushchev concluded with a warning that "your holding of nuclear weapons tests underground or in the atmosphere, in space or under water, will force the Soviet Union to hold tests of its own nuclear weapons so that the defense of the countries of socialism . . . will be at an appropriate level."

Neutrals Urge A-Inspection. The 8 neutral delegations to the Geneva conference submitted a joint appeal Apr. 16 for a nuclear test ban agreement that would be supervised by an international commission of eminent scientists, preferably drawn from the non-aligned countries.

According to the neutrals' draft, the commission would have at its disposal a monitoring network composed of the national test detection systems currently in operation plus such additional detection facilities as might be established by agreement. The international commission would consult with any power on whose territory a suspected clandestine test had occurred and would carry out the necessary investigation. Other parties to the agreement would be informed of the commission's findings, or of any interference with its work, and would be free to take whatever action might be provided for by the final treaty.

The neutrals' proposal was promised careful study by the U.S. and British envoys but was not seriously discussed by either East or West. It was, however, used by Zorin as a major weapon in the Soviet effort to mobilize criticism of the U.S.' planned atmospheric tests. Zorin told the conferees Apr. 19 that the USSR accepted the neutral draft as a basis for further test-ban negotiations, but only on condition the West agreed to an immediate uninspected moratorium on tests.

U.S. Arms Draft Presented. A detailed "outline of basic provisions" of a comprehensive 3-stage treaty for general disarmament was presented to the conference Apr. 18 by the U.S. delegation. The U.S. document was the first detailed exposition of the disarmament plan promised to the UN General Assembly by Pres. Kennedy in 1961. Mr. Kennedy, commenting on the proposal at a Washington news conference later Apr. 18, described it as "the most comprehensive and specific series of proposals the United States or any other country has ever made on disarmament." He declared that it represented a "major effort" by the U.S. to "achieve a breakthrough on disarmament negotiations."

The U.S. plan, submitted with the support of the other Western delegations to the conference, was rejected by Zorin Apr. 25 as "utterly unacceptable" to the USSR.

Summary of the U.S. disarmament plan, as issued by the White House:

GOALS. First—General and complete disarmament: The disbanding of all armed forces and the destruction of all arms except those needed for keeping order within each nation and for a United Nations peace force. 2d—Gradual replacement of the armed power of single nations by a strengthened United Nations, strong enough to settle disputes and to suppress conflict.

PRINCIPLES. (A) The disarming process would be balanced to prevent any state from gaining a military advantage. (B) Compliance with all obligations would be effectively verified.

PROCESS. The process of disarming would be verified by an International Disarmament Organization (IDO) to be established within the United Nations when the treaty becomes effective. The process would be divided into 3 stages—the first to take 3 years, the 2d 3 years and the 3d to be completed as soon as possible thereafter.

Transition from stage to stage would take place when the IDO Control Council determined all measures in the last stage had been carried out and all preparations for the next stage had been made. If one or more of the permanent members of the IDO Control Council should declare that these conditions did not exist, the transition could take place only by a decision of a special session of the United Nations Security Council.

Major actions to be completed under the treaty through the 3 stages are:

(1) Arms reductions. Most categories of arms—including all non-nuclear arms and delivery systems for nuclear weapons—would be reduced by 30% in Stage I, by 50% of the remaining levels in Stage II, and eliminated in Stage III. . . .

During Stage I only, production of armaments would be limited to an agreed allowance for specified categories, but there would be compensating destruction of armaments to ensure that reductions would not be impaired. In Stage II production would be halted, except for spare parts. In Stage III, all production, testing, research and development of armaments would be ended except for support of the United Nations peace force and maintenance of order within nations.

(2) Nuclear weapons reductions. In Stage I, production of weapons-grade fissionable material would be stopped and agreed quantities transferred to non-weapons purposes (the United States has proposed an initial transfer of 50,000 kilograms of U-235). Nuclear powers would agree not to transfer control over nuclear weapons to any non-nuclear state, nor to aid such a state in making nuclear weapons.

In Stage II, remaining stocks of weapons-grade fissionable material would be reduced. During the last 6 months of this stage, all nations would register with the IDO an inventory of their remaining nuclear weapons and fissionable material stocks, preparatory to destroying them in Stage III.

In Stage III, the nations would eliminate all nuclear weapons remaining at their disposal and would dismantle all plants for producing them.

(3) Manpower reductions. Stage I: Armed forces of the United States and the USSR would be reduced to 2,100,000 men each, with the same level for other "specified parties." Other nations would reduce to 100,000 men or 1% of their population, whichever is higher, but no nation could exceed present levels.

Stage II: The United States and the USSR would reduce to levels 50% below those agreed for the end of Stage I. Forces of other states would be reduced by agreed percentages.

Stage III: National armed forces would be reduced to levels sufficient for keeping internal order, with international peace-keeping taken over by the United Nations.

(4) Reduction of military bases. Certain military bases would be dismantled in Stage II. All others, except those needed to maintain internal order, would be eliminated in Stage III.

(5) Reducing the risks of war. In Stage I, certain measures could be taken immediately—even before any arms reductions are agreed—to cut the risk of war by accident, miscalculation or surprise attack:

(A) Advance notification of major military maneuvers.

(B) Observation posts at agreed locations, such as ports, railway centers, highways and air bases, to report military movements.

(C) Establishment of rapid and reliable communications among heads of government and with the [UN] Secretary General. . . .

(D) Setting up an international commission to examine and recommend further measures to .educe war risks.

(6) **Outer space.** The parties would agree in Stage I to cooperate in the peaceful use of outer space and not to place in orbit weapons of mass destruction. Production, stockpiling and testing of boosters for space vehicles would be limited.

(7) **United Nations peacekeeping.** Stage I: The parties would prepare for the setting up of a United Nations peace force in Stage II by supporting a United Nations General Assembly study of such matters as the composition and strength, command and control, training, logistical support and financing of the force. The United Nations Peace Observation Corps would be established to check on possible conflicts. Nations would use all available means for peaceful settlement of disputes, including forums in and outside the United Nations and regional organizations, and would accept the compulsory jurisdiction of the International Court of Justice.

Stage II: The United Nations Peace Force would come into being during the first year of Stage II and would be progressively strengthened during this stage. The parties would agree to accept rules of international conduct which would become effective 3 months after circulation to all parties unless a majority disapproved.

Stage III: The United Nations Peace Force reaches full strength with such power that no single nation can challenge it.

(8) **Verification.** The International Disarmament Organization would apply inspection during each stage to the extent required in relation to the amount of disarmament being undertaken. This might be done, for example, through a "zonal inspection" arrangement, under which each party would divide its territory into zones.

An agreed number of these zones would be progressively inspected by the IDO on the ground and from the air during Stage I. Once a zone had been inspected, it would remain open for further inspection while verification was being extended to additional zones. By the end of Stage III, inspection would have been extended to all parts of the territory of parties to the treaty.

U.S. Begins Pacific Tests

Air Bursts Announced. The U.S. Apr. 25 carried out its first atmospheric nuclear test since 1958.

A brief announcement of the test, the first of a series, was made by the Atomic Energy Commission. It said:

"A nuclear test detonation took place at 10:45 a.m. EST today [Apr. 25] in the vicinity of Christmas Island. The detonation was in the intermediate-yield range. The device was dropped from an airplane. The test was the first detonation in Operation Dominic, now under way in the Pacific."

Description of the device tested as of "intermediate yield" meant that it produced an explosive force equivalent to that yielded by between 20,000 and 1,000,000 tons of TNT. A supplementary AEC statement said the tests would be conducted "under conditions which will restrict the radioactive fall-out to a minimum, far less than that from the Soviet Union's series of nuclear weapons tests in the fall of 1961."

Pres. Kennedy's order to begin the tests had been announced Apr. 24 by the AEC. The announcement said: "Pres. Kennedy has authorized the commission and the Department of Defense to proceed with a series of nuclear tests in the atmosphere over the Pacific. The tests, conducted by Joint Task Force 8 under the command of Maj. Gen. A[lfred] D[odd] Starbird, will begin as soon as is operationally feasible."

The Apr. 25 detonation was followed by 2 more tests in the Christmas Island test zone Apr. 27 and May 2. The May 2 detonation was of a device officially described as in the "low megaton yield range." It was the first U.S. detonation since 1958 to exceed a megaton in force. The atmospheric tests were to be supplemented by a series of high-altitude missile-borne tests over Johnson Island in the Central Pacific.

(*For list of atmospheric nuclear tests in 1962, see table at end of this section.*)

Reaction to Tests. The U.S.' resumption of atmospheric testing was supported as militarily necessary by U.S. Congressional and other political leaders of both parties. It was backed in most allied countries as justified in view of the prior Soviet tests. It was opposed by Asian and neutralist political leaders and by small pacifist groups in the West as a tension-provoking act that would add to the threat to human health from radioactive fallout. The USSR denounced the opening test as an aggressive act and warned that it might be forced to start new tests.

Senate Democratic leader Mike Mansfield (Mont.) and GOP leader Everett M. Dirksen (Ill.) Apr. 25 issued statements supporting the tests. Mansfield asserted that "the President has shown great forbearance," and "I fully concur in his decision." Dirksen said: "We want it to be done and we applaud the decision."

Acting UN Secy. Gen. U Thant, speaking at a UN correspondents' luncheon Apr. 24, a few hours before the U.S.' announcement that the start of the tests had been ordered, had made a new appeal "to all powers concerned to refrain from tests on the basis of the resolutions adopted at the 16th session of the General Assembly."

Tass, the Soviet news agency, in the first Russian comment on the U.S. test, denounced it as "the gravest crime against mankind." It asserted that the U.S. test had opened a new round in the nuclear weapons race.

The most severe reaction was reported in Japan. 2,000 leftist students battled police near the U.S.' Tokyo embassy Apr. 27, and 3,000 anti-test marchers paraded through Tokyo streets Apr. 28. The Japanese government had protested the tests formally in a note delivered to the U.S. Apr. 26. A U.S. reply delivered Apr. 30 defended the tests as militarily necessary but declared that the U.S. was prepared to halt all testing "if the Soviet Union changes its previous position and now concludes a test-ban treaty."

In London, 25,000 demonstrators had presented petitions against the planned Pacific tests to British government officials and the U.S. embassy Apr. 23 after a rally ending the Campaign for Nuclear Disarmament's annual 4-day Easter march from the nuclear weapons laboratories at Aldermaston. 350 CND members were arrested in London Apr. 26 during a demonstration outside the U.S. embassy.

3,000 members of the U.S. group Women Strike for Peace marched to the UN's headquarters in New York Apr. 26 to protest the tests. Pickets opposed to the tests marched near the White House in Washington Apr. 28. (They included Dr. Linus C. Pauling, biochemist, who was a guest at a White House dinner given the next day by Pres. & Mrs. Kennedy for 49 Nobel Prize laureates and other scientists.)

Talks Continue. Both the U.S. and the Soviet Union made it clear Apr. 26 that they intended to continue their participation in the Geneva disarmament talks despite the new U.S. tests and the USSR's repeated threats to resume such tests.

The U.S.' "test-and-talk" policy was reasserted by State Secy. Rusk Apr. 26 in a prepared statement read at a Washington news conference. Rusk declared that the U.S. was proceeding on the basis of 2 decisions: (1) "On the one side, . . . we shall conduct, in the absence of an adequate treaty, a series of selected and sophisticated nuclear tests." (2) "We shall make every possible effort to achieve a nuclear test ban treaty at the earliest occasion." "We . . . will continue the negotiations looking toward the possibility of such a treaty."

The Soviet position was disclosed in a vituperative address delivered in Geneva Apr. 26 by Zorin. Zorin's speech was made in the conference subcommittee devoted to study of nuclear tests. It stressed that, in view of the West's new tests, the USSR "will ever more persistently struggle for general and complete disarmament, for the cessation of the nuclear arms race."

French Test in Sahara. The French government confirmed May 8 that it had carried out a nuclear test underground in the Sahara May 1. The announcement, made by the Armed Forces Ministry, gave no details, but it was reported from Paris that it had taken place in the Hoggar Mountains, 500 miles south of the usual French atomic test site at Reggan, in the central Sahara. The test was France's 5th.

Reports of the French test, apparently based on U.S. detection of the explosion, had circulated in Washington several hours before the French announcement. Administration officials said May 8 that the explosion had been on the order of tens of kilotons. Their comments were elicited in response to *N.Y. Times* reports the previous day that the test had been of a one-kiloton device; it was feared that the USSR would cite the allegedly erroneous report as a proof of its argument that existing national detection networks were capable of spotting nearly all clandestine underground nuclear tests.

Conference Recesses. The Geneva talks continued through May and the first half of June with no significant progress on any proposal before them. The conference was recessed for one month June 15.

Major proposals and debate:

▶ The question of France's refusal either to participate in the conference or to halt its tests was raised May 9 by Zorin, who made French participation a condition for Soviet acceptance of a test-ban agreement. Zorin said: "There is another power now testing nuclear weapons. This power is refusing to take part in the negotiations and has never said it would adhere to a nuclear test ban treaty. The Soviet Union will not sign any treaty on banning nuclear tests unless France is a party to it."

▶ The U.S.' rejection of the disarmament measures proposed in the Soviet draft treaty presented to the conference was reiterated by Dean May 11. Dean declared that the USSR's insistence on the liquidation within 18 months of all foreign military bases and missiles and other nuclear weapons delivery systems would "prejudice the Western military position at a time when disarmament was only in the first stage." He asserted that any effective agreement must provide for a balanced reduction of both sides' forces. He said the U.S. could counterbalance the USSR's Eurasian military power "only by having sizable contingents of its forces join . . . its allies on their respective territories, and by maintaining a strategic deterrent."

▶ An appeal for conference action to prevent the extension of the East-West arms race into outer space was made May 14 by Charles C. Stelle, acting head of the U.S. delegation. Urging conferees to begin negotiations on demilitarization of space during their discussion of general disarmament needs, Stelle elaborated on the U.S. disarmament plan's provision forbidding the orbiting of mass destruction weapons.

▶ The USSR's rejection of Western suggestions for the demilitarization of outer space was delivered May 16 by Zorin. The Soviet delegate declared that the USSR would not accept controls over its missile forces or facilities as long as the threat posed by foreign bases and the existence of nuclear weapons remained. Zorin reiterated that only the total liquidation of foreign bases and nuclear weapons delivery systems would assure Soviet and world security.

▶ British proposals June 6 that the USSR join in discussion of measures for checking that steps toward elimination of nuclear weapons had been carried out were rejected June 7 by

Zorin. (British delegate Godber had said June 6: modern nuclear warheads measured no more than 5 feet in length and 24 inches in diameter; "no responsible government" could accept the Soviet plan, which called for destruction of all nuclear weapons in the 2d stage but contained no inspection measures until the 3d stage.) Zorin asserted June 7 that such technical studies would complicate the conference and would delay a decision on the "political" question of eliminating nuclear weapons.

▶ The 8 neutral disarmament delegations called on the U.S., Britain and USSR June 8 to review their positions and make a fresh attempt to reach agreement at least on the banning of nuclear weapons tests. The neutrals made clear their disappointment at the 3 nuclear powers' failure to begin negotiations on their plan for use of national detection systems as a basis for supervision of a test ban.

U.S. High Altitude Shots

The U.S. began a series of high-altitude tests of nuclear warheads mounted on Thor intermediate-range ballistic missiles in June and July. The missile-borne warheads, intended to be detonated over Johnston Island in the central Pacific at altitudes of from 30 to 500 miles, were to test whether such explosions would black out military radar and communications systems. It also had been suggested that nuclear explosions at great heights might neutralize warheads and guidance systems of attacking missiles.

The disclosure of plans for the high-altitude tests was made Apr. 29 by Dr. Harrison Brown, director of Defense Department research and engineering. It brought an immediate series of protests from prominent scientists, among them Sir Bernard Lovell, director of Britain's Jodrell Bank Radio Observatory, who de-

clared his "dismay" May 1 that nuclear tests should be extended to "a region of space which is at present the subject of detailed study." However, Dr. James A. Van Allen, discoverer of the radiation belt (or belts) bearing his name, declared May 2 that the planned tests were a "magnificent experiment" that would add to man's knowledge of the universe.

The Soviet government, in a statement published June 3 by the Tass news agency, declared that the USSR would be forced to respond with "measures to assure its security" if the U.S. carried out the tests. The statement called the projected tests "new confirmation" of U.S. preparations for a first-strike nuclear war. Noting that the tests were intended to assess their effect on military communications, it charged: "This is tantamount to admitting that the United States is searching in advance for an opportunity to paralyze the defenses of peace-loving nations, thereby safeguarding itself from a retaliatory nuclear blow."

The first 2 high-altitude tests attempted by scientists at the Johnston Island center failed June 4 and June 19 when the Thor rocket carriers had to be destroyed due to malfunctions after launching. The 3d test was carried out successfully July 9. A 4th launching, attempted July 19, ended in failure when the Thor rocket burst into flames before lift-off and was blown up by the range safety officer.

U.S. H-Blast in Space. A missile-borne thermonuclear device was fired high over the central Pacific July 9 by U.S. scientists and military personnel. The detonation produced spectacular auroral displays that were visible for thousands of miles.

The hydrogen device, reportedly of between one and 2 megatons in explosive power, was sent up from the Johnston Island test center aboard a

Thor intermediate range ballistic missile. It was reliably reported to have been detonated in the upper level of the earth's ionosphere at an altitude of about 200 miles. The official announcement of the detonation, issued by Joint Task Force 8, the combined AEC-Defense Department unit carrying out the U.S.' Pacific tests, said only: "A nuclear device carried aloft by a Thor booster was detonated at an altitude of hundreds of kilometers over Johnston Island. . . . The detonation was in the megaton yield range. . . ."

The explosion lighted the Pacific skies for hundreds of miles despite the late hour (11 p.m. July 8 in Hawaii).

In Honolulu, 750 miles to the northwest, the brilliance was visible for 7 minutes. The burst of electrical energy from the blast caused an unparalleled auroral display visible from Hawaii to the Samoan Islands and in places as far distant as Auckland, New Zealand, 3,000 miles to the southwest.

Although no official information was made public regarding the explosion's effect on radar and military communications systems, it was reported that it had disrupted trans-Pacific radio transmissions far less than had been expected. Radio "blackouts" of from 3 to 30 minutes were reported between Japan, Australia, Hawaii and other Pacific points and between them and stations in the U.S. and Europe. Commercial radio facilities reported that these temporary breaks in communications had not appreciably affected their work.

The reported objectives of the test were: (1) to ascertain its "jamming" effects on radio and radar; (2) to determine whether the blast, heat and radioactivity generated by nuclear detonations at high altitudes were capable of destroying, neutralizing or diverting missiles.[*]

(5 other major nuclear tests had been carried out by the U.S. at missile heights: 2 conducted from the Johnston Island test center in 1958 and 3 Project Argus detonations performed at a 300-mile height over the south Atlantic later the same year.)

Nevada H-Test. The first hydrogen device known to have been tested in the continental U.S. was set off at the AEC's Nevada proving grounds July 6. It was followed July 7 by the first atmospheric nuclear test to be carried out in the U.S. since the series ended in Oct. 1958.

The thermonuclear device set off July 6 was planned as part of the Project Plowshare program to test the use of nuclear explosions for peaceful purposes. It was fired in a chamber 650 feet under the test site, 65 miles northwest of Las Vegas. Of 100-kiloton intensity—equivalent to 100,000 tons of TNT—it produced the largest known man-made explosion ever set off in the U.S. According to the AEC, the detonation threw dirt and rocks 7,000 feet into the air and left a crater measuring 300 feet in depth and 1,200 feet in diameter. The radioactive cloud that followed the blast was estimated by the AEC to have reached a height of 12,000 feet, but newsmen outside the test site said it had reached twice that height. AEC spokesmen asserted that 95% of the blast's radioactivity had been trapped in the earth or quickly returned to earth in the heavier portion of the debris thrown skyward by the explosion.

Khrushchev Vs. U.S. Tests. The U.S.' nuclear tests in the atmosphere and in space were denounced by Khrushchev July 10 in an address

[*] The revised 1962 edition of The Effects of Nuclear Weapons, issued May 8 by the Atomic Energy Commission and Defense Department, confirmed that a megaton-range nuclear device detonated over Johnston Island Aug. 1, 1958 had blacked out military communications for up to and beyond 1,000 miles from the detonation point. It disclosed that nuclear explosions at such heights could disrupt missile-tracking radar networks for several hours and shorten the range of search radar systems used to detect incoming missiles or bombers.

to a World Congress on General Disarmament & Peace, meeting in Moscow.

Khrushchev declared that the "new major series of nuclear tests that the United States government is carrying out jointly with the British government is a challenge to mankind." The U.S., he charged, was "carrying out nuclear weapon tests in outer space, disregarding the fact that these experiments may have very dangerous consequences for the conditions of man's life." Khrushchev noted Pres. Kennedy's assurances that the U.S. tests constituted no danger to human health. But he added: "Mr. Kennedy has not told the truth. . . . Modern scientific data show that the American tests bring great harm to the health of people."

Referring to the USSR's resumption of tests prior to the U.S. series, Khrushchev said that it had been necessary to "cool some hot heads who proposed to finish off Russia with one blow" at the height of the 1961 Berlin crisis.

Geneva Talks Resume. The 17-nation Geneva disarmament conference resumed its meetings July 16 after a one-month recess. France, which had boycotted the conference since its inception, did not attend.

An appeal for Soviet cooperation in a "creative search for ways to end the arms race and to devote our common skills and resources to the enlargement of the peaceful opportunities of mankind" had been made by Pres. Kennedy in a statement issued July 14 on the eve of the resumption of talks. The President said that although he did not "underestimate the difficulties" posed by "the Soviet Union's resistance to the minimum inspection necessary to insure effective disarmament," he hoped the arms negotiations would prove to the USSR that "in a nuclear age, all nations have a common interest in preserving their mutual security against the growing perils of the arms race."

The USSR, as an "act of good-will" on the resumpiton of the conference July 16, offered to compromise with the West by accepting its proposals for a 30% reduction in conventional arms during the first stage of disarmament if the West accepted Soviet demands for the total abolition of nuclear weapons delivery systems in the first stage. The Soviet proposal was rejected by Arthur Dean July 18 on the ground that "it would create an early disequalibrium of military power detrimental to peace."

Dean urged the conference July 19 to begin immediate work on measures to curtail the threat of war by "accident, miscalculation or failure of communications." His suggestions for study: advance notice of military maneuvers; exchanges of military missions and establishment of inspection posts at major port and rail centers; a system of rapid communications among heads of government.

USSR Resumes Tests

The Soviet Union announced July 22 that the U.S.' nuclear tests had forced the USSR to resume testing.

The Soviet announcement, published in Russian newspapers, said: "In reply to the series of nuclear tests by the United States, the Soviet government has ordered tests to be held of the newest types of Soviet nuclear weapons." "On it [the U.S.], and on it alone, depended whether the tests to which the Soviet Union had had to resort in the fall of 1961 would be the last or whether our planet would be swept by a new wave of nuclear tests. And the . . . United States made its choice. The explosions of American nuclear bombs . . . have produced their echo—they have made . . . tests by the Soviet Union inevitable."

The U.S.' official response to the Soviet announcement was limited to a State Department expression of regret. But it was disclosed Aug. 1 by Pres. Kennedy that the U.S. had reversed a key part of its policy on detection and control of a nuclear test ban treaty and was willing to accept, in modified form, the neutralist proposal for self-inspection with national detection systems.

Russia resumed nuclear testing Aug. 5.

JFK Accepts National Policing. The U.S.' acceptance of proposals for national monitoring of an international treaty banning nuclear tests was announced by Pres. Kennedy at his news conference in Washington Aug. 1.

The President's announcement represented a basic revision of the previous American position: that only an internationally-manned detection system would provide adequate protection against clandestine nuclear tests.

The new U.S. policy in effect accepted the major provisions of the test-monitoring system suggested by the 8 neutral nations at the Geneva talks and already accepted by the USSR as a basis for negotiations.

Mr. Kennedy's acceptance of monitoring by nationally-manned control posts—subject to international supervision and on-site inspection of suspected nuclear tests—was not stated explicitly in the opening statement on nuclear tests that he read at his news conference. It was, however, described as the U.S.' policy in his replies to requests for clarification of the opening statement. Mr. Kennedy's statement and clarifying responses all emphasized the need for international supervision of any detection system used to monitor a test-ban treaty.

The President's prepared statement said: ". . . We are completing a careful review of the technical problems associated with an effective test-ban treaty. This review was stimulated by important new technical assessments. These assessments give promise that we can work towards an internationally-supervised system of detection and verification for underground testing which will be simpler and more economical than the system which was contained in the treaty which we tabled in Geneva in Apr. 1961.° I must emphasize that these new assessments do not affect the requirement that any system must include provision for on-site inspection of unidentified underground events. It may be that we shall not need as many as we have needed in the past. But we find no justification for the Soviet claim that a test-ban treaty can be effective without on-site inspection."

Asked whether his statement meant that the U.S.' new assessments had "affected our position on the need for international control stations on Soviet territory," Mr. Kennedy answered: "No, I think that our position, which Mr. Dean will elaborate, has been that national control posts should be internationally monitored, supervised." Asked again for clarification, he declared: "I think that the language I used . . . was carefully chosen and is precise: . . . internationally monitored supervised national control posts."

(A Defense Department statement made public July 7 with the approval of the White House had said that the U.S.' Project Vela underground detection research program had "begun

---

*The draft treaty, presented at the U.S.-British-Soviet A-test conference in Geneva Apr. 18, 1961, had called for a worldwide network of 180 test detection stations of which approximately 20 each would be situated in the U.S. and USSR. These posts were to have been internationally-manned and subject to an international control commission on which the Western and Soviet blocs each would have 4 seats and neutral nations 3 seats. The detection network's findings were to be investigated by international inspection teams not including nationals of the country on whose territory the inspection was being carried out (except in the case of the USSR, which was to be given the right to assign observers to the inspection team). On-site investigations were to be limited to a quota of 20 on the territory of each of the 3 major nuclear powers.

to bear fruit." It said new data had shown that there might be "substantially fewer" earthquakes producing seismic signals similar to those of underground nuclear tests than previously was thought. Thus, according to the statement, "there will be fewer earthquakes that might be mistaken for possible underground nuclear explosions of a given size." The defense report asserted that these developments might make it possible to detect and identify low kiloton-range nuclear detonations underground "with some reliability" at distances of 1,500 to 3,000 miles.)

(The recommendation for a change in U.S. detection policy reportedly had been made July 26 by the Committee of Principals, a body created during the Eisenhower Administration to advise the President on the conduct of nuclear test-ban negotiations.† The committee's findings were taken up at a White House meeting held by the President July 27 with Vice Pres. Johnson, State Secy. Dean Rusk, Defense Secy. Robert S. McNamara, AEC Chrmn. Glenn T. Seaborg, Gen. Lyman L. Lemnitzer, chairman of the Joint Chiefs of Staff, Director William C. Foster of the Arms Control & Disarmament Agency and Jerome B. Wiesner, Presidential science advisor. A 2d White House meeting on the subject, held July 30, included Johnson, Rusk, McNamara, Foster, Seaborg, Lemnitzer and Arthur Dean, who had been summoned from Geneva to take part in the talks.)

U.S. Offer Rejected. The Kennedy offer to negotiate a test ban agreement policed by nationally-manned detection systems under international supervision was rebuffed Aug. 6 by the Soviet delegation at the conference.

The American proposal had been transmitted to Valerian Zorin by Arthur Dean in Geneva Aug. 5. Zorin, addressing the conference Aug. 6,

declared that the new U.S. proposal did not constitute a change "in principle" from the previous Western position. Zorin said that he saw "no great hope" that it would meet Soviet objections to international supervision and on-site inspection of suspected clandestine nuclear tests, both measures previously rejected by the USSR as tantamount to international espionage. Zorin delivered the USSR's formal rejection of Pres. Kennedy's offer in an address to the conference Aug. 9.

USSR Resumes Tests. The detonation of a powerful Soviet thermonuclear device over Novaya Zemlya, the USSR's Arctic island test site, was monitored Aug. 5 by Japanese, Swedish and U.S. scientists. Although the detonation initially was thought to have been the first in a new Soviet test series, the U.S. reported Aug. 6 that it had been preceded by a series of low-yield tests.

The Aug. 5 detonation was the first Soviet atmospheric test to be reported publicly since Nov. 4, 1961.* Scientists of the Seismological Institute of Uppsala University, Sweden, reported that the detonation had been of 40-megaton intensity, but the U.S. Atomic Energy Commission estimated Aug. 6 that the detonation had been on "the order of magnitude of 30 megatons"; in either case the Soviet test was 2d in power only to the 58-megaton test carried out by the USSR Oct. 30, 1961.

The U.S. report that the 30-megaton test had been preceded by other tests was made Aug. 6 in an AEC

---

† Membership of the Committee of Principals: the Secretaries of State and Defense, the chairman of the Atomic Energy Commission, the director of the Central Intelligence Agency and the President's science advisor.

* The AEC had reported Feb. 2 that a clandestine Soviet nuclear test apparently had been conducted underground earlier that day in the Semipalatinsk region of central Asia. Although the AEC, which said the test had been indicated by seismic signals, had no proof the detonation was nuclear in origin, it estimated its force as in the 20-kiloton range.

statement that said: "There are indications that the Soviet Union had resumed atmospheric nuclear testing a few days prior to the nuclear detonation announced as having occurred at Novaya Zemlya on Aug. 5." It reported that the earlier tests (no total was given) apparently were of detonations in the "low-kiloton range" carried out in Siberia.

A State Department statement issued Aug. 5 said that "the Soviet Union's initiation of yet another series of atmospheric tests—the 2d such series in less than a year—can only be regarded as a somber episode."

The Soviet test series continued with mounting intensity throughout the autumn. Many of the nuclear devices tested were multi-megaton weapons, all of which were detonated in the atmosphere. The Russian tests were halted Nov. 17, 3 days before a Nov. 20 deadline pledged by Khrushchev Nov. 7 in remarks to newsmen at a Kremlin reception marking the 45th anniversary of the Bolshevik Revolution. They were, however, resumed briefly with a series of detonations monitored Dec. 18-25.

(For list of Soviet nuclear tests during 1962, see table at end of this section.)

Soviet Tests Protested. News of the Soviet test resumption on the eve of the 17th anniversary of the Aug. 6, 1945 atomic bombing of Hiroshima, was broadcast and published everywhere in the world except in the USSR and possibly some other Communist nations.

Demonstrations and parades commemorating the Hiroshima bombing victims took place in New York, London, The Hague, Stockholm and Copenhagen Aug. 6; many participants carried signs protesting the Soviet test resumption.

3 members of a Japanese Zengakuren student delegation to a Moscow meeting of the International Union of Students reportedly were beaten by police when they sought Aug. 6 to unfurl a banner in Red Square protesting the Soviet test.

Mayor Shinzo Hamai said at a dawn prayer meeting in Hiroshima Aug. 6 that the Soviet action was "callous and cynical" in its intent and timing. In Tokyo, Socialists and some leftist Zengakuren factions withdrew from the 8th World Congress Against Atomic & Hydrogen Weapons after Communist delegates had refused to vote on a resolution condemning the Soviet tests.

In Helsinki, 100 Western delegates to a meeting of the Communist-dominated World Youth Festival were prevented by force from displaying anti-test slogans as they marched in the festival's concluding parade; an anti-test demonstration apparently had been approved by festival officials but was canceled after news of the Soviet tests.

West Offers 2 Plans. The U.S. and British governments Aug. 27 offered the USSR its choice of 2 contrasting plans for halting the current wave of nuclear weapons tests.

The Western offer was made in a special joint statement issued by Pres. Kennedy and Prime Min. Macmillan and in draft treaties embodying the 2 plans, presented to the 17-nation Geneva disarmament conference by Arthur Dean. The USSR's rejection of the offer was made clear within 24 hours.

The new Western initiative offered the Soviet Union a choice between the following test-ban proposals:

▶ An international treaty banning all nuclear tests in the earth's atmosphere, in outer space, underground and under water. The treaty would be monitored by a system of nationally-manned detection posts, which would be operated under the supervision of an international control commission consisting of 4 Western representatives, 4 Communists and 7 representatives of neutral or non-aligned states. Unidentified seismic events suspected of arising from clandestine nuclear tests would be subjected to on-site inspection by international scientific teams; however, only a few inspections would be permitted each year on the territories of the 3 participating nuclear powers.

▶ A limited treaty banning nuclear tests in the atmosphere, in outer space and under water, but leaving open the question of underground tests. This proposal, favored by the West as a feasible "first step" toward a treaty banning all tests, was advanced on the grounds that it could be monitored easily by existing detection networks and would not require the on-site inspection machinery that might be needed to check for suspected underground tests. Negotiations would continue on extending the treaty to provide an inspected ban on underground tests.

The joint statement of Pres. Kennedy and Macmillan, made public in London and Newport, R.I. Aug. 27, emphasized the 2 leaders' "strong preference" for an inspected ban on all nuclear tests. It added: "We are also prepared to conclude an early agreement on the basis of the 2d document, that covering a more limited field"; "such a treaty would result in a definite downward turn in the arms race . . . [and] would make it easier to prevent the spread of nuclear weapons to countries not now possessing them."

The Western proposals were rejected categorically by Soviet Deputy Foreign Min. Vasily V. Kuznetsov in a address Aug. 28 at the Geneva conference. Kuznetsov declared that the West's plan for a ban on all nuclear tests was unacceptable because it was conditional on mandatory on-site inspection of suspected underground tests. He repeated previous Soviet arguments that this provision would open the USSR to legalized espionage; he said on-site inspection was "guided by political and military considerations that have nothing to do with a test ban." With respect to the alternate proposal for a limited test ban, Kuznetsov declared that the West's draft treaty, in effect, would sanction continued underground tests.

USSR Asks Test Cut-Off. A Soviet formula for a cut-off of all nuclear testing by Jan. 1, 1963 was presented at the talks by Kuznetsov Aug. 29.

The Soviet plan was submitted as a counter-offer to the U.S.-British proposals of Aug. 27. It called for the cessation by Jan. 1, 1963 of all nuclear tests in the earth's atmosphere, in space and underwater, and for an unpoliced moratorium, effective the same date, on all underground tests. It provided for extension of the moratorium until such time as a "permanent solution" could be negotiated for measures to detect and thus prevent clandestine underground tests. The Soviet proposal contained no measures for mandatory on-site inspection of suspected tests, but Kuznetsov said that if a treaty was signed the USSR would be willing to invite inspection of any suspicious seismic shock originating on its territory.

The Soviet proposal was supported Aug. 29 by M. T. Mbu of Nigeria and Sept. 3 by James Barrington of Burma and Haddis Alemayeho of Ethiopia.

(The Geneva conference recessed Sept. 7 to permit the UN General Assembly to take up again the questions of disarmament and a nuclear test ban.)

JFK Backs Plan. Pres. Kennedy announced Aug. 29 his support in principle for the Soviet proposal. The President made it clear, however, that the U.S. would not participate in another unpoliced test moratorium to obtain agreement on a cut-off date.

Reading a prepared statement at his news conference, Mr. Kennedy said: "In Geneva . . . The Soviet representative proposed [today] that agreement should be reached on a cut-off time for all nuclear weapons tests and that this date should be set as of Jan. 1, 1963. I'm happy to say that the United States . . . regards this as a reasonable target date. . . . The world will welcome an agreement that a way should be found to stop all nuclear testing at the end of this year. But I must point out again that in order to . . . end testing, we must have workable international agreements. Gentlemen's agreements and moratoria do not provide the type of guarantees that are necessary. . . . This is the lesson of the Soviet government's tragic decision to renew testing just a year ago. . . . That is why we must have a definite agreement with reasonable and adequate assurance."

U.S. Resumes Pacific Shots. The Defense Department and the Atomic Energy Commission announced jointly Sept. 10 that the U.S. planned to resume both atmospheric and high altitude (missile warhead) nuclear tests in the vicinity of Johnston Island in the Pacific.

It had been assumed that the atmospheric tests had been completed July 12, when the U.S. announced the termination of the "Christmas Island phase" of its 1962 Pacific tests. But the joint announcement said the new tests would include "a few high-altitude events and a few in which the devices will be dropped from an airplane." The high-altitude tests referred to were those remaining to be carried out when the Johnston Island missile launching installation had been damaged by a malfunctioning missile July 26.

The new series was reopened Oct. 2 with the detonation of an intermediate-yield device airdropped near Johnston Island.

5 missile-borne tests were attempted during the high-altitude phase of the new series, but only 4 of them were successful. The first, attempted Oct. 16, failed when the Thor missile carrier veered off course after launching and was destroyed, together with its warhead.

The 2d and 3d tests, conducted Oct. 19 and 26, were described officially as successful. In the Oct. 19 test, a device with an estimated yield of less than 20 kilotons was carried up 20 to 30 miles by a modified Sergeant rocket and exploded. In the Oct. 26 experiment, a warhead described as of less than megaton power was launched atop a Thor missile and detonated at a reported height of 30 to 40 miles.

The 4th and 5th missile-borne devices of the new series were detonated successfully Nov. 1 and 4. The Nov. 1 detonation was of a "submegaton" device fired at an unknown altitude. The Nov. 4 shot was of a device of less than 20 kilotons carried aloft by a Nike-Hercules rocket and detonated at a reported height of 30 miles.

The completion of the 2d phase of the U.S. atmospheric tests in the Pacific was announced by Pres. Kennedy in a statement issued Nov. 4. The statement made it clear, however, that the U.S. would continue its underground tests in Nevada until agreement had been reached on a cessation of tests.

New Moves Toward A-Ban

Optimism Grows. Leading Soviet and Western statesmen expressed optimism in October and November that agreement could be found on terms for a new halt to nuclear tests. This optimism was generated largely as a result of the successful resolution of the U.S.-Russian confrontation over missile bases in Cuba. It was felt that the flexibility and moderation exhibited by Pres. Kennedy and Krushchev in the Cuban crisis could be extended to the questions of nuclear tests and disarmament.

The 2 leaders themselves had expressed such feelings in a series of notes exchanged Oct. 28.

Premier Khrushchev, in his Oct. 28 letter to Mr. Kennedy on the Cuban affair, had declared: "We should like to continue the exchange of views on the prohibition of atomic and thermonuclear weapons, on general disarmament and other problems relating to the relaxation of international tension."

Mr. Kennedy, replying to Khrushchev the same day, had agreed that "perhaps now, as we step back from danger, we can make some real progress in this vital field. I think we should give priority to questions relating to the proliferation of nuclear weapons, on the earth and in outer space, and to the great effort for a nuclear test ban. . . ."

UN Assembly Asks Action. The UN General Assembly called Nov. 6 for immediate great-power action to halt all nuclear tests by Jan. 1, 1963. The Assembly's appeal was made in 2 rival resolutions, one presented by 37 non-aligned and non-nuclear powers, the 2d submitted by the U.S. and Britain. Both resolutions called for immediate negotiations to end the nuclear weapons test race, but the U.S.-British draft demanded that any new test ban be subjected to strict on-site verification.

The 2 resolutions and their major provisions:

▶The 37-nation draft, adopted by the Assembly by a vote of 75-0, with 21 abstentions (principally the 4 nuclear powers and their allies), condemned all nuclear weapons tests and called for: (a) the cessation of all tests immediately or by Jan. 1, 1963; (b) a settlement of East-West differences on terms of a treaty to halt further testing; (c) in the event this was not feasible, an "immediate [East-West] agreement prohibiting nuclear weapons tests in the atmosphere, underwater and in outer space, accompanied by an interim arrangement suspending all underground tests . . . [with] adequate assurances for effective detection and identification of seismic events by an international scientific commission."

▶The U.S.-British draft, approved by a vote of 51-10 (Soviet bloc opposed), with 40 abstentions, called for: (a) negotiation by the Geneva conference of "a treaty with effective and prompt international verification which prohibits nuclear weapons tests in all environments for all time"; (b) if this was not possible, "an interim treaty prohibiting nuclear weapons tests in those environments where radioactive fallout is a matter of international concern and where nuclear weapons tests can be detected and identified without international controls, namely, the atmosphere, the oceans and space."

The principal difference between the 2 resolutions was the insistence in the Western draft that a test-ban treaty be subject to strict verification or that an interim agreement be limited to atmospheric and other forms of testing that could be supervised without inspection.

The question of disarmament had been taken up by U.S. delegate Adlai E. Stevenson Sept. 20 and Soviet Foreign Min. Andrei A. Gromyko Sept. 21 in the general debate at the opening of the Assembly session.

Stevenson's remarks:

"The most overwhelming danger" to peace remained "the onrushing arms race. . . . It goes on because no nation, confronted by hostile nations, can neglect its defenses. No great power can risk unilateral disarmament. There is a system of complete and general disarmament under which all nations progressively tear down—in plain view of the international community and with suitable safeguards—their own capacity to wage war. . . . But, just as it takes at least 2 to make an arms race, it takes at least 2 to stop an arms race. No one in his senses would expect one side to abandon the means of self-defense unless it knew for sure that the other side was giving up its arms as well. This means that practical verification is the essence of any workable agreement for general disarmament. It need not be total verification. . . . We are prepared to take certain risks to lessen the chance of an intensified arms race. But we are not prepared to risk our survival."

Gromyko's remarks:

The USSR's proposals on general disarmament had been rejected by the U.S. because of their provisions for "the elimination, at the first stage of disarmament, of all nuclear weapons delivery vehicles," because "states embarking on disarmament would for some time allegedly need some sort of 'protective umbrella.' . . . Taking account of the stand of the Western powers, the Soviet government agrees that in the process of destroying nuclear weapons delivery vehicles at the first stage exception be made for a strictly limited and agreed number of global missiles, anti-missile missiles and anti-aircraft missiles, . . . which would remain at the disposal of the USSR and the United States alone. Thus for a definite period the means of defense would remain in case someone . . . ventures to violate the treaty and conceal missiles or aircraft."

'Black Boxes' Proposed. The Soviet Communist party newspaper *Pravda* suggested Nov. 10 that the East-West impasse over on-site inspection might be solved by an agreement to use sealed automatic seismic stations—"black boxes"—that would be installed on the territories of the nuclear powers to record any seismic movements produced by clandestine underground tests. The automatic devices would be linked to an international network of data systems and would be removed periodically for inspection and servicing by the proposed international commission for supervision of the test ban.

The Soviet proposal was rejected informally by Arthur Dean Nov. 24 on his arrival in Geneva for the resumption of the arms talks. Dean said that although the U.S. was ready to examine any such proposal on "a scientific basis," it believed that the use of "black boxes" would be impractical because "many hundreds or thousands" would be required to cover the USSR and they could be fed false signals to screen clandestine tests. Other U.S. officials said the installation and servicing of an adequate network of "black boxes" would require a far greater opening of Soviet territory than that demanded by the West under its proposals for limited on-site inspection.

Geneva Talks Resume. The UN Disarmament Committee resumed its work in Geneva Nov. 26 in the wake of the nuclear war scare generated by the crisis over Cuba.

Amb. Arthur Dean, in his opening address at the meeting Nov. 26, declared that the conference should redouble its efforts, especially in view of the "recent [Cuban] events that brought civilization so close to the abyss of nuclear war." Dean asserted that the apparent solution of the Cuban crisis had demonstrated that "the earth's 2 great military powers can reach agreement based on reason when a sufficient incentive to reach agreement exists on both sides." He warned, however, that these same Cuban events had shown that "the world cannot rest agreements involving national security on good faith" because "falsification of facts may be made at very high levels of government." Dean reiterated that the U.S. would accept a pact to ban nuclear weapons tests only if it contained adequate "international arrangements for detection, identification, location and inspection."

Soviet Amb. Semyon K. Tsarapkin, chief of the USSR's delegation, said Nov. 26 that the Soviet Union was prepared to make major concessions. His description of proposed concessions, however, disclosed none considered major by the Western delegation. The Tsarapkin proposals were a restatement of an offer made by Soviet Foreign Min. Gromyko, in an address Sept. 21 before the UN General Assembly, to permit the U.S. and USSR to retain a limited number of ICBMs, anti-missile missiles and anti-aircraft missiles until the end of the 2d stage of a 3-stage disarmament treaty. (This retention had been demanded by the West to assure itself of continued protection against aerial or missile attack during the preliminary stages of disarmament.)

(U.S., British and Soviet negotiators had continued discussions on proposals for a ban on nuclear tests during the 17-nation committee's recess. They had met as a 3-nation subcommittee of the conference. The interim negotiations were ended without result Nov. 20 after 19 sessions.)

The neutral delegations, in a plan advanced Nov. 30 by Arthur S. Lall of India, urged the nuclear powers to accept a test ban system under which inspectors from neutral states would carry out an agreed number of inspections annually on their territories. Lall said that although inspection would remain voluntary under the proposal, any state refusing to admit the inspectors would face public blame for violating the anti-test accord.

The USSR Dec. 3 rejected the various neutral proposals for a new temporary ban on underground tests. Tsarapkin said the USSR would accept nothing less than a "permanent" ban on all tests, above and beneath the earth.

The USSR announced Dec. 10 that it was prepared to accept an inspected test ban—one that would be policed by a network of automatic seismic detection stations operated under international supervision. The Soviet proposal, submitted by Tsarapkin as a substantial concession to the West's position, called for the placing of 3 unmanned seismic stations on the territory of each of the nuclear powers. These stations would be supplemented by a network of other seismic detectors situated immediately adjacent to the nuclear powers' borders. The instruments located within their territories would be installed and periodically replaced for servicing and examination by foreign personnel of the proposed international test-ban control commission.

The Soviet proposal was welcomed by Charles C. Stelle of the U.S. and Sir Michael Wright of Britain Dec. 11 as a step toward the minimum test-ban terms envisaged by the West. They were unsuccessful, however, in efforts to obtain further details from Tsarapkin on technical features of the Soviet proposal.

U.S.-USSR Phone Link. The installation of a direct phone or teletype connection between the Kremlin and the White House was proposed formally by the U.S. Dec. 12 at the Geneva conference. The idea was given strong support by Pres. Kennedy at his news conference later the same day.

The proposal was made in a working paper on prevention of war by accident or miscalculation, submitted in Geneva by Amb. Dean. The proposal, known popularly as the "hot telephone" plan, also had been advanced by the USSR.[*]

Mr. Kennedy, questioned on the U.S.' intentions in proposing the Kremlin-White House link, said at his news conference that the Cuban crisis had shown the need for rapid communications between world leaders in the nuclear age. The President said: "There was a delay . . . in the communications back and forth in the Cuban affair. In some degree . . . it was necessary to rely on open broadcasts of messages, rather than sending them through the coding procedure, which took a number of hours. . . . In a nuclear age speed is very desirable. So we are hoping that . . . we can get instantaneous communication, or at least relatively instantaneous communication." Reminded by newsmen that he once had indicated opposition to the use of a direct Kremlin-White House phone line, he added: "I am not convinced that telephoning would have speeded . . . a solution of the Cuban crisis. Teletype I think might have made it a safer situation."

[*] Moscow sources had reported July 23 that the USSR favored the establishment of a direct phone link between the Kremlin and the White House. Questioned about the idea, Pres. Kennedy said at his news conference July 23 that he had no plans for a phone link with Khrushchev because the basic difficulty between them was one of comprehension rather than of communication.

1963 Moratorium Seen. By the year's end officials in Soviet and in Western capitals were predicting that an informal moratorium on nuclear tests would be in effect by Jan. 1, 1963 despite the U.S.-Soviet disagreement on terms for a formal pact.

A new moratorium was viewed as probable despite the USSR's carrying out of a brief series of atmospheric nuclear tests Dec. 18-25 and the Geneva conference's recess without success Dec. 21.

Soviet Premier Khrushchev, in an interview granted the *London Daily Express* and made public on New Year's Eve by the Tass news agency, repeated the USSR's offer to abide by an unpoliced moratorium if the Western powers did so. U.S. Amb. Dean had formally rejected the Soviet moratorium proposal at the Geneva conference Dec. 19, but it was believed likely that the U.S. would refrain at least temporarily from further atmospheric tests.

At the final 1962 session of the Geneva conference Dec. 20, Dean and Semyon Tsarapkin traded charges of bad faith against each other's government; both were accused by neutral delegates of having harmed the conference by their suspicion and inflexibility.

1962 Nuclear Tests

More than 130 nuclear detonations were reported in 1962. All but 3 were carried out by the U.S. and Soviet Union.

The principal authoritative information about these tests was supplied to the press by the U.S. Atomic Energy Commission. The AEC's data on Soviet tests was gathered by the U.S.' seismic and atmospheric monitoring systems.

The AEC specifically reported 89 U.S. nuclear tests (including 2 of British nuclear devices, tested jointly by U.S. and British scientists) and 37 Soviet tests during the year. The AEC's announcements of Soviet tests included the information that the Russian test series known to have been begun Aug. 5 had been preceded by an unspecified number of low-yield nuclear detonations in Siberia and that "a number of" Soviet tests—at least 3—had been conducted Dec. 23 to 25 in the vicinity of Novaya Zemlya, the USSR's main atomic test cen-

ter. (Sweden's Uppsala University Seismological Institute reported that the Dec. 23-25 Soviet tests included 3 detonations, of 8, 10 and 19 megatons, respectively, Dec. 24 and one, of 11 megatons, Dec. 25. The AEC specifically reported only one of these, apparently the largest, in an announcement that a 20-megaton test had taken place at Novaya Zemlya Dec. 24.) Added to these U.S., British and Soviet tests was a single French nuclear detonation in the Sahara.

The following table includes all nuclear detonations specifically reported by the AEC during 1962. Tests described as low-yield or low-range°° are those that produced an explosive force of 20 kilotons or less. Intermediate-range tests were those producing a detonation force of from 20 to 500 kilotons. Megaton tests were those of 1,000-kiloton or greater force. (One kiloton measures the equivalent of the energy released by the explosion of 1,000 tons of TNT.)

U.S. Explosions

Date	Force	Site
Jan. 9‡	Low yield	Nevada test site, 65 miles north-west of Las Vegas
Jan. 18‡	Low yield	Nevada test site
Jan. 30‡	Low yield	Nevada test site
Feb. 8‡	Low yield	Nevada test site
Feb. 9‡	Low yield	Nevada test site
Feb. 15‡	Low yield	Nevada test site
Feb. 19‡	Low yield	Nevada test site
Feb. 19‡	Low yield	Nevada test site
Feb. 23‡	Low yield	Nevada test site
Feb. 24‡	Low yield	Nevada test site
Mar. 5‡	Low yield	Nevada test site
Mar. 8‡	Low yield	Nevada test site
Mar. 15‡	Low yield	Nevada test site
Mar. 28‡	Low yield	Nevada test site
Mar. 31‡	Low yield	Nevada test site
Apr. 5‡	Low yield	Nevada test site
Apr. 6‡	Low yield	Nevada test site
Apr. 12‡	Low yield	Nevada test site
Apr. 14‡	Low yield	Nevada test site
Apr. 21‡	Low yield	Nevada test site
Apr. 25*	Intermediate yield	Christmas Island area in central Pacific
Apr. 27*	Intermediate yield	Christmas Island
Apr. 27‡	Low yield	Nevada test site
May 2*	Low yield	Christmas Island
May 4*	Intermediate yield	Christmas Island
May 6§	500-kiloton Polaris missile warhead	Christmas Island
May 7‡	Low yield	Nevada test site
May 8*	Intermediate yield	Christmas Island
May 9*	Intermediate yield	Christmas Island
May 11*	Intermediate yield	Christmas Island
May 11†	Low yield	Eastern Pacific
May 12‡	Low yield	Nevada test site

(Continued on next page)

Date	Force	Site
May 12*	Intermediate range	Christmas Island
May 14*	Intermediate range	Christmas Island
May 19*	Intermediate range	Christmas Island
May 19‡	Low yield	Nevada test site
May 25‡	Low yield	Nevada test site
May 25*	Low yield	Christmas Island
May 27*	Intermediate	Christmas Island
June 1‡	Low yield	Nevada test site
June 6‡	Low yield	Nevada test site
June 8*	Intermediate range	Christmas Island
June 9*	Intermediate range	Christmas Island
June 10*	Low yield	Christmas Island
June 12*	Intermediate range	Christmas Island
June 13‡	Low yield	Nevada test site
June 15*	Intermediate range	Christmas Island
June 17*	Intermediate range	Christmas Island
June 19*	Low yield	Christmas Island
June 21‡	Low yield	Nevada test site
June 22*	Intermediate range	Christmas Island
June 27*	Megaton range	Christmas Island
June 27‡	Intermediate range	Nevada test site
June 28‡	Low yield	Nevada test site
June 30‡	Low yield	Nevada test site
June 30*	Low yield	Christmas Island
July 6‡	100-kiloton peace-ful-use H-test	Nevada test site
July 7*	Low yield	Nevada test site
July 9¶	1.4 megatons	Johnston Island test side in central Pacific
July 10*	Intermediate range	Christmas Island
July 11*	Low yield	Christmas Island
July 11‡	Low yield	Nevada test site
July 13‡	Low yield	Nevada test site
July 14*	Low yield	Nevada test site
July 17*	Low yield	Nevada test site
July 27‡	Low yield	Nevada test site
Aug. 24‡	Low yield	Nevada test site
Aug. 24‡	Low yield	Nevada test site
Sept. 14‡	Low yield	Nevada test site
Sept. 20‡	Low yield	Nevada test site
Sept. 29‡	Low yield	Nevada test site
Oct. 2*	Intermediate yield	Johnston Island
Oct. 5‡	Intermediate range	Nevada test site
Oct. 6*	Low yield	Johnston Island
Oct. 12‡	Low yield	Nevada test site

Date	Force	Site
Oct. 18*	Low megaton range	Johnston Island
Oct. 19‡	Low yield	Nevada test site
Oct. 20¶	Less than 20 kilotons	Johnston Island
Oct. 26¶	20 kilotons to one megaton	Johnston Island
Oct. 27‡	Low yield	Nevada test site
Oct. 27*	Intermediate range	Johnston Island
Oct. 30*	Megaton yield	Johnston Island
Nov. 1*	Submegaton yield range	Johnston Island
Nov. 4¶	Less than 20 kilotons	Johnston Island
Nov. 27‡	Low yield	Nevada test site
Dec. 12‡	Low yield	Nevada test site
Dec. 12‡	Low yield	Nevada test site

Soviet Explosions

Date	Force	Site
Feb. 2‡	20 kiloton range	Semipalatinsk area (Siberia)
Aug. 5*	30-40 megatons	Novaya Zemlya area (Arctic islands between Barents and Kara Seas)
Aug. 7*	Low kiloton range	Central Siberia
Aug. 10*	Less than one megaton	Novaya Zemlya
Aug. 20*	10-12 megatons	Novaya Zemlya
Aug. 22*	9 megatons	Novaya Zemlya
Aug. 25*	Several megatons	Novaya Zemlya
Aug. 27*	Several megatons	Novaya Zemlya
Sept. 2*	Intermediate range	Novaya Zemlya
Sept. 8*	Megaton	Novaya Zemlya
Sept. 15*	15 megatons	Novaya Zemlya
Sept. 16*	Several megatons	Novaya Zemlya
Sept. 18*	"A few megatons"	Novaya Zemlya
Sept. 19*	Multimegaton	Novaya Zemlya
Sept. 21*	"A few megatons"	Novaya Zemlya
Sept. 25*	Multimegaton range	Novaya Zemlya
Sept. 27*	Nearly 30 megatons	Novaya Zemlya
Oct. 7*	Intermediate range	Novaya Zemlya
Oct. 14*	Low yield	Semipalatinsk
Oct. 22*	"A few hundred kilotons"	Central Asia
Oct. 22*	Several megatons	Novaya Zemlya
Oct. 27*	Intermediate range	Novaya Zemlya
Oct. 28*	Intermediate range	Central Asia
Oct. 28*	Low yield	Semipalatinsk
Oct. 29*	Intermediate range	Novaya Zemlya
Oct. 30*	Intermediate range	Novaya Zemlya
Nov. 1*	Intermediate range	Central Asia
Nov. 1*	Intermediate range	Novaya Zemlya
Nov. 3*	Intermediate range	Novaya Zemlya
Nov. 3*	Intermediate range	Novaya Zemlya
Nov. 4*	Intermediate range	Semipalatinsk
Nov. 17*	Low yield	Semipalatinsk
Dec. 18*	Intermediate yield	Novala Zemlya
Dec. 18*	Intermediate yield	Novaya Zemlya
Dec. 20*	Low yield	Novaya Zemlya
Dec. 22*	Intermediate range	Novaya Zemlya
Dec. 24*	20 megatons	Novaya Zemlya

Other Explosions

Date	Force	Site
Mar. 1 (U.S.-British)‡	"Low kiloton range"	Nevada test site
May 1 (French)‡	Not given	Hoggar Mountains in Sahara
Dec. 7 (U.S.-British)‡	Low yield	Nevada test site

*Atmospheric test.   ‡Underground test.
†Underwater test, reportedly of an anti-submarine weapon detonated several hundred miles south-west of Southern California.
¶Missile-borne tests (8 of these tests, of nuclear devices carried to high-altitude detonation points in missile warheads, were attempted in 1962; 4 were successful, 4 were failures. The 4 failures, all attributed to defects in the carrier missiles and related equipment, occurred June 4, June 19, July 26 and Oct. 16).
§ test of nuclear warhead reportedly carried to the target by a Polaris missile. Official announcements described the test only as the first of a nuclear-armed U.S. long-range missile. Press reports said, however, that the test had been of a Polaris missile, with a 500-kiloton warhead, launched 1,200 miles from the target area by the nuclear submarine Ethan Allen. The AP reported from Washington May 7 that the Ethan Allen had launched the missile while cruising submerged under simulated battle conditions.
**"Yield" and "range" were used interchangeably to describe the force produced by nuclear detonations.

The 3 major atomic powers agreed in 1963 to halt nuclear tests in the earth's atmosphere, under the sea and in space. The treaty, signed in Moscow, was welcomed by many nations of both East and West as a first step toward international disarmament. The 18-nation Geneva disarmament conference, which had set the stage for the Moscow treaty, faltered through its 2d year; but it was the scene of successful negotiations for establishing a 'hot line' emergency communications system between Moscow and Washington.

Moscow A-Test Negotiations

An East-West agreement for a fresh start in negotiating a treaty banning nuclear weapons tests was announced by Pres. John F. Kennedy June 10. The announcement confirmed reports that a series of messages exchanged by Mr. Kennedy with British Prime Min. Harold Macmillan and Soviet Premier Nikita S. Khrushchev beginning Apr. 24 had been devoted to the question of new talks on the nuclear test question.

The 3 major nuclear powers had been negotiating fruitlessly on the test problem since Oct. 1958. These negotiations, pursued intermittently in Geneva, had always stalemated on the question of detection and inspection to insure that clandestine tests could not be carried out. The U.S. and Britain had contended that any effective treaty must provide for seismic detection posts on the territory of each of the nuclear powers and for on-site inspection of any earth shocks suspected as produced by nuclear explosions. The USSR had held that modern detection techniques made this unnecessary and that on-site inspection would be used by the West to spy out Soviet defenses.

It was apparent by early 1963 that both sides (a) were eager for an agreement that would halt testing and the concomitant growth of radioactive fallout levels and (b) were willing to "freeze" nuclear weapons development at the rough balance that apparently existed. The major question remaining unanswered was whether East and West would permit their differences over detection and inspection to wreck new negotiations or whether their desire for a test-ban agreement would lead to a formula that would by-pass these differences; a possible solution that had been suggested was a ban that exempted underground tests, which the West held could be carried out secretly unless there were rigid detection and inspection procedures.

The matter was dealt with successfully at a conference opened in Moscow July 15 by U.S., British and Soviet negotiators.

Conference Arranged. Pres. Kennedy announced June 10 that the U.S., British and Soviet governments had agreed to convene new negotiations in Moscow on a treaty to ban nuclear weapons tests. He said that as a sign of American good faith, the U.S. had halted nuclear tests in the earth's atmosphere and would not resume them unless another country did so.

The President's announcements were made in an address devoted to elaborating "a strategy of peace" to prevent a world nuclear holocaust. His speech, regarded as a major statement of U.S. hopes for a relaxation of the cold war, was given wide attention, especially in the USSR, where it was published in full June 11 by the government newspaper *Izvestia*. The address was delivered at the American University in Washington.

Mr. Kennedy offered these 2 decisions as preliminary but important steps toward a lessening of East-West tension, disarmament and an eventual world order capable of resolving international conflict without war. He called on Americans to support this aim by re-examining their attitudes toward peace, the USSR and the cold war. He said U.S. cold war policies must be conducted "in such a way, that it becomes in the Communists' interest to agree on a genuine peace."

"We are both caught up in a vicious and dangerous cycle," he said, "with suspicion on one side breeding suspicion on the other, and new weapons begetting counter-weapons." "Both

the United States and its allies, and the Soviet Union and its allies, have a mutually deep interest in a just and genuine peace and in halting the arms race. Agreements to this end are in the interests of the Soviet Union as well as ours—and even the most hostile nations can be relied upon to accept and keep those treaty obligations . . . which are in their own interest."

The President warned: "Today, should total war ever break out again —no matter how—our 2 countries will be the primary targets. It is an ironic but accurate fact that the 2 strongest powers are the 2 most in danger of devastation. All we have built, all we have worked for, would be destroyed in the first 24 hours."

Khrushchev for 2 Pacts. Soviet Premier Khrushchev called July 2 for the simultaneous signing of an East-West nonaggression pact and an agreement banning all nuclear weapons tests except those conducted underground.

This was the first time that Khrushchev had linked the nuclear-test question to repeated Soviet proposals for a nonaggression treaty between the NATO and Warsaw Treaty powers.

Khrushchev's proposal was made in the course of an address at an East Berlin rally. His speech reaffirmed that the USSR would not accept the on-site inspection demanded by the West for a treaty banning all nuclear tests, including those hidden under the earth's surface. He offered a partial nuclear ban as a feasible way to end prolonged disagreement on the on-site inspection problem.°

Excerpts from Khrushchev's address:
▶ "Carefully analyzing the situation, the

NOBEL PEACE PRIZE. The Nobel Peace Prize Committee of the Norwegian Storting (parliament) announced Oct. 10 the award of the 1962 Nobel Peace Prize, withheld in 1962, to Dr. Linus Carl Pauling, 62, California Institute of Technology chemist. It simultaneously announced that the 1963 Nobel Peace Prize would be shared by the International Committee of the Red Cross and the League of Red Cross Societies, both of Geneva. The 1962 prize carried a cash award of $49,465, the 1963 prize a $53,000 award.

Pauling, a controversial figure, had been accused of being a Communist but had denied the charge under oath. He had been in the forefront of the campaign to ban nuclear tests and had warned since 1950 of the harmful effects of radio-active fallout. Pauling had won a Nobel Prize for Chemistry in 1954 and was the first person to win 2 entire Nobel awards. (Mme. Marie Curie, co-discoverer of radium, had won one Nobel Prize and had shared a 2d.) Pauling was the 13th American to win the Peace Prize.

---

*A limited nuclear test ban—one excluding those underground tests considered by the West to be undetectable without international detection and on-site inspection procedures—had been proposed and rebuffed repeatedly by each side in the course of the 5-year U.S.-British-Soviet negotiations on a test ban. Most recently it had been offered by Pres. Kennedy and British Prime Min. Macmillan as a way to end the inspection impasse but had been rejected by Khrushchev as an attempt to obtain an agreement that would permit the West to continue underground testing.

Soviet government . . . expresses its willingness to conclude an agreement banning nuclear tests in the atmosphere, in outer space and under water. If the Western powers now accept this proposal, the question of inspection no longer arises. For the Western powers declare that no inspections whatever are needed to check the states' fulfillment of their commitments to stop nuclear tests in the atmosphere, in outer space and under water."

▶ ". . . The Soviet government believes that already, at the conclusion of a test-ban agreement, it is necessary to take also another big step toward easing international tension and strengthening confidence between states: to sign a nonaggression pact between the 2 main military groups of states—the NATO countries and the Warsaw Treaty states. . . . A test-ban agreement, combined with the simultaneous signing of a nonaggression pact between the 2 groups of states, will create a fresh international climate more favorable for a solution of major problems of our time, including disarmament."

Moscow Negotiations. The new 3-power talks on a nuclear test treaty were opened in Moscow July 15 by representatives of the U.S., British and Soviet governments. The 3 delegations met technically as the nuclear test subcommittee of the 18-nation UN Disarmament Committee, whose Geneva conference was in recess during the Moscow talks.

The conference convened in the Kremlin office of Soviet Premier Khrushchev, who had assumed temporary leadership of the Soviet delegation. (His action, given wide publicity in the USSR, was interpreted as a gesture demonstrating the seriousness with which the USSR approached the new negotiations.) The U.S. and British delegations were led, respectively, by State Undersecy. (for Political Affairs) W. Averell Harriman and Science Min. Lord Hailsham.†

A joint statement issued after the 3½-hour opening session stated that the 3 delegations had discussed a nuclear test ban and "other questions of mutual interest."

The talks were resumed July 16 for what was described as the conference's first working session. Harriman, Hailsham and their aides met for 3 hours with a Soviet delegation headed by Foreign Min. Gromyko at the Foreign Ministry's Spiridonovska Palace. Following the 3d session, held July 17, the delegation issued a joint communiqué in which they announced "progress in drafting some of the provisions of a test-ban treaty covering tests in the atmosphere, outer space and under water." The communiqué's unusually specific wording made it clear by omission that the question of underground tests—on which all previous nuclear negotiations had foundered—would not be dealt with by the draft treaty under discussion.

The USSR's draft of an East-West nonaggression pact was submitted to the conference July 17 by Gromyko. Harriman and Hailsham agreed to discuss the Soviet proposal but made it clear they were not authorized to conduct substantive negotiations on it nor would their governments do so without consultation with the other NATO states. They also reportedly informed Gromyko that a nonaggression pact would be acceptable only if it did not involve recognition of Communist East Germany since such recognition would make it impossible to obtain West German agreement to the pact. The USSR was reported to have indicated its readiness to accept a formula that would avoid the question of East Germany's recognition.

The Moscow negotiations were re-

†Harriman was accompanied by U.S. Amb.-to-USSR Foy D. Kohler, Deputy Director Adrian S. Fisher of the U.S. Arms Control & Disarmament Agency and Carl Kaysen, a special assistant to Pres. Kennedy for national security affairs. Lord Hailsham was accompanied by British Amb.-to-USSR Sir Humphrey Trevelyan, Foreign Office Undersecy. Sir Duncan Wilson, and Sir Solly Zuckerman and Sir William Penney, advisers on nuclear weapons and disarmament matters. The Soviet delegation included Foreign Min. Andrei A. Gromyko, Deputy Foreign Min. Valerian Zorin and Semyon K. Tsarapkin, the USSR's chief delegate at the Geneva disarmament conference.

ported to have reached tentative agreement on a draft nuclear test treaty July 20. The draft then was referred by the delegates to their respective governments. Minor amendments apparently were requested by both sides, and these were incorporated in the text by a 3-power drafting subcommittee July 22 before the completed draft was referred back to the conference later the same day.

The final major obstacle to initialing the treaty, the question of whether the USSR would insist on the signing of a nonaggression pact with the test-ban treaty, was overcome July 24. It was settled by Gromyko's acceptance of a Western commitment to discuss a nonaggression treaty in good faith after the conclusion of the nuclear test talks.

Nuclear Test Curb Signed

3 Powers Agree on Pact. The 3 Moscow delegations July 25 initialed a treaty prohibiting nuclear weapons tests in the earth's atmosphere, in space or under water. The treaty was initialed in the Soviet government's Spiridonovska Palace by Harriman, Hailsham and Gromyko, the 3 chief delegates.

Excluded from the treaty were those nuclear tests carried out underground and considered by the West to be undetectable without inspection provisions unacceptable to the USSR. A later accord covering such tests was envisaged by the text.

The pact did not include measures for disarmament and did not bind other nations. But hope was expressed that the treaty would serve as a step toward disarmament and eventually would be accepted by all states.

A joint communiqué issued by the 3 delegations July 25, together with the text of the treaty, confirmed that the participants had agreed to pursue negotiations toward a nonaggression treaty between the NATO and War-

saw Treaty powers. It said: "The heads of the 3 delegations . . . discussed the Soviet proposal relating to a pact of nonaggression between the participants in the North Atlantic Treaty Organization and the . . . Warsaw Treaty. The 3 governments have agreed fully to inform their respective allies . . . concerning these talks and to consult with them about continuing discussions on this question. . . ."

The communiqué confirmed that the 3 delegations also had discussed "other measures directed at a relaxation of tension." This was taken as an allusion to Soviet proposals, outlined by Khrushchev in a radio-TV speech from the Kremlin July 19, for the settling of East-West differences in central Europe, inspection measures to reduce the danger of surprise attack and a possible reduction of Western and Soviet bloc military contingents in Germany. Harriman confirmed to newsmen July 25 that these had been discussed, particularly the proposal for fixed-site inspectors at key military centers, airfields, ports, rail and road centers.

Treaty Signed in Moscow. The nuclear test treaty was signed in Moscow Aug. 5 by State Secy. Dean Rusk, Soviet Foreign Min. Gromyko and British Foreign Secy. Lord Home.

The signing ceremony took place in Catherine Hall in the Kremlin's Great Palace. It was witnessed by Khrushchev, Soviet Pres. Leonid I. Brezhnev, UN Secy. Gen. U Thant and about 70 U.S., Soviet and British officials.

In a joint communiqué issued after the treaty was signed, the 3 signatory nations expressed agreement "that this treaty is an important initial step toward the lessening of international tension and the strengthening of peace." They expressed "the hope that other nations will accede to the treaty."

Rusk warned in a brief speech after the signing that the treaty "is only a first step. It does not end the threat of nuclear war. . . .It does not halt the production of nuclear weapons. It does not restrict their use in time of war." He asserted that "the signature of this treaty represents the readiness of the United States to join with the 2 other original signatories . . .in a determined and sustained effort to find practical means by which tensions can be reduced. . . ."

Khrushchev, in a talk at a reception that followed the signing ceremony, paid tribute to the U.S. and British governments for accepting "the [nuclear ban] proposal advanced by the Soviet government." "A kind of referendum is now taking place on all continents," he said, "and its results are already known: The peoples of the world have firmly come out in support of the treaty banning nuclear weapon tests."

JFK Hails Pact. Pres. Kennedy reported to the American people by radio and TV July 26 on the successful conclusion of the Moscow test-ban negotiations. He described the treaty as a "victory for mankind," "a shaft of light" into the dark threat of thermonuclear war.

Speaking from the White House, Mr. Kennedy explained what the treaty meant for the U.S. and for the world. "This treaty," he said, "is not the millenium. It will not resolve all conflicts, or cause the Communists to forego their ambitions, or eliminate the dangers of war. It will not reduce our need for arms or allies or programs of assistance to others. But it is an important first step—a step toward peace—a step toward reason—a step away from war."

The President added: "A war today or tomorrow, if it led to nuclear war, would not be like any war in history. A fullscale nuclear exchange, lasting less than 60 minutes, could wipe out more than 300 million Americans, Europeans and Russians, as well as untold numbers elsewhere. And the survivors, as Chrmn. Khrushchev warned the Communish Chinese, 'would envy the dead.' "

Khrushchev Support. Khrushchev made clear his personal approval of the test-ban treaty in an interview granted to the Soviet newspapers *Pravda* and *Izvestia* July 26.

Khrushchev declared that the treaty was "an event of . . . great international significance" and "a good beginning" to further efforts to ameliorate East-West differences and liquidate the cold war. He pledged that if the West was prepared to join in such efforts, there would be "no shortage of good will from the Soviet side."

Khrushchev declared: "We address the Western powers with the proposal: Let us come to terms on all these questions. . . . Let us now advance further toward the easing of international tension, the liquidation of the cold war."

France Rejects Pact. French Pres. Charles de Gaulle declared July 29 that France—already building its own national nuclear force—would not sign the Moscow test-ban treaty. He similarly rejected, as an unwarranted intervention in Europe's affairs, the Anglo-U.S. agreement to discuss with the USSR an East-West nonaggression pact.

Addressing an audience of 900 at his news conference, de Gaulle said: The Moscow treaty had left "nothing . . . changed in the terrible threat which the nuclear armaments of the 2 rivals suspends over the world, in particular over those peoples which do not have them." Under these conditions, "the situation of the world with regard to this threat being in no way changed, it is quite natural that a country like France, which is beginning to have the means [nuclear weapons] to free itself . . . from this permanent terror, should use these means."

Support Pledged. The Moscow treaty won enthusiastic acceptance in most countries of the world. France and Communist China were the only 2 nations to object publicly to the agreement.

Pope Paul VI sent a congratulatory message Aug. 5 to Pres. Kennedy, Premier Khrushchev, Prime Min. Macmillan and UN Secy. Gen. Thant. The pope said he considered the treaty "a token of goodwill, a pledge of con-

cord, a promise of a more serene future."

Indian Prime Min. Jawaharlal Nehru said in a statement to Tass Aug. 5 that the treaty was "the first breaking of the ice presented by the cold war" and that "every lover of peace must welcome it."

Aside from the 3 "original parties," approximately 100 countries signed the pact by the end of 1963.

Peiping Condemns Talks. The Moscow test-ban negotiations were denounced by Communist China even before their completion.

The Chinese CP newspaper *Jenmin*

Treaty Banning Nuclear Weapons Tests In Atmosphere, In Outer Space & Under Water

(Partial Text)

Preamble: The governments of the United States of America, the United Kingdom of Great Britain & Northern Ireland, and the Union of Soviet Socialist Republics, hereinafter referred to as the "original parties,"

Proclaiming as their principal aim the speediest possible achievement of an agreement on general and complete disarmament under strict international control in accordance with the objectives of the United Nations, which would put an end to the armaments race and eliminate the incentive to the production and testing of all kinds of weapons, including nuclear weapons,

Seeking to achieve the discontinuance of all test explosions of nuclear weapons for all time, determined to continue negotiations to this end, and desiring to put an end to the contamination of man's environment by radioactive substances,

Have agreed as follows:

Article I: 1. Each of the parties to this treaty undertakes to prohibit, to prevent, and not to carry out any nuclear weapon test explosion, or any other nuclear explosion at any place under its jurisdiction or control:

A. In the atmosphere, beyond its limits, including outer space, or under water, including territorial waters or high seas; or

B. In any other environment if such explosion causes radioactive debris to be present outside the territorial limits of the state under whose jurisdiction or control such explosion is conducted. It is understood in this connection that the provisions of this subparagraph are without prejudice to the conclusion of a treaty resulting in the permanent banning of all nuclear test explosions including all such explosions underground, the conclusion of which, as the parties have stated in the preamble to this treaty, they seek to achieve.

2. Each of the parties to this treaty undertakes furthermore to refrain from causing, encouraging, or in any way participating in, the carrying out of any nuclear weapon test explosion, or any other nuclear explosion, anywhere which would take place in any of the environments described, or have the effect referred to in Paragraph 1 of this article.

Article II: 1. Any party may propose amendments to this treaty. The text of any proposed amendment shall be submitted to the depositary governments which shall circulate it to all parties to this treaty. Thereafter, if requested to do so by 1/3 or more of the parties, the depositary governments shall convene a conference, to which they shall invite all the parties, to consider such amendment.

2. Any amendment to this treaty must be approved by a majority of the votes of all parties to this treaty, including the votes of all of the original parties. The amendment shall enter into force for all parties upon the deposit of instruments of ratification by a majority of all the parties, including the instruments of ratification of all the original parties.

Article III: 1. This treaty shall be open to all states for signature. Any state which does not sign this treaty before its entry into force in accordance with Paragraph 3 of this article may accede to it at any time.

2. This treaty shall be subject to ratification by signatory states. Instruments of ratification and instruments of accession shall be deposited with the governments of the original parties. . . .

3. This treaty shall enter into force after its ratification by all the original parties and the deposit of their instruments of ratification.

4. For states whose instruments of ratification or accession are deposited subsequent to the entry into force of this treaty, it shall enter into force on the date of the deposit of their instruments of ratification or accession. . . .

Article IV: This treaty shall be of unlimited duration.

Each party shall in exercising its national sovereignty have the right to withdraw from the treaty if it decides that extraordinary events, related to the subject matter of this treaty, have jeopardized the supreme interests of its country. It shall give notice of such withdrawal to all other parties to the treaty 3 months in advance.

Article V: This treaty, of which the English and Russian texts are equally authentic, shall be deposited in the archives of the depositary governments. . . .

Jih Pao declared July 20 that "such talks [as in Moscow] amount to saying that there is no alternative to capitulation in the face of imperialist nuclear blackmail." Reiterating Red China's rejection of Soviet fears of nuclear war, the paper said: "Some people believe that if nuclear war breaks out all mankind will perish"; but Mao Tse-tung had "pointed out that mankind will definitely not be destroyed even if the imperialists insist on a nuclear war with the sacrifice of hundreds of millions of people"; "the future of mankind will nevertheless be a bright one [under communism]."

A Communist Chinese government statement issued July 31, after the treaty had been initialed, called for an immediate summit meeting by all heads of government to "discuss the . . . complete prohibition and thorough destruction of nuclear weapons," the dismantling of all foreign bases and the creation of nuclear-free zones covering most of the world. The Chinese statement denounced the Moscow treaty as a "dirty fraud" perpetrated by the U.S., Britain and USSR to "consolidate their nuclear monopoly and bind the hands of all peace-loving countries subjected to the nuclear treaty." It charged that the Soviet government had made an "about face" in accepting the treaty and had "sold out" the interests of the Soviet bloc.

A Soviet government statement Aug. 3 denounced the July 31 Chinese attack on the treaty and charged that the Chinese were "trying to cover up their refusal to sign a nuclear test-ban treaty." It said: "Trying to discredit . . . the assured success in the struggle for diminishing the war danger, to vilify the peace-loving foreign policy of the Soviet Union, the leaders of China have shown . . . that their policy leads . . . to the further stepping up of the nuclear arms race.

. . . This position is tantamount to actual connivance with those who advocate world thermonuclear war."

Jenmin Jih Pao countered in an Aug. 3 editorial that the test-ban treaty was "a U.S.-Soviet alliance against China, pure and simple." It charged that Khrushchev had betrayed the Soviet people by agreeing to the treaty, and it predicted that he would be overthrown.

(Communist Chinese Premier Chou En-lai warned Aug. 6, in a message to the 9th World Conference Against Nuclear Weapons, that "the danger of nuclear war, instead of being reduced, has [been] increased" by the pact. The conference, which had opened in Hiroshima, Japan Aug. 5, served as forum for the competing Soviet and Chinese views. The 14-member Soviet delegation and delegates from India, Czechoslovakia, Hungary, Rumania and Yugoslavia walked out Aug. 5 when Chao Pu-chu, leader of the Chinese delegation to the conference, rose to speak. Chao charged that the test-ban treaty "allows the aggressor the right of massacre and denies the victims the right of self-defense.")

Ratification Completed. The treaty entered into force Oct. 10 with the exchange of instruments of ratification in Washington, London and Moscow.

American ratification had been completed Oct. 7, when Pres. Kennedy, acting after the Senate had consented to the pact, signed the U.S. instrument of ratification at ceremonies in the White House.

The Presidium of the USSR's Supreme Soviet had completed Soviet ratification Sept. 25. Tass reported that the treaty had been presented at a Presidium meeting that day by First Deputy Foreign Min. Vasily V. Kuznetsov and that the 25 Presidium members attending, including Soviet Pres. Brezhnev, unanimously gave their approval.

Britain did not require approval of the treaty by Parliament; the British ratification, legally carried out by the foreign secretary with the assent of the queen, became effective with Lord Home's signing of the London instruments of ratification Oct. 10.

U.S. Ratification of Treaty

Pact Sent to Senate. The Moscow treaty was submitted to the U.S. Senate by Pres. Kennedy Aug. 8 with the request that it act swiftly to consent to the treaty's ratification.

In a special message sent to the Senate together with a certified copy of the treaty, the President declared that the treaty was "the first concrete result of 18 years of effort by the United States to impose limits on the nuclear arms race." "There is hope," he said, "that it may lead to further measures to arrest and control the dangerous competition for increasingly destructive weapons."

The President's message contained this assessment of the treaty:

"This treaty advances, though it does not assure, world peace; and it will inhibit, though it does not prohibit, the nuclear arms race. . . .

"While it will not end the threat of nuclear war or outlaw the use of nuclear weapons, it can reduce world tensions, open a way to further agreements and thereby help to ease the threat of war.

"While it cannot wholly prevent the spread of nuclear arms to nations not now possessing them, it . . . [is] an important opening wedge in our effort to 'get the genie back in the bottle'."

Hearings Probe Effects. The treaty was submitted to Senate scrutiny in hearings opened Aug. 12. The principal hearings were conducted by the Senate Foreign Relations Committee with the participation of members of the Senate Armed Services Committee and the Joint Congressional Committee on Atomic Energy. Parallel hearings on the treaty were held by the Preparedness Subcommittee of the Senate Armed Services Committee.

Testifying on the treaty and its possible effect on U.S. national security were leading members of the Kennedy Administration as well as the U.S.' senior military officers and several scientific experts in the field of nuclear weapons testing and technology. The testimony (including that taken at open hearings and that taken at closed sessions but subsequently published) was overwhelmingly in favor of ratification of the treaty, although a few witnesses opposed the pact on the ground it would be detrimental to U.S. superiority in the East-West nuclear arms balance.

Principal testimony heard by the Senate committees:

State Secy. Rusk—The Administration's case for ratification of the treaty was opened by Rusk Aug. 12 as the first witness to be heard by the Foreign Relations Committee. Rusk called the pact "one of the most significant" treaties ever to be brought before the Senate. He said: The treaty was limited in scope and related only to the problem of nuclear testing, but it represented an important departure from past East-West failures to cope with the problem and might open new paths to East-West cooperation on disarmament. He added: "The hard fact is that a full-scale nuclear exchange could erase all that man has built over the centuries. War has devoured itself because it can devour the world."

Defense Secy. McNamara—"Unequivocal support" for the treaty was voiced Aug. 13 by Defense Secy. Robert S. McNamara before the Foreign Relations Committee. He based his approval of the treaty on these grounds: (a) The U.S.' nuclear forces were "manifestly superior" to the USSR's; the U.S. arsenal of nuclear warheads numbered in "the tens of thousands"; the U.S. was "clearly superior" to the Soviet Union in the "yield-to-weight ratio" of its small and intermediate weapons; (b) the treaty would help the U.S. maintain this superiority since the only type of testing it permitted was that conducted underground, a technique in which the U.S.

had "substantially more experience than the USSR"; (c) the U.S. would almost certainly detect any attempts by the Soviet Union to test clandestinely; (d) the U.S. planned to maintain its readiness to initiate "a major atmospheric series" if the Soviet Union did break the treaty and renewed testing; (e) proliferation of nuclear weaponry would be retarded and hence the danger of war by escalation from minor incidents was reduced; (f) "sheer multiplication" of nuclear armaments would "not necessarily produce a net increase" in a nation's security.

JCS Chrmn. Taylor—Gen. Maxwell D. Taylor, chairman of the Joint Chiefs of Staff, testified before the Preparedness Subcommittee Aug. 14 that the JCS supported the treaty as "compatible with the security interests of the United States." Taylor's testimony, in closed session, was based on a JCS memo (released later in censored form) that made this assessment of the military reasons for ratifying the treaty:

(1) Multi-megaton weapons—The USSR was ahead of the U.S. in the development of such weapons, which could be tested effectively only in the atmosphere, but the JCS did not consider "important the attainment of weapons in the 100-megaton range."

(2) Anti-missile defense—the USSR might have made more progress toward an operational anti-missile weapon, but both sides could continue their current search for such a weapon through underground testing, a process in which the U.S. had superior experience and techniques.

(3) Diversity of arsenal—The U.S. had a wide range of nuclear weapons of all types, both tactical and strategic, and this arsenal was considered superior to the USSR's atomic armament; a cessation of atmospheric testing would make it difficult for the USSR to catch up to this over-all U.S. superiority.

The JCS memo said: ". . . the Joint Chiefs have reached the determination that while there are military disadvantages to the treaty, they are not so serious as to render it unacceptable. . . ."

Edward F. Teller—Nuclear scientist Edward F. Teller, director of the University of California's AEC-run Livermore nuclear laboratory, told the Foreign Relations Committee Aug. 20 that he was totally opposed to the Moscow treaty. Teller, who had campaigned against any limitation on nuclear testing, said: "I say that the signing was a mistake. If you ratify the treaty, you will have committed an enormously greater mistake. You will have given away the future safety of our country and increased the dangers of war." The principal objection to the treaty voiced by

Teller was its prohibition on atmospheric nuclear tests. Teller asserted that atmospheric tests were absolutely required to bring "a reliable conclusion" to research on an effective anti-missile system and to "practice" the techniques acquired. He rejected CIA and Administration estimates that the USSR lacked a substantial lead in anti-missile missile development. He said that the USSR had progressed "far ahead" of the U.S.' program in its 1961-62 atmospheric test series and that "they have had 10 times, 20 times more opportunity to find out about missile defense" than the U.S. He charged that American atmospheric tests carried out at the same time had been curtailed by the Kennedy Administration in order to placate "popular opinion" and anti-test sentiment.

(Pres. Kennedy, meeting with newsmen later Aug. 20, rebutted Teller's arguments and denied that he had permitted tests to be halted for political reasons. Mr. Kennedy said that each test had been studied carefully before it was carried out and that several more tests were conducted than originally had been planned. Confronted with Pres. Kennedy's remarks later Aug. 20, at the Foreign Relations Committee's hearings, Teller said: the President's "information is mistaken"; "we could have and should have carried out more tests in the atmosphere; the Administration didn't want more tests.")

SAC, Service Chiefs—Gen. Thomas S. Power, Strategic Air Command chief, became the first major military leader to oppose the treaty. Testifying at a closed session of the Preparedness Subcommittee Aug. 19, Power reportedly urged the Senate to reject the pact as not in the best interests of the U.S. He reportedly warned that the pact would hamper the U.S.' development of essential nuclear weapons, jeopardize the U.S. nuclear lead and, ultimately, lead to reversal of the East-West military balance.

The JCS' position in support of the treaty was reiterated before the Foreign Relations Committee Aug. 19 by the 4 uniformed service chiefs, Gen. Curtis E. LeMay, Air Force chief of staff, Gen. Earle G. Wheeler, Army chief of staff, Adm. David L. McDonald, chief of naval operations, and Gen. David M. Shoup, Marine Corps commandant. (The JCS was composed of the 4 service chiefs and the JCS chairman, Gen. Taylor.) Wheeler, Shoup and McDonald unanimously supported the treaty. They said they had favored the pact before it was signed. But LeMay said that although he had not pressed his opposition to the treaty before it was signed, his testimony "would have been against it" if the pact had not already been signed.

Committee Backs Pact. The Foreign Relations Committee voted by 16-1 Aug. 29 to recommend that the Senate consent the treaty's ratification.

The lone committee member to oppose the treaty was Sen. Russell B. Long (D., La.). All other members, 11 Democrats and 5 Republicans, approved the recommendation.

The committee report on the treaty was submitted to the Senate Sept. 4. The report recommended only one major "interpretation" of the treaty's text—a statement making clear the committee's view that the pact would not bar the use of nuclear weapons in the event of war.

Debate. Senators debated the treaty for 2 weeks (Sept. 9-20) before putting it to a vote. The overwhelming majority of the Senators taking part in the debate supported the pact, but the members opposed to it refused to relent in the hope that they could force through amendments that would soften the pact's meaning or defer its coming into force.

Highlights of the debate:

Chrmn. Fulbright of the Foreign Relations Committee formally opened the debate Sept. 9 with an address in which he asserted that the treaty might be the first step toward preventing a nuclear war that would destroy the U.S. and USSR as "organized societies." He said: "The essential purpose of the . . . treaty is to bring an element of sanity and restraint into the relations of great nations which know, but do not always seem to . . . act as though they know, that a decision made in anger or fear, or a simple mistake, could result in the grisly incineration of millions of good people who are helpless against nuclear bombs, and the complete destruction of human society."

Bipartisan support for the treaty was emphasized Sept. 11 by Senate GOP leader Everett M. Dirksen (Ill.), who read to the Senate a personal letter in which Pres. Kennedy had given him an 8-point statement of U.S. safeguards against the risks posed by the treaty. Dirksen reviewed all the reasons given for ratification and, as Senate GOP leader, added one more: that the Republican Party had advocated such a treaty in its 1960 platform. Referring to his age (67), Dirksen said: "I wouldn't like to have it written on my stone: 'He knew what happened at Hiroshima, but he didn't take a first step.'"

Chrmn. John Stennis (D., Miss.) of the Armed Services Subcommittee on Preparedness declared Sept. 13 that he opposed the treaty because of secret testimony by the Joint Chiefs of Staff. Stennis said: The JCS had made "a clear case against ratification of the treaty from the professional military viewpoint, which . . . is their real field of competence"; the JCS had been "driven into . . . foreign policy" to support the treaty against their judgment.

Sen. Barry Goldwater (R., Ariz.), in one of the major statements of opposition to the treaty, said he would "vote against this treaty because in my heart, mind, soul and conscience, I feel it detrimental to the strength of my country." Goldwater said his principal reason for opposing the pact was that it was "a political ambush, baited by the necessity of the Soviet to ease the many pressures upon its tyranny." The 2d and major reason was his view that "it will erode our military strength." He said: "I will vote against this treaty because it preserves the enemy's advances in high-yield weaponry while freeing them to overtake our lead in low-yield weaponry. We pay a price; they do not."

Senate Gives Consent. The Senate voted by 80 to 19 Sept. 24 to consent to ratification of the nuclear test treaty.

The Senate gave its consent unconditionally after attempts to attach reservations to the treaty were defeated by overwhelming majorities. The Kennedy Administration had sought unconditional approval of the treaty to preclude amendments that might have required renegotiation.

The final vote on the treaty:

For ratification: 55 D. — Anderson (N.M.), Bartlett (Alaska), Bayh (Ind.), Bible (Nev.), Brewster (Md.), Burdick (N.D.), Cannon (Nev.), Church (Idaho), Clark (Pa.), Dodd (Conn.), Douglas (Ill.), Edmondson (Okla.), Ellender (La.), Ervin (N.C.), Fulbright (Ark.), Gore (Tenn.), Gruening (Alaska), Hart (Mich.), Hartke (Ind.), Hayden (Ariz.), Hill (Ala.), Holland (Fla.), Humphrey (Minn.), Inouye (Hawaii), Jackson (Wash.), Johnston (S.C.), Jordan (N.C.), Kennedy (Mass.), Long (Mo.), Magnuson (Wash.), Mansfield (Mont.), McCarthy (Minn.), McGee (Wyo.), McGovern (S.D.), McIntyre (N.H.), McNamara (Mich.), Metcalf (Mont.), Monroney (Okla.), Morse (Ore.), Moss (Utah), Muskie (Me.), Nelson (Wis.), Neuberger (Ore.), Pastore (R.I.), Pell (R.I.), Proxmire (Wis.), Randolph (W.Va.), Ribicoff (Conn.), Smathers (Fla.), Sparkman (Ala.), Symington (Mo.), Walters (Tenn.), Williams (N.J.), Yarborough (Tex.), Young (Ohio). **25 R.**—Aiken (Vt.), Allott (Colo.), Beall (Md.), Boggs (Del.), Carlson (Kan.), Case (N.J.), Cooper (Ky.), Cotton (N.H.), Dirksen (Ill.), Dominick (Colo.), Fong (Hawaii), Hickenlooper (Ia.), Hruska (Neb.), Javits (N.Y.), Keating (N.Y.), Kuchel (Calif.), Miller (Iowa), Morton (Ky.), Mundt (S.D.), Pearson (Kan.), Prouty (Vt.), Saltonstall (Mass.), Scott (Pa.), Williams (Del.), Young (N.D.).

Vs. ratification: 11 D.—Byrd (Va.), Byrd (W.Va.), Eastland (Miss.), Lausche (Ohio), Long (La.), McClellan (Ark.), Robertson (Va.), Russell (Ga.), Stennis (Miss.), Talmadge (Ga.), Thurmond (S.C.). **8 R.**—Bennett (Utah), Curtis (Neb.), Goldwater (Ariz.), Jordan (Idaho), Mechem (N.M.), Simpson (Wyo.), Smith (Me.), Tower (Tex.).

Not voting because of absence due to illness, but announced as favoring ratification: Engle (D., Calif.).

One "understanding" and 3 "reservations" were considered by the Senate Sept. 23, in its last full day of debate on the treaty; all, attempts to make ratification contingent on other matters, such as a Soviet withdrawal from Cuba or the USSR's payment of its UN debts, were defeated.

JFK Signs Ratification. U.S. ratification of the treaty was completed Oct. 7 when Pres. Kennedy signed the documents of ratification at a White House ceremony attended by members of the U.S. delegation that had negotiated it and by leading Senators of both parties who had worked for its approval.

'Hot Line' Communications Pact

U.S.-Soviet Link Agreed. Proposals for a radio or teletype network that would assure rapid and private communications between the U.S. and Soviet governments in the event of a sudden crisis had been advanced repeatedly in past years, but they had received little impetus until a communications failure forced Pres. Kennedy and Premier Khrushchev to publicly broadcast several of the diplomatic messages by which they settled the 1962 crisis over Soviet missile bases in Cuba.

The proposals were turned over to the U.S. and Soviet delegations to the 17-nation Geneva disarmament conference, and discussion of a possible treaty setting up the "hot line" network were begun in April by Charles C. Stelle and Semyon K. Tsarapkin, the chief U.S. and Soviet delegates to the arms conference. Technical details of the network were worked out in Geneva in the next few months by Brig. Gen. George P. Sampson, deputy director of the Defense Department Defense Communications System, and Ivan Kokov, Soviet communications minister.

A "Memorandum of Understanding" on creation of a direct Washington-Moscow teletype system was signed in Geneva June 20 by Stelle and Tsarapkin. An annex to the memo set out in detail the technical aspects of the system and the procedures for its use in case of a grave international emergency requiring rapid and direct communication between the heads of the 2 governments.

The system's primary circuit was to consist of a duplex cable, permitting simultaneous transmission in both directions, between Washington and Moscow via London, Copenhagen, Stockholm and Helsinki. A standby radio circuit was to be established between the 2 capitals by way of Tangier, Morocco. The primary cable circuit between Moscow and Washington would be 4,883 miles in length.

Teletype System Operative. The "hot line" between Washington and Moscow was declared operational Aug. 30. The teletype system was to be kept open 24 hours a day but was to be used for emergency messages only. The Washington terminus of the line was located in the National Military Command Center in the Pentagon offices of the Joint Chiefs of Staff. The Moscow terminus was in a Kremlin site adjacent to Khrushchev's office. Messages originating in Washington were to be sent in English; those sent from Moscow were to be in Russian. All messages were to be encoded to protect the secrecy of their contents.

Contacts Continue. The U.S.-Soviet contacts that had led to the test ban treaty were continued intermittently following the signing of the pact.

State Secy. Rusk, who had gone to Moscow to sign the treaty, conferred with Premier Khrushchev Aug. 9 at Khrushchev's summer home in Gagra, on the Black Sea coast. The talks were attended by Soviet Foreign Min. Gromyko and the U.S. and Soviet ambassadors in Moscow and Washington.

Rusk returned to Washington Aug. 11 to launch the Administration's campaign for Senate ratification of the treaty. He disclosed Aug. 16, at a news conference, that the current East-West discussions probably would take up proposals for an agreement to prevent surprise attacks. Rusk said that the measures envisaged included mutual "control posts at key ports and railway stations, highway centers and airfields."

UN Space A-Ban. The discussion of further measures to lessen East-West tensions was carried forward by Rusk, Gromyko and Lord Home in a series of informal meetings begun in New York Sept. 28 in conjunction with the opening of the annual session of the UN General Assembly.

The New York talks produced an agreement in principle on the banning of nuclear weapons from space and from orbiting earth satellites. The

---

The U.S.-Soviet 'Hot Line' Agreement

(Partial text)

Memorandum of understanding . . . regarding the establishment of a direct communications link signed on June 20, 1963 at Geneva, Switzerland.

For use in time of emergency, the government of the United States of America and the government of the Union of Soviet Socialist Republics have agreed to establish as soon as technically feasible a direct communications link between the two governments.

Each government shall be responsible for the arrangements for the link on its own territory. Each government shall take the necessary steps to insure continuous functioning of the link and prompt delivery to its head of government of any communications received by means of the link from the head of government of the other party.

Arrangements for establishing and operating the link are set forth in the annex which is attached hereto and forms an integral part hereof. . . .

Annex to the memorandum . . .

The direct communications link between Washington and Moscow . . . and the operation of such link shall be governed by the following provisions.

(1) The direct communications link shall consist of:

A. 2 terminal points with telegraph-teleprinter equipment between which communications shall be directly exchanged;

B. One full-time duplex wire telegraph circuit, routed Washington-London-Copenhagen-Stockholm-Helsinki-Moscow, which shall be used for the transmission of messages;

C. One full-time duplex radio-telegraph circuit, routed Washington-Tangier-Moscow, which shall be used for service communications and for coordination of operations between the 2 terminal points.

If experience in operating the direct communications link should demonstrate that the establishment of an additional wire telegraph circuit is advisable, such circuit will be established by mutual agreement between authorized representatives of both governments.

(2) In case of interruption of the wire circuit, transmission of messages shall be effected via the radio circuit, and for this purpose provision shall be made at the terminal points for the capability of prompt switching of all necessary equipment from one circuit to another.

(3) The terminal points of the link shall be so equipped as to provide for the transmission and reception of messages from Moscow to Washington in the Russian language and from Washington to Moscow in the English language. In this connection, the USSR shall furnish the United States 4 sets of telegraph terminal equipment, including page printers, transmitters, and reperforators, with one year's supply of spare

accord, announced Oct. 3 by spokesmen for the 3 foreign ministers, was not made public in a textual form; the announcement said only that it was clear, from the addresses made to the UN Assembly by Pres. Kennedy and Foreign Min. Gromyko, that the U.S. and Soviet governments had accepted the principle that nuclear arms should be barred from space. It was noted that since the U.S. and the USSR currently were the only 2 powers capable of orbiting such weapons, there was no need to go beyond a statement of their intentions to refrain from doing so.

(The U.S.-Soviet agreement was made the subject of a joint resolution adopted by the UN Assembly Oct. 17 by acclamation.)

The label "inconclusive" was applied to the ministers' discussion of the other major disarmament proposals currently under examination: a nonaggression pact between the NATO and Warsaw Treaty powers and measures for inspection to guard against surprise attacks.

Assembly Actions. Major actions taken by the UN Assembly before its adjournment:

Space A-ban—A resolution calling on all states to refrain from placing nuclear arms in space was adopted by the Assembly Oct. 17 by acclamation.

The draft was sponsored jointly by the 17 active members of the Geneva Disarmament Committee (France not participating). Submitted to the Assembly's Political Committee Oct. 16 by Luis Padilla Nervo of Mexico, chairman of the Disarmament Committee, the draft declared the Assembly's determination "to take steps to prevent the spread of the arms race to outer space." In its operative clauses, the resolution said that the Assembly:

"1. Welcomes . . . expressions by the United States of America and the Union of Soviet Socialist Republics of their in-

---

parts and all necessary special tools, test equipment, operating instructions and other technical literature, to provide for transmission and reception of messages in the Russian language. The United States shall furnish the Soviet Union 4 sets of telegraph terminal equipment, including page printers, transmitters, and reperforators, with one year's supply of spare parts and all necessary special tools, test equipment, operating instructions and other technical literature, to provide for transmission and reception of messages in the English language. . . .

(4) The terminal points of the direct communications link shall be provided with encoding equipment. For the terminal point in the USSR, 4 sets of such equipment . . . shall be furnished by the United States to the USSR against payment of the cost thereof by the USSR.

The USSR shall provide for preparation and delivery of keying tapes to the terminal point of the link in the United States for reception of messages from the USSR. The United States shall provide for the preparation and delivery of keying tapes to the terminal point of the link in the USSR for reception of messages from the United States. . . .

(5) The United States and the USSR shall designate the agencies responsible for the arrangements regarding the direct communications link, for its technical maintenance, continuity and reliability, and for the timely transmission of messages.

Such agencies may, by mutual agreement, decide matters and develop instructions relating to the technical maintenance and operation of the direct communications link and effect arrangements to improve the operation of the link.

(6) The technical parameters of the telegraph circuits of the link and of the terminal equipment, as well as the maintenance of such circuits and equipment, shall be in accordance with CCITT [International Telephone & Telegraph Consultative Committee] and CCIR [International Radio Consultative Committee] recommendations.

Transmission and reception of messages over the direct communications link shall be effected in accordance with applicable recommendations of international telegraph and radio communications regulations, as well as with mutually agreed instructions.

(7) The costs of the direct communications link shall be borne as follows:

A. The USSR shall pay the full cost of leasing the portion of the telegraph circuit from Moscow to Helsinki and 50% of the cost of leasing the portion of the telegraph circuit from Helsinki to London. The United States shall pay the full cost of leasing the portion of the telegraph circuit from Washington to London and 50% of the cost of leasing the portion of the telegraph circuit from London to Helsinki.

B. Payment of the cost of leasing the radio telegraph circuit between Moscow and Washington shall be effected without any transfer of payments between the parties. The USSR shall bear the expenses relating to the transmission of messages from Moscow to Washington. The United States shall bear the expenses relating to the transmission of messages from Washington to Moscow.

tention not to station any objects carrying nuclear weapons or other kinds of weapons of mass destruction in outer space;

"2. Solemnly calls upon all states: (A) To refrain from placing in orbit around the earth any objects carrying nuclear weapons or any other kinds of weapons of mass destruction, installing such weapons on celestial bodies, or stationing such weapons in outer space in any other manner. . . ."

Disarmament action—The Assembly acted Nov. 27 to approve 4 resolutions dealing with the problems of nuclear tests and disarmament. The 4 drafts:

▶ A resolution on general and complete disarmament, adopted by acclamation, calling on the 18-nation UN Disarmament Committee "to resume with . . . determination its negotiations on general and complete disarmament under effective international control." (Although the vote was not recorded, Albania's delegation had announced that it would not vote because the draft was insufficient.)

▶ A request for an international conference to examine a comprehensive prohibition of the use of nuclear weapons. The resolution was adopted by 64-18 vote (25 abstentions and several nations absent). The U.S., Britain and France, which had opposed such a prohibition as meaningless except within the framework of a general disarmament agreement, were among those abstaining.

▶ A call for the suspension of all nuclear and thermonuclear tests, including those underground and thus currently permissible under the Moscow test-ban treaty of July. The resolution was approved by 104-1 vote (3 abstentions). Albania cast the negative vote; France, Cuba and the Central African Republic were the abstainers. The resolution called on all states to adhere to the Moscow treaty and urged the 18-nation Disarmament Committee to begin work on extending the ban to underground tests.

▶ A resolution calling on all Latin American governments to examine measures that would ban nuclear arms from their territories and turn the continent into a "nuclear-free zone." The draft was adopted by 91-0 vote (15 abstentions). Among the abstaining nations were all Soviet-bloc nations except Rumania; Rumanian Deputy Foreign Min. Mircea Malitza explained that the vote expressed Rumania's support for the principle of nuclear-free zones and was no indication of Soviet-bloc differences on the question.

East-West Arms Estimates. The Institute of Strategic Studies, in its annual survey of world military strength, reported Nov. 6 that the NATO countries had outspaced the Soviet bloc by 5 to 1 in numbers of intercontinental ballistic missiles (ICBMs) and that they outnumbered Soviet bloc countries in conventional armed forces, even if Communist China were included in the figures.

The institute, a nongovernmental research organization centered in London, reported that the USSR's "slow buildup" of ICBMs "is continuing," with "stress on high-yield warheads for the smaller number of missiles available." It held that "the Soviet claim that a true Polaris-type missile which can be fired from a submerged submarine has been successfully developed must be treated with caution." It noted, however, that the USSR had a 400-mile range naval rocket that could be fired from surfaced submarines. As for intermediate and medium-range ballistic missile (IRBM & MRBM) forces, it estimated

Institute estimates of East-West military strength early in 1964:

	Western Alliance	Communist Bloc
ICBMs (over 2,500-mile range)	475	100+
Fleet ballistic missiles	192	100
IRBMs and MRBMs (600-1,200-mile range)	None	800
Medium-range land-based bombers (over 2,000 mile)	780	1,400
Carrier-based bombers (over 2,000 mile range)	600	None
Carriers (including commando and escort)	38 (37)*	None
Cruisers	33 (125)*	10 (2)*
Escorts	742 (358)*	124 (248)*
Nuclear submarines	33	23
Conventional submarines	219 (42)*	446 (55)*
Armies (men)	5,696,300	6,035,000
Navies	1,211,269	661,800
Air forces	1,658,775	771,000
Armed forces total	8,566,344	7,467,800

*Figures in parentheses refer to ships in reserve.

that the USSR had 800 such rockets while the U.S., currently dismantling its Thor and Jupiter IRBM sites in Britain, Turkey and Italy, would have none by 1964. But the U.S. would have 192 Polaris IRBM missiles in 12 operational nuclear submarines by the time it finished withdrawing IRBMs from Europe.

USSR Cuts Arms Budget. A reduction in the USSR's publicly-reported military budget was announced by Khrushchev in an address in which he linked the measure to Russia's disarmament proposals and will to peace. The measure was introduced in the USSR Supreme Soviet (parliament) Dec. 16 by Khrushchev's government.

Khrushchev's announcement was made in a speech delivered Dec. 13 at the close of a 5-day meeting in Moscow of the Central Committee of the Soviet Communist Party. His address, published the next day in the government newspaper *Izvestia*, coupled the planned cut in arms expenditures with proposals to reduce Soviet military manpower. The latter proposals, however, were not made part of the budgetary measures submitted to the Supreme Soviet 2 days later.

Khrushchev challenged the West to match the planned Soviet arms cuts. Citing a recent assessment of East-West strength in which U.S. Defense Secy. McNamara had declared that the West had superiority in conventional and nuclear armaments, Khrushchev said: "So you now think, gentlemen, that the number of troops under NATO is larger than under the Warsaw Pact countries? Then why do you not agree now to a reduction of forces? Why do you not agree now to a reduction of foreign forces in . . . [Germany]? The Soviet Union is still standing by its proposal. . . . In addition, as is known, we propose to establish control posts in the territories of

states belonging to both groupings for the purpose of preventing secret concentration of armed forces and averting surprise attack."

The reduction in military expenditures was outlined in the 1964 state budget submitted to the Supreme Soviet Dec. 16 by Finance Min. Vasily F. Garbuzov. The budget's publicly-announced allocation for defense was 13.3 billion rubles ($14.6 billion), a reduction of 600 million rubles ($660 million) from the expenditure budgeted for 1963. The military budget represented 14.6% of the total expenditures of 91.3 billion rubles ($100.4 billion) foreseen in 1964.

It was assumed by many Western experts that the publicly-announced Soviet military budget represented only a part of the sums that actually were spent on military purposes but were concealed under other budgetary categories.

(The *N.Y. Times* reported from London Dec. 17 that the U.S. and Britain were prepared to examine with the USSR the possibility of a mutual reduction of up to 10% in the 3 countries' military budgets. The proposal was said to have been discussed by the 3 powers during 1963, but Foreign Min. Gromyko was reported to have rejected Western demands that each of the 3 open its budget to independent examination of its spending on arms.) *

---

*Kennedy Administration officials had indicated in June and July that the U.S. was considering a cutback in its production both of nuclear weapons and of fission materials for weapons use. A detailed report on the problem appeared June 30 in the N.Y. Times in an article by John W. Finney. According to the Times, Administration and Congressional leaders had voiced concern over the growth of the U.S. nuclear weapons stockpile to tens of thousands of bombs, projectiles and warheads. It was felt that the stockpile had grown excessively in the past 5 years and had reached a point where it contained many times—"tens" or "hundreds" of times—the number of weapons that conceivably could be used in an atomic war. Finney reported that Pentagon spokesmen recently had informed newsmen at a "background meeting" that it might be possible to cut $1 billion from the AEC's $1.8 billion annual budget for weapons production.

NATO Backs New Talks. The winter ministerial meeting of the NATO Council, concluded in Paris Dec. 17, upheld the U.S.' search for new negotiations with the USSR on the lessening of East-West tensions.

The alliance's backing had been asked by State Secy. Rusk in an address at the Council's opening session Dec. 16. Rusk asserted that the current state of Communist-bloc politics presented the West with an unusual opportunity for fruitful negotiations with the USSR. He based his argument on the assessment that the Soviet-Chinese ideological rift mirrored a fundamental conflict between the 2 nations and could not be resolved. Rusk reportedly asserted that in the conflict between Chinese militancy and Soviet hopes for peaceful coexistence, the West logically should encourage and respond to the Soviet view. He asserted that no matter how unsatisfactory the USSR's goal of peaceful coexistence might seem to the West, it was a relatively moderate course and presented an opportunity for negotiation of potentially threatening situations.

The Council's final communiqué, made public Dec. 17, indorsed Rusk's call for negotiations and expressed the hope they would lead to "a genuine and fundamental improvement in East-West relations."

Geneva Disarmament Talks

The Moscow test-ban treaty and the U.S.-Soviet "hot line" pact were outgrowths of the work of the 18-nation UN Disarmament Committee, which had been meeting intermittently in Geneva since Mar. 12, 1962.

The conference, reduced to 17 nations by France's refusal to send a delegation,* had given little indica-

*Participating nations at the Geneva talks: West— U.S., Britain, Italy and Canada; Soviet bloc—USSR, Poland, Czechoslovakia, Rumania and Bulgaria; neutral—Brazil, Burma, Ethiopia, India, Mexico, Nigeria, Sweden and the UAR.

tion of progress until the seemingly sudden U.S.-Soviet decision to come to terms on nuclear tests and the Washington-Moscow teletype link. It was clear that the Geneva meetings, despite their failure to make progress on their stated goal—a general disarmament treaty—were being used as a forum for the communication of ideas and attitudes on limited but specific disarmament matters. The meetings also were credited with having clarified many of the differences remaining to be resolved before agreement could be reached on an effective disarmament pact.

17-Nation Talks Resumed. The UN Disarmament Committee, reconvening in Geneva Feb. 12, was given a Soviet plan for the barring of foreign missile and nuclear submarine bases.

The Soviet proposal, in the form of a declaration submitted by First Deputy Foreign Min. Vasily V. Kuznetsov, called for: (1) dismantling of foreign bases for nuclear submarines and renunciation of the use of foreign ports for such vessels; (2) withdrawal from foreign bases of aircraft armed with nuclear bombs or weapons; (3) dismantling of foreign missile bases and withdrawal to their home territory of missiles (with their nuclear warheads) in the 1,500-kilometer (935-mile) range. Kuznetsov said it was "completely unfounded" to regard the substitution of Polaris submarines for land-based missiles as a "solution of the problem of foreign rocket bases."

State Min. Joseph B. Godber, leader of the British delegation, called the Soviet proposal a "political maneuver" favorable to the Communist bloc because of its large land mass. Godber recommended instead acceptance of the Western proposal of a 30% reduction in all weapons as the first step toward disarmament.

The USSR Feb. 20 tabled a draft

of a proposed NATO-Warsaw Pact nonaggression treaty. Kuznetsov requested the negotiation of a treaty providing for: (1) a resolution committing signatories to refrain from attack, threat or use of force; (2) negotiated settlement of all disputes; (3) special consultations on dangerous situations that might arise; (4) enforcement of the pact for the duration of the Warsaw and NATO treaties.

Charles C. Stelle, the U.S.' chief negotiator in Geneva, offered a Western plan Mar. 13 that made concessions to the Soviet terms for the policing of a proposed treaty banning nuclear tests. Stelle said that the U.S. was prepared to: (a) reduce the area of Soviet territory subject to on-site inspection from 700 to 500 square kilometers (270 to 190 square miles) for each inspection and (b) exclude "sensitive defense installations" from the policed area. (The U.S. and Great Britain Feb. 23 had reduced their proposed on-site inspection quota requirement from 8 to 7 or fewer yearly "if there was a clear understanding on the set of principles governing . . . procedures.")

Semyon K. Tsarapkin, successor to Kuznetsov as leader of the Soviet delegation, submitted proposals Mar. 27 for a missile disarmament pact that would include international inspection of missile stockpiles at launching sites. The 3-stage plan provided for a "minimal" number of missiles retained after the first stage and for destruction of all launching sites and missiles after the 2d stage. Western delegates objected that the proposal would permit inspection of launching areas only. The plan, which called for the elimination of Polaris submarines as well as land-based delivery systems, was rejected by the West Mar. 29.

The Geneva meetings during April, May and June were devoted largely to negotiation of the proposed U.S.-Soviet "hot line" agreement. They were recessed June 21, after the signing of the agreement, to permit the U.S., Britain and USSR to begin the Moscow negotiations that resulted in the limited treaty to ban nuclear weapons tests. The conference resumed its work Aug. 12.

Stelle disclosed Aug. 14 that the USSR had rejected these 2 proposals for relaxation of the nuclear arms race: (a) an immediate halt to the production of fissile materials for weapons purposes, and (b) the transfer from military to peaceful uses of 132,000 pounds of U.S. nuclear materials and of 88,000 pounds of equivalent Soviet materials. Tsarapkin replied that "the Soviet Union cannot accept any control without disarmament." The U.S. offer, he said, "was not disarmament."

Stelle announced at the conference Aug. 16 that the U.S. was ready to negotiate on Soviet proposals for the establishment of observation posts in Germany to prevent surprise attacks. Stelle said, however, that the U.S. was not willing to negotiate on the USSR's simultaneous proposals for reduction of Soviet and Western troops in Germany. Tsarapkin stressed Aug. 16 that the USSR's proposals against surprise attack were conditional on a negotiated withdrawal of troops from Germany.

The Geneva talks were recessed Aug. 29 to permit the UN General Assembly to take up the disarmament question. Spokesmen for the UN Disarmament Committee, parent body of the conference, announced Nov. 22 that the meetings would be resumed in Geneva Jan. 21, 1964.

Chinese-Soviet Differences: Issue of War & Peace Disputed

The Soviet Communist Party's dramatic 1956 denunciation of Stalin's rule had set the stage for a division of the Communist world between "have-not" parties committed to advancing their interests by armed revolution and "bourgeois" parties desirous of maintaining world peace in order to consolidate their gains.

This division led to a confrontation of the Soviet and Chinese Communist Party leaderships. Initially confined to ideological matters—questions of internal party administration and of revolutionary principles—the 2 nations' differences spread into the sphere of state policy. Russia's leaders, disavowing policies of terror and revolution, proclaimed their readiness to accept "peaceful coexistence" with the capitalist West. China rejected the new Russian stand and summoned all revolutionaries to renew their struggles under Peiping's guidance.

The most fundamental questions of Communist policy and world peace were debated by the 2 powers in 1963 as they vied for the leadership of world communism.

Peiping Assails Khrushchev. The leaders of the Chinese Communist Party proclaimed anew their total rejection of Soviet Premier Nikita S. Khrushchev's policies in a year-end statement published Dec. 31, 1962 in the official party newspaper *Jenmin Jih Pao* (the *Peiping People's Daily*).

The Chinese statement, reported from Hong Kong Jan. 1, made it clear that Communist China intended to champion its interpretation of Marxist-Leninist policy even though this meant a fundamental ideological conflict with the USSR.

The statement, especially critical of Soviet professions of "peaceful coexistence" with the West, was viewed as Communist China's reply to an address Dec. 12, 1962 in which Khrushchev had condemned Chinese intransigeance as a threat to peace.

Ostensibly written to answer an attack recently mounted against Chinese views by Palmiro Togliatti, secretary general of the Italian Communist Party, the statement repeatedly referred to Togliatti and "other comrades" or "certain others." It was clear from the context—and from the fact that Khrushchev's remarks were quoted and criticized although not attributed to him—that these "others" were Khrushchev.

Points made by the Chinese statement, entitled "The Differences Between Comrade Togliatti and Us":

Imperialism a 'paper tiger'—"Comrade Togliatti and certain other comrades have strongly opposed the Marxist-Leninist proposition of the Chinese Communist Party that 'imperialism and all reactionaries are paper tigers.' . . . Togliatti said that it 'is wrong to state that imperialism is simply a paper tiger which can be overthrown by a mere push of the shoulder.' Then there are other persons who assert that today imperialism has nuclear teeth, so how can it be called a paper tiger? [Khrushchev's words in his Dec. 12, 1962 speech] . . .

"The possession of nuclear weapons by imperialism has not changed by one iota the nature of imperialism, which is rotten to the core and declining, inwardly weak though outwardly strong. . . . When in his talk with Anna Louise Strong Comrade Mao Tse-tung first put forward the proposition that imperialism and all reactionaries are paper tigers, the imperialists already had nuclear weapons. In this talk Comrade Mao Tse-tung pointed out: 'The atom bomb is a paper tiger which the U.S. reactionaries use to scare people. It looks terrible, but in fact it is not. Of course, the atom bomb is a weapon of mass slaughter, but the outcome of a war is decided by the people, not by one or 2 types of weapons.' . . .

"In the final analysis, neither nuclear teeth nor any other kind of teeth can save imperialism from its fate of inevitable extinction."

Coexistence & imperialism—"Even more absurd is the allegation that 'a world without war' can be achieved through peaceful coexistence. In the present situation, it is possible to prevent imperialism from launching a new world war if all the peace-loving forces of the world unite . . . and fight together. But it is one thing to prevent a world war and another to eliminate all wars. . . .

"The principle of peaceful coexistence can apply only to relations between countries with different social systems, not to relations between oppressed and oppressor nations, nor to relations between oppressed and oppressing classes. . . .

"But Togliatti and those attacking China extend their idea of 'peaceful coexistence' to cover relations between the colonial and semicolonial people . . . and the imperialists. . . .

"They do not like the sparks of revolution among the oppressed nations and peoples. They say that a tiny spark may lead to a world war. Such a way of speaking is really asking the oppressed nations to 'coexist peacefully' with their colonial rulers . . . rather than to resist or wage struggles for independence, much less to fight wars of national liberation."

Soviet policy toward Cuba—"Those who accuse China of opposing peaceful coexistence also attack the Chinese people for supporting the just stand of the Cuban people in their struggle against U.S. imperialism. . . .

". . . On more than one occasion we have made it clear that we neither called for the establishment of missile bases in Cuba nor obstructed the withdrawal of the so-called 'offensive weapons' from Cuba. We have never considered that it was a Marxist-Leninist attitude to brandish nuclear weapons as a way of settling international disputes. . . . What we did strongly oppose . . . is the sacrifice of another country's sovereignty as a means of reaching a compromise with imperialism. A compromise of this sort can only be regarded as 100% appeasement, a 'Munich' pure and simple."

Need for revolution — "Marxist-Leninists, while favoring struggle for reforms, resolutely oppose reformism."

"Whenever the possibility for peaceful transition appears in a given country, the Communists should strive for its realization. After all, possibility and reality . . . are 2 different things. Hitherto, history has not witnessed a single example of peaceful transition from capitalism to socialism. Communists should not pin all their hopes for the victory of the revolution on peaceful transition. The bourgeoisie will never step down from the stage of history of its own accord."

"Communists must . . . be prepared to repel the assaults of counter-revolution and to overthrow the bourgeoisie by armed force at the critical juncture of the revolution. . . ."

Moscow Warns China. The Soviet Communist Party rejected the Chinese ideological thesis and political attack Jan. 7. It warned that if Red China continued its attack on Soviet-bloc policies, it could split the world Communist movement.

The Soviet reply to China was made in an article published by the Moscow CP newspaper *Pravda* and given prominent publicity in other major Soviet newspapers and broadcasts. As the Chinese article had done, *Pravda* began by excoriating secondary Communist leaders rather than its true target (*Pravda* attacked the Albanians) but ended by condemning positions whose more powerful advocates were clearly identifiable.

Experts considered the following Soviet warning the most important part of the statement:

"Communists cannot but feel gravely concerned over the thesis launched recently that there is a 'temporary majority' in the international movement which 'persists in its mistakes,' and a 'temporary minority' which

.'boldly and resolutely upholds the truth.' . . . To insist on this thesis would in effect mean to lead matters to the fragmentation of the international Communist movement, to undermine the ideology on which it is built. . . . This thesis only serves to substantiate the split of the Communist movement and renunciation of the common positions of the Marxist-Leninist parties."

The statement rejected Chinese contentions that Soviet actions during the Cuban crisis constituted a Communist-bloc "Munich." It denounced the "home-made thesis on the 'paper tiger,' which is an underestimation of the forces of imperialism."

Albania (by implication, China) had rejected the principles of peaceful coexistence, *Pravda* said. "But what, then, is the general line? War? If so, where, then, is the difference between such an approach . . . and the viewpoint of the adventurist circles of imperialism." "Which Marxist-Leninist would agree that the way to the victory of communism lies through a thermonuclear war? The dogmatists . . . do not understand that competition in peaceful conditions is one of the most important battlegrounds between socialism and capitalism. As regards the struggle against imperialism proclaimed by the dogmatists, it boils down to mere high-sounding phrases and foul language."

Rift Debated in Berlin. The Russian-Chinese differences were debated Jan. 15-21 by Khrushchev and other high-ranking Communists, including representatives of Peiping, at a gathering in East Berlin of delegations from 70 national Communist parties.

The East Berlin gathering technically was held for the 6th Congress of the East German Socialist Unity (Communist) Party. But the guest delegations transformed the congress into a forum for discussing the Sino-Soviet disagreements.

The congress' purpose was confirmed Jan. 15, when East German CP First Secy. Walter Ulbricht convened the meeting with an address in which he attacked China for invading India. Ulbricht's address was followed by major speeches by Khrushchev Jan. 16 and by Wu Hsiu-chuan, Chinese CP Central Committee member, who was jeered by the congress Jan. 18 when he attempted to reply.

Major addresses and the congress' reaction to them:

Khrushchev — Addressing the congress for 2½ hours Jan. 16, Khrushchev appealed for an end to the ideological debate. Although he defended his views on peaceful coexistence and again warned of the dangers of nuclear war, Khrushchev urged other Communist leaders to agree to an ideological truce and avert a split in the Communist movement. His words were directed at Albania, but in the context, China was his target.

Excerpts from Khrushchev's speech, as reported Jan. 16 by the USSR's Tass news agency:

▶ "No doubt that as a result of a world thermonuclear war, . . . the warbreeding capitalists would inevitably perish. But would the Socialist countries . . . benefit by a worldwide thermonuclear catastrophe? . . . [Marxists-Leninists] cannot conceive the creation of a Communist civilization on the ruins of the world cultural centers, upon an earth deserted and poisoned by thermonuclear fallout."

▶ "I will tell you a secret: Our scientists have worked out a 100-megaton bomb. But according to our scientists' calculations, a 100-megaton bomb must not be used in Europe. Should our probable enemy unleash war, then where should we drop it? Over West Germany or France? But the explosion of such a bomb . . . would affect you [East Germany] and several other countries. Therefore we can use such a weapon only outside the confines of Europe. . . . And a 100-megaton bomb is not the limit." "Comrades, to put it in a

nutshell, . . . it is not advisable to be in a hurry for the other world."

▶ "As it is said, blessed is he who chatters about war and does not understand what he is chattering about. The Albanian leaders chatter much about rocket-nuclear war. . . . Except for chatter they have nothing to their name and . . . do not dispose of any real means. As you see, in these matters we have different positions and different responsibilities."

Wu Hsiu-chuan—Communist China's reply to the charges against it was jeered and reviled from the floor of the congress Jan. 18. Delegates shouted, whistled and stamped their feet as Wu, Chinese delegation chief, assailed Yugoslavia's "revision" of Marxist doctrine in terms that were recognized as directed at the USSR.

According to Reuters correspondent Jack Altman, the only Western reporter permitted to attend the congress after Jan. 16, the Chinese spokesman was subjected to public humiliation unprecedented in recent Communist history. Wu was silenced several times by the reaction from the floor. His address was concluded in silence, without applause.

Key points of Wu's address:
▶ "More and more people in the world have come to realize that U.S. imperialism is the center of world reaction, the most ferocious enemy of the people of the world, and the most ferocious enemy of world peace."

▶ "The Communist Party of China is consistent in safeguarding the unity of the socialist camp. . . . This is why, when the practice of publicly attacking another fraternal party by name—the Albanian Party of Labor — first emerged more than a year ago, . . . the Communist Party of China expressed its resolute opposition. . . ."

▶ "The modern revisionists represented by the renegades to the working class, the Tito group of Yugoslavia, have surrendered to imperialist pressure, are willingly serving imperialism and are . . . undermining the international unity of the working class. . . ."

(Yugoslav Pres. Tito, in a speech at a youth congress in Belgrade Jan. 23, had charged that China was following a "Genghis Khan policy" that threatened world peace. Tito said: "With a population of 700 million in China, they estimate that at least 300 million Chinese would survive a nuclear war, whereas there would be very few survivors among other nations. They said that the capitalists would perish; but what about workers and peasants in America, Europe and elsewhere, as well as the people of the socialist countries? They do not think that it matters in the least if they too perish.")

Chinese Letter Assails 'Coexistence.' The Chinese Communist Party Central Committee assailed Khrushchev and the Soviet leadership publicly June 16 for pursuing policies of "peaceful coexistence" at the expense of the revolutionary aims of the world Communist movement.

The new attack came in a 60,000-word letter addressed to the Soviet party's Central Committee June 14 and publicized 2 days later by the Peiping press and radio.

The letter warned that over-emphasis on policies of peaceful coexistence had led "certain persons in the international Communist movement" to neglect their duty to advance communism by whatever means were necessary: "peaceful and armed, open and secret, legal and illegal, parliamentary struggle and mass struggle." If this error was perpetuated, Peiping warned, the "proletarian party will paralyze the revolutionary will of the proletariat, disarm itself ideologically and sink into a totally passive state of unpreparedness . . . and . . . bury its proletarian revolutionary cause."

The Chinese declared that peaceful coexistence already had led some Communist leaders to take a "passive or scornful or negative attitude toward the struggles of the oppressed peoples for liberation." "Certain persons," they charged, "now go so far as to deny the

great international significance of anti-imperialist, revolutionary struggles of Asian, African and Latin American peoples . . . and to hold down those struggles." The letter declared that coexistence "cannot replace the revolutionary struggles of the people." There was "no historical precedent for a peaceful transition" to socialism, the document warned.

The letter denounced as "erroneous" the view that (1) "the contradiction between the proletariat and the bourgeoisie can be resolved without proletarian revolution in each country," and (2) "the contradiction between oppressed nations and imperialism can be resolved without revolution by the oppressed nations."

Women's Congress Disrupted. The Chinese-Russian rift disrupted the meetings of a World Women's Congress held in Moscow June 24-29 under the sponsorship of the Communist-dominated Women's International Democratic Federation.

The congress, opened by Khrushchev in the Kremlin's Palace of Congresses, was marked immediately by dissention when the Italian delegation, led by Mrs. Baldina Victoria, a Communist member of Italy's Parliament, walked out June 24 and 25 during speeches in which Japanese and Cuban delegates attacked the U.S. as the main threat to world peace. The dissention became more specifically ideological June 25 when Mrs. Yang Yun-yu, leader of the Chinese delegation, violently attacked the U.S. and declared that "at no time is it possible for oppressed people to coexist peacefully with imperialists."

The Congress' June 26 meeting was adjourned in disorder after Chinese delegates invaded the speaker's platform. The meeting resumed later June 26 to hear Dolores Ibarruri, leading Communist participant in the Spanish

Civil War, declare that "we want to come to terms with Mrs. Kennedy too . . . if she is ready to defend her children from the danger of nuclear war."

The Moscow women's meeting ended in an uproar June 29, after the Chinese and Albanian delegations were shouted down as they opposed a final statement that approved Soviet policies based on peaceful coexistence.

Reply to Chinese Letter. The Soviet Communist Party replied July 14 to the Chinese party's June 14 letter. The Soviet reply was made in the form of an open letter from the Central Committee to all party members and organizations in the Soviet Union. It was published in the Soviet press together with the text of the original Chinese letter, considered the most violent Marxist critique of Russian policy published in the USSR since the 1920s.

The open letter rejected the Chinese message's attacks on Khrushchev's coexistence policies and denounced the Chinese leaders for their apparent willingness to see millions die in a nuclear war if this would advance their own aims.

The Central Committee declared: "We are sure that all of our party and the entire Soviet people support us in that we can not share the views of the Chinese leadership on the creation of a '1,000 times higher civilization' on the corpses of hundreds of millions of people."

Major points made by the Russian party's letter:

Nuclear war—"Our party in the decisions of the 20th and 22d Congresses, the world Communist movement, in the declaration and the statement, set before Communists as a task of extreme importance the task of struggling for peace, for averting a world thermonuclear catastrophe. . . .

"The Chinese comrades obviously underestimate all the danger of thermonuclear war. 'The atomic bomb is a paper tiger; it is not terrible at all,' they contend.

"The main thing, don't you see, is to put an end to imperialism as quickly as possible; but how—with what losses—this will be achieved seems a secondary question.

"To whom, it is right to ask, is it secondary? To the hundreds of millions of people who are doomed to death in the event of the unleashing of a thermonuclear war? To the states that will be erased from the face of the earth . . .?

"No one, including big states, has the right to play with the destinies of millions of people. Those who do not want to exert efforts to exclude world war from the life of the peoples—to avert a mass annihilation of people and the destruction of the values of human civilization—deserve condemnation.

"The letter of the CPC Central Committee of June 14 says much about 'inevitable sacrifices,' ostensibly in the name of the revolution. Some responsible Chinese leaders have also declared that it is possible to sacrifice hundreds of millions of people in war. The anthology 'Long Live Leninism!,' approved by the CPC Central Committee, asserts: 'On the ruins of destroyed imperialism, the victorious peoples will create with tremendous speed a civilization a thousand times higher than under the capitalist system, will build their really bright future.' . . .

"We would like to ask the Chinese comrades —who suggest building a bright future on the ruins of the old world destroyed by a thermonuclear war—if they have consulted the working class of the countries where imperialism dominates. The working class of the capitalist countries would be sure to ask them, 'Do we ask you to trigger a war and destroy our countries while annihilating imperialists?'

"Is it not a fact that . . . the bulk of the population of the capitalist countries consists of the working class, working peasantry, working intelligentsia. The atomic bomb does not distinguish between the imperialists and the working people; it hits big areas, and therefore millions of workers would be destroyed for each monopolist."

Dispute over Cuban crisis—"The Chinese comrades allege that in the period of the Caribbean crisis we made an 'adventurist' mistake by introducing rockets in Cuba, and then 'capitulated to American imperialism' when we removed the rockets from Cuba. (Such allegations were made in the leading article in Jenmin Jih Pao on Mar. 8, 1963. 'On the Statement of the Communist party of the USA').

"Such assertions utterly contradict the facts.

"What was the actual state of affairs? The CPSU Central Committee and the Soviet government possessed trustworthy information that an armed aggression of United States imperialism against Cuba was about to start. We realized with sufficient clarity that the most resolute steps were needed to rebuff aggression, to defend the Cuban Revolution effectively. . . .

"The delivery of missiles to Cuba signified that an attack on her would meet a resolute rebuff, with the employment of rocket weapons against the organizers of the aggression. Such a resolute step . . . was a shock to the American imperialists, who felt for the first time in their history that in case they undertook an armed invasion on Cuba, a shattering retaliatory blow would be dealt on their own territory.

"Inasmuch as the point in question was not simply a conflict between the United States and Cuba but a clash between two major nuclear powers, the crisis in the area of the Caribbean Sea would have turned from a local one into a world one. A real danger of world thermonuclear war arose.

"There was one alternative in the prevailing situation: either to follow in the wake of the 'madmen' . . . and embark upon the road of unleashing a world thermonuclear war or, profiting by the opportunities offered by the delivery of missiles, . . . to reach an agreement on the peaceful solution of the crisis and to prevent aggression against the Cuban Republic.

"We have chosen, as is known, the 2d road, and are convinced that we have done the right thing. . . ."

Revolution & 'liberation' wars — "The Chinese comrades regard as the main criterion of revolutionary spirit the recognition of an armed uprising always, in everything, everywhere. Thereby the Chinese comrades actually deny the possibility of using peaceful forms of struggle for the victory of the socialist revolution, whereas Marxism-Leninism teaches that the Communists must master all forms of revolutionary class struggle—both violent and nonviolent. . . ."

"As depicted by the Chinese comrades, the differences on this question appear as follows: One side—they themselves—stands for the world revolution, while the other—the CPSU, the Marxist-Leninist parties—have forgotten the revolution, even 'fear' it, and instead of revolutionary struggle is concerned with things 'unworthy' of a real revolutionary, such as peace, the economic development of the Socialist countries, . . . such as struggling for the democratic rights and vital interests of the working people of the capitalist countries. . . .

"The question arises: What is the explanation for the incorrect propositions of the CPC leadership on the basic problems of our times? It is either the complete divorce of the Chinese comrades from actual reality, a dogmatic, bookish approach to problems of war, peace and the revolution, their lack of understanding of the concrete conditions of the modern epoch, or the fact that behind the rumpus about the 'world revolution,' raised by the Chinese comrades, are other goals that have nothing in common with revolution."

Inter-Party Talks Begun. Delegations representing the Central Committees of the Soviet and Chinese Communist parties began talks in Moscow July 5 on the 2 parties' differences on Communist policy and ideology.

While invective filled Russian and Chinese newspapers and radio broadcasts, the 2 governments were exchanging a series of messages aimed at convening inter-party talks on their ideological differences.

The proposal for negotiations had been made by the Chinese earlier in the year and had been rejected by Soviet Premier Khrushchev. But the plan was revived and made the subject of a Chinese note, transmitted to the USSR Mar. 9, in which it was suggested that Khrushchev come to Peiping for direct talks with Chinese leaders. This idea was rejected by the Soviet leader, but it was proposed instead that the Chinese send a dele-

gation to Moscow for talks on a high, but not summit, level. The Russian suggestion was accepted by the Chinese party's Central Committee May 9, and the Moscow meetings were scheduled to begin July 5.

The talks were opened amidst an exchange of propaganda attacks in which the 2 sides accused each other of political and ideological betrayal and of attempts to use the world Communist movement for national ends.

The Chinese delegation, headed by Central Committee Secy. Gen. Teng Hsiao-ping, arrived in Moscow by plane July 5. Met at the airport by CP Central Committee Secy. Mikhail A. Suslov, the leader of the Soviet delegation, the Chinese emissaries were driven into Moscow, where, after a brief delay, the 2 sides opened their conference with a private dinner at a Soviet government villa overlooking the city.

The 2 sides began working sessions at the Moscow villa July 6 under conditions of maximum security and total secrecy. The talks were recessed July 7, resumed the next day and recessed again July 9, apparently to permit the Chinese to communicate with Peiping. The meetings resumed July 10 with a 5-hour session reportedly to have intensified the differences between the 2 sides. The delegates conferred again July 11 and 12, the latter session attended by Soviet First Deputy Premier Anastas Mikoyan. Further meetings were held July 15, 17, 19 and 20.

Failure Conceded. The Moscow talks were recessed July 20 without having lessened the ideological differences separating the 2 powers.

Following the final session July 20, the Chinese went to the Kremlin, where they were received by Khrushchev (for the first time since the talks were opened) for a farewell dinner in what Moscow radio described as "a friendly atmosphere." After the Kremlin dinner, the Chinese were escorted to the Moscow airport by the Soviet delegation. According to Western newsmen, the 2 delegations remained "frigidly" apart except for a perfunctory handshake and a few words exchanged by Suslov and Teng, leader of the Chinese group, immediately before the Chinese boarded their plane for home. (The Chinese were given a mammoth public reception on their return to Peiping July 21.)

A joint communiqué published in Moscow and Peiping July 21 indicated that the 2 sides had failed even to begin negotiations of the differences between them. The communiqué said only that the delegations had "set forth their views and positions" on "important questions of principles concerning contemporary world developments, the international Communist movement and Soviet-Chinese relations."

A-Bomb Aid Withdrawn. A Chinese government statement broadcast Aug. 15 by Peiping radio charged that the USSR had offered in 1957 to help China produce nuclear bombs but had withdrawn its offer in 1959 to placate the U.S.

The Chinese statement said, in part: "It is no new story that Soviet leaders, in collusion with American imperialism, plot to bind China hand and foot." "On June 20, 1959, when there was no hint of the so-called nuclear test ban treaty, the Soviet government unilaterally scrapped the Oct. 15, 1957 agreement concerning new defense technology [and] refused to supply China with atomic bomb samples and technical materials for the manufacture of atomic bombs, apparently as a gift for . . . [Khrushchev] to take to Eisenhower when visiting the United States in September."

The USSR replied with a lengthy statement issued Aug. 21 through the Tass news agency. The Russian statement defended the nuclear test ban treaty and charged that China's opposition to the pact proved that its leaders did not care "how nuclear arms spread among the capitalist states as long as the Chinese leaders got a chance to lay their hands on a nuclear bomb and see what it is like."

China responded with a 10,000-word statement issued in Peiping Sept. 1. The Chinese statement, rejecting Russia's "gross and fantastic lies" about Chinese policy, said: "Apparently the Soviet leaders have already become so degenerate that they now depend on telling lies for a living." "The Soviet leaders are perhaps too hasty in deriding China for its backwardness . . . [But] even if we Chinese people are unable to produce an atom bomb for 100 years, we will neither crawl to the baton of the Soviet leaders nor kneel before the nuclear blackmail of the U.S. imperialists."

Russia Scores Mao View. The Chinese position on the question of nuclear armaments and war was rejected in its totality by the USSR Sept. 21. A Soviet government statement, issued in reply to China's Sept. 1 denunciation of Russian "lies," declared that Chinese leaders "have set the aim of discrediting at any cost the . . . Soviet Union, of splitting the Communist movement and undermining the unity of anti-imperialist forces."

Turning to the nuclear war views proclaimed by China, the USSR said:

"The authors of the [Chinese] statement quote a . . . version of Mao Tse-tung's pronouncement at the 1957 Moscow meeting that differs substantially from the genuine text. For the sake of truth we shall quote from the records of the meeting the words actually uttered by Mao Tse-tung. . . .

" 'Can one guess,' he said, 'how great will be the toll of human casualties in a future war? Possibly it would be a 3d of the 2.700 billion inhabitants of the entire world—i.e., only 900 million people. I consider this to be even low, if atomic bombs would actually fall.'

" 'Of course it is most terrible. But even a half would not be so bad. Why? Because it was not we that wanted that, but they. It is they who are imposing war on us. If we fight, atomic and hydrogen weapons will be used. Personally, I think that in the entire world there will be such suffering that a half of humanity, and perhaps even more than a half, will perish.'

" 'I had an argument about this with [Indian Prime Min.] Nehru. In this respect, he is more pessimistic than I am. I told him that if a half of humanity were destroyed, the other half would still remain but imperialism would be destroyed entirely and there would be only socialism in all the world, and within half of a century or a whole century the population would again increase even by more than a half.' "

1963 Nuclear Tests

U.S. Detonations. More than 24 nuclear tests were officially reported to have been carried out by the U.S. Atomic Energy Commission during 1963. All were of devices detonated underground at the AEC's Nevada proving grounds; most were of low-yield intensity, although a few were of intermediate-yield range. A few of the devices were tested under the AEC's Project Plowshare program for research in the peaceful uses of nuclear explosions, but most of the tests were for unspecified purposes, and it was assumed that they were of weapons or of weapons prototypes.

The U.S. tests reported:

Date	Strength	Date	Strength
Feb. 8*	.. Intermediate	Sept. 13	...... Low yield
Feb. 21	...... Low yield	Sept. 13	.. Intermediate
Feb. 21†	... Low yield	Oct. 11..	.... Low yield
Mar. 29	...... Low yield	Oct. 11†	.... Low yield
Apr. 5	.... Low yield	Oct. 16	.. Intermediate
May 23	.. Intermediate	Oct. 26‡	.... 12 kilotons
June 5	.... Low yield		(low yield)
June 6	.... Low yield	Nov. 14	...... Low yield
June 14	...... Low yield	Nov. 15	...... Low yield
June 25	..... Low yield	Nov. 22	...... Low yield
Aug. 12	...... Low yield	Dec. 4	...... Low yield
Aug. 15	...... Low yield	Dec. 12	...... Low yield
Aug. 23	...... Low yield		

Soviet Tests Doubted. The Atomic Energy Commission reported June 20 that it had "inconclusive" evidence that the Soviet Union had secretly carried out several low-yield nuclear tests. But a subsequent AEC announcement, issued Sept. 20, said there had been no further confirmation of the tests.

French Test Protested. The Algerian government asserted Mar. 19 that France had carried out an underground nuclear test Mar. 18 near In-Ekker, in the Hoggar region of the Sahara. The French Armed Forces Ministry refused Mar. 19 to confirm that the detonation had taken place.

The Paris newspaper *Le Monde*, reporting Mar. 15 that a Sahara test was planned, had said that it would be France's 8th nuclear detonation—all carried out in the Sahara—and its 4th underground one.

France's reported plans for the test had been protested by the Algerian government in a communiqué issued Mar. 16.

(The *N.Y. Herald Tribune* reported Nov. 4 that France had secretly carried out a new series of underground nuclear tests in the Sahara in October. The detonations were said to have been devoted primarily to testing an atomic trigger that presumably would be used in a hydrogen bomb scheduled to be tested by France in the Pacific in 1967. The newspaper also reported that France had carried out 2 small underground detonations in secret in March immediately after the March 18 test.)

Fallout Rise Reported. The U.S.' Federal Radiation Council reported May 31 that U.S. and Soviet nuclear tests carried out in 1962 had doubled the amount of radioactive debris in the earth's atmosphere and had caused a commensurate rise in the intensity of test-caused fallout and radioactivity in food supplies. The council asserted, however, that even with the increased fallout, "the health risks from radioactivity in foods . . . are too small to justify countermeasures."

---

*According to the AEC, a number of intermediate-range detonations were set off at the Nevada test site, 65 miles northwest of Las Vegas, Feb. 8; the number was not specified.
†Project Plowshare detonations. ‡Detonation set off near Fallon, Nev. under AEC-Defense Department Project Vela program for improvement of underground test-detection techniques.

INDEX

Index entries refer to text by page number usually followed by the letter **L** or **R** to indicate whether the item appears in the Left or Right column

A

ADENAUER, Dr. Konrad—48L
AEC—see ATOMIC Energy Commission
AFRICA—68R, 71
AIKEN, Sen. George D(avid) (R., Vt.)—101L
AILLERET, Maj. Gen. Charles—27L
ALBANIA—104L, 109-110, 112L
ALEMAYEHO, Haddis—83R
ALGERIA—26R-28L, 62R, 76L, 89R, 90R, 115R
ALLOT, Sen. Gordon L(lewellyn) (R., Colo.)—101L
ALTMAN, Jack—110R
AMERICAN Association for the Advancement of Science—29R-30L
AMERICAN University (Washington, D.C.)—92L
ANDERSON, Sen. Clinton P(resba) (D., N.M.)—22R, 101L
ARGENTINA—15R
ARGUS, Project—78R
ARMS Control & Disarmament Agency (U.S.)—61, 93R
ASIA—71L; see also specific country
ATOMIC Energy, Joint Congressional Committee on (U.S.)—45, 67L, 98L
ATOMIC Energy Commission (AEC) (U.S.)—20, 22R, 25R, 28L, 29L, 45, 48, 52L, 53L, 54L, 59, 60L, 62, 66L, 74, 78, 81R, 84L, 89, 115
ATOMIC & Hydrogen Weapons, 8th World Congress Against—82R
ATOMIC Radiation & Fallout—see RADIATION & Fallout
ATOMIC Test Detection—20R-21L, 23R, 24R-25L, 59R, 80-81, 86
ATOMIC Tests: Britain—55L, 89L, 90R. France—26R-28R, 41L, 42R, 52L, 62, 76L, 90R, 115R. International—23R. Radiation & Fallout—see under 'R.' USSR—46-48, 51R-54L, 59L, 62, 79R-80L, 81R-82L, 88R-90R, 115. U.S.—22R, 23R-24R, 25R, 45R, 48R-49L, 51, 54R-55L, 59, 62, 65R-68R, 74, 77-78, 84, 89-90, 115L,
ATOMIC Tests, Prohibition or Suspension of—19R-26R, 32R-33L, 35L, 40, 41R-46R, 56R-58R, 63R-64R, 66, 68R, 69L, 70L-73L, 75R, 80-81, 82R-88R, 91L-101L, 103R-104R
ATOMIC Tests, Protests & Demonstrations Against—47R-48L, 49L-54L, 74R-75R, 78R-79L, 82, 115R
ATOMIC Weapons (Misc.)—7L, 28R-30L
ATOMIC Weapons, Prohibition or Control of—9-10, 12, 13L, 14, 15R, 16R, 18L, 37R, 40R, 58, 68R, 103R-104R
AUSTRALIA—50R, 67R, 78L

B

BARRINGTON, James—83R
BARTLETT, Sen. Edward Lewis (Bob) (D., Alaska)—101L
BAYH, Sen. Birch E(vans) (D., Ind.)—101L
BEALL, Sen. J(ames) Glenn (R., Md.)—101L

BELGRADE Conference of Non-Aligned Nations—49L-51L
Ben-GURION, David—29L
BENNETT, Sen. Wallace F(oster) (R., Utah)—101L
BERKNER, Dr. Lloyd V.—24L
BETHE, Dr. Hans—22R
BIBLE, Sen. Alan (D., Nev.)—101L
BOGGS, Sen. J(ames) Caleb (R., Del.)—101L
BOHLEN, Charles E.—69R
BOLAND, Frederick H(enry)—38R
BOULAY, Robert—36R
BRAZIL—60L, 69R, 71L, 106L
BREWSTER, Sen. Daniel B(augh) (D., Md.)—101L
BREZHNEV, Leonid I.—94R
BROWN, Dr. Harrison—77L
BUCHALET, Brig. Gen. Albert—27L
BULGARIA—7L, 60L, 69R, 106L
BURDICK, Sen. Quentin N(orthrop) (D., N.D.)—101L
BURMA—60L, 69R, 71, 83R
BURNS, Gen. E. L. M.—7L, 69R
BYRD, Sen. Harry F(lood) (D., Va.)—101L
BYRD, Sen. Robert C(arlyle) (D., W. Va.)—101L

C

CAMPAIGN for Nuclear Disarmament (Britain)—48L, 75
CANADA—7L, 8R, 30L, 54L, 55L, 56L, 60L, 67R, 69R, 106L
CANNON, Sen. Howard W(alter) (D., Nev.)—101L
CARLSON, Sen. Frank (R., Kan.)—101L
CASE Jr., Sen. Clifford P(hilip) (R., N.J.)—101L
CASTRO Ruz, Fidel—40L, 50R
CAVALETTI, Francesco—11L
CENTRAL African Republic—104L
CENTRAL Intelligence Agency (CIA) (U.S.)—22R, 30R, 67L, 81R
CEYLON—15R
CHAO Pu-chu—97R
CHEN Yi, Marshal—6R
CHINA (Communist), People's Republic of—6, 30L, 55R-56L, 96-97, 107R-115L
CHOU En-lai—97R
CHURCH, Sen. Frank (Forrester) (D., Idaho)—101L
CLARK Jr., Sen. Joseph S(ill) (D., Pa.)—101L
COAST & Geodetic Survey—59R
COMMITTEE for Non-Violent Action—51R-52L
COMMITTEE of 100 (Britain)—53R
COMMITTEE of Principals, U.S.—81L
COMMUNIST Bloc—107R-115L; see also specific country
COMMUNIST Party Congress, 22d Soviet—52L, 54R
COOPER, Sen. John Sherman (R., Ky.)—101L
CONGRESS, U.S.—20R, 45, 61, 67L, 98L-101L
COTTON, Sen. Norris (R., N.H.)—101L
CUBA—40L, 50R, 54L, 56R, 85R, 104L

116

DISARMAMENT & NUCLEAR TESTS 1960-63

Contents:

FACTS ON FILE, 119 W. 57th St., NEW YORK, N.Y. 10019

INTERIM HISTORY

The Bridge Between Today's News and Tomorrow's History